Hands-On Music Generation with Magenta

Explore the role of deep learning in music generation and assisted music composition

Alexandre DuBreuil

BIRMINGHAM - MUMBAI

Hands-On Music Generation with Magenta

Copyright © 2020 Packt Publishing

Commissioning Editor: Mrinmayee Kawalkar
Acquisition Editor: Ali Abidi
Content Development Editor: Nazia Shaikh
Senior Editor: Ayaan Hoda
Technical Editor: Joseph Sunil
Copy Editor: Safis Editing
Project Coordinator: Aishwarya Mohan
Proofreader: Safis Editing
Indexer: Tejal Daruwale Soni
Production Designer: Deepika Naik

First published: January 2020

Production reference: 1300120

Published by Packt Publishing Ltd.
Livery Place
35 Livery Street
Birmingham
B3 2PB, UK.

ISBN 978-1-83882-441-9

www.packt.com

Contributors

About the author

Alexandre DuBreuil is a software engineer and generative music artist. Through collaborations with bands and artists, he has worked on many generative art projects, such as generative video systems for music bands in concerts that create visuals based on the underlying musical structure, a generative drawing software that creates new content based on a previous artist's work, and generative music exhibits in which the generation is based on real-time events and data. Machine learning has a central role in his music generation projects, and Alexandre has been using Magenta since its release for inspiration, music production, and as the cornerstone for making autonomous music generation systems that create endless soundscapes.

About the reviewer

Gogul Ilango has a bachelor's degree in electronics and communication engineering from Thiagarajar College of Engineering, Madurai, and a master's degree in VLSI design and embedded systems from Anna University, Chennai, where he was awarded the University Gold Medal for academic performance. He has published four research papers in top conferences and journals related to artificial intelligence. His passion for music production and deep learning led him to learn about and contribute to Google's Magenta community, where he created an interactive web application called DeepDrum as well as DeepArp using Magenta.js, available in Magenta's community contribution demonstrations. He is a lifelong learner, hardware engineer, programmer, and music producer.

Packt is searching for authors like you

If you're interested in becoming an author for Packt, please visit authors.packtpub.com and apply today. We have worked with thousands of developers and tech professionals, just like you, to help them share their insight with the global tech community. You can make a general application, apply for a specific hot topic that we are recruiting an author for, or submit your own idea.

Table of Contents

Section 4: Making Your Models Interact with Other Applications

Preface

The place of machine learning in art is becoming more and more strongly established because of recent advancements in the field. Magenta is at the forefront of that innovation. This book provides a hands-on approach to machine learning models for music generation and demonstrates how to integrate them into an existing music production workflow. Complete with practical examples and explanations of the theoretical background required to understand the underlying technologies, this book is the perfect starting point to begin exploring music generation.

In *Hands-On Music Generation with Magenta*, you'll learn how to use models in Magenta to generate percussion sequences, monophonic and polyphonic melodies in MIDI, and instrument sounds in raw audio. We'll be seeing plenty of practical examples and in-depth explanations of machine learning models, such as **Recurrent Neural Networks (RNNs)**, **Variational Autoencoders (VAEs)**, and **Generative Adversarial Networks (GANs)**. Leveraging that knowledge, we'll be creating and training our own models for advanced music generation use cases, and we'll be tackling the preparation of new datasets. Finally, we'll be looking at integrating Magenta with other technologies, such as **Digital Audio Workstations (DAWs)**, and using Magenta.js to distribute music generation applications in the browser.

By the end of this book, you'll be proficient in everything Magenta has to offer and equipped with sufficient knowledge to tackle music generation in your own style.

Who this book is for

This book will appeal to both technically inclined artists and musically inclined computer scientists. It is directed to any reader who wants to gain hands-on knowledge about building generative music applications that use deep learning. It doesn't assume any musical or technical competence from you, apart from basic knowledge of the Python programming language.

What this book covers

Chapter 1, *Introduction to Magenta and Generative Art*, will show you the basics of generative music and what already exists. You'll learn about the new techniques of artwork generation, such as machine learning, and how those techniques can be applied to produce music and art. Google's Magenta open source research platform will be introduced, along with Google's open source machine learning platform TensorFlow, along with an overview of its different parts and the installation of the required software for this book. We'll finish the installation by generating a simple MIDI file on the command line.

Chapter 2, *Generating Drum Sequences with the Drums RNN*, will show you what many consider the foundation of music—percussion. We'll show the importance of RNNs for music generation. You'll then learn how to use the Drums RNN model using a pre-trained drum kit model, by calling it in the command-line window and directly in Python, to generate drum sequences. We'll introduce the different model parameters, including the model's MIDI encoding, and show how to interpret the output of the model.

Chapter 3, *Generating Polyphonic Melodies*, will show the importance of **Long Short-Term Memory (LSTM)** networks in generating longer sequences. We'll see how to use a monophonic Magenta model, the Melody RNN—an LSTM network with a loopback and attention configuration. You'll also learn to use two polyphonic models, the Polyphony RNN and Performance RNN, both LSTM networks using a specific encoding, with the latter having support for note velocity and expressive timing.

Chapter 4, *Latent Space Interpolation with MusicVAE*, will show the importance of continuous latent space of VAEs and its importance in music generation compared to standard **autoencoders (AEs)**. We'll use the MusicVAE model, a hierarchical recurrent VAE, from Magenta to sample sequences and then interpolate between them, effectively morphing smoothly from one to another. We'll then see how to add groove, or humanization, to an existing sequence, using the GrooVAE model. We'll finish by looking at the TensorFlow code used to build the VAE model.

Chapter 5, *Audio Generation with NSynth and GANSynth*, will show audio generation. We'll first provide an overview of WaveNet, an existing model for audio generation, especially efficient in text to speech applications. In Magenta, we'll use NSynth, a Wavenet Autoencoder model, to generate small audio clips, that can serve as instruments for a backing MIDI score. NSynth also enables audio transformation like scaling, time stretching and interpolation. We'll also use GANSynth, a faster approach based on GAN.

Chapter 6, *Data Preparation for Training*, will show how training our own models is crucial since it allows us to generate music in a specific style, generate specific structures or instruments. Building and preparing a dataset is the first step before training our own model. To do that, we first look at existing datasets and APIs to help us find meaningful data. Then, we build two datasets in MIDI for specific styles—dance and jazz. Finally, we prepare the MIDI files for training using data transformations and pipelines.

Chapter 7, *Training Magenta models*, will show how to tune hyperparameters, like batch size, learning rate, and network size, to optimize network performance and training time. We'll also show common training problems such as overfitting and models not converging. Once a model's training is complete, we'll show how to use the trained model to generate new sequences. Finally, we'll show how to use the Google Cloud Platform to train models faster on the cloud.

Chapter 8, *Magenta in the browser with Magenta.js*, will show a JavaScript implementation of Magenta that gained popularity for its ease of use, since it runs in the browser and can be shared as a web page. We'll introduce TensorFlow.js, the technology Magenta.js is built upon, and show what models are available in Magenta.js, including how to convert our previously trained models. Then, we'll create small web applications using GANSynth and MusicVAE for sampling audio and sequences respectively. Finally, we'll see how Magenta.js can interact with other applications, using the Web MIDI API and Node.js.

Chapter 9, *Making Magenta Interact with Music Applications*, will show how Magenta fits in a broader picture by showing how to make it interact with other music applications such as DAWs and synthesizers. We'll explain how to send MIDI sequences from Magenta to FluidSynth and DAWs using the MIDI interface. By doing so, we'll learn how to handle MIDI ports on all platforms and how to loop MIDI sequences in Magenta. We'll show how to synchronize multiple applications using MIDI clocks and transport information. Finally, we'll cover Magenta Studio, a standalone packaging of Magenta based on Magenta.js that can also integrate into Ableton Live as a plugin.

To get the most out of this book

This book doesn't require any specific knowledge about music or machine learning to enjoy, as we'll be covering all the technical aspects regarding those two subjects throughout the book. However, we do assume that you have some programming knowledge using Python. The code we provide is thoroughly commented and explained, though, which makes it easy for newcomers to use and understand.

The provided code and content works on all platforms, including Linux, macOS, and Windows. We'll be setting up the development environment as we go along, so you don't need any specific setup before we start. If you already are using an **Integrated Development Environment** (IDE) and a DAW, you'll be able to use them during the course of this book.

Download the example code files

You can download the example code files for this book from your account at www.packt.com. If you purchased this book elsewhere, you can visit www.packtpub.com/support and register to have the files emailed directly to you.

You can download the code files by following these steps:

1. Log in or register at www.packt.com.
2. Select the **Support** tab.
3. Click on **Code Downloads**.
4. Enter the name of the book in the **Search** box and follow the onscreen instructions.

Once the file is downloaded, please make sure that you unzip or extract the folder using the latest version of:

- WinRAR/7-Zip for Windows
- Zipeg/iZip/UnRarX for Mac
- 7-Zip/PeaZip for Linux

The code bundle for the book is also hosted on GitHub at https://github.com/PacktPublishing/Hands-On-Music-Generation-with-Magenta. In case there's an update to the code, it will be updated on the existing GitHub repository.

We also have other code bundles from our rich catalog of books and videos available at https://github.com/PacktPublishing/. Check them out!

Download the color images

We also provide a PDF file that has color images of the screenshots/diagrams used in this book. You can download it here: http://www.packtpub.com/sites/default/files/downloads/9781838824419_ColorImages.pdf.

Conventions used

There are a number of text conventions used throughout this book.

`CodeInText`: Indicates code words in text, database table names, folder names, filenames, file extensions, pathnames, dummy URLs, user input, and Twitter handles. Here is an example: "Each time the step operation is called, the RNN needs to update its state, the hidden vector, `h`."

A block of code is set as follows:

```
import os
import magenta.music as mm

mm.notebook_utils.download_bundle("drum_kit_rnn.mag", "bundles")
bundle = mm.sequence_generator_bundle.read_bundle_file(
    os.path.join("bundles", "drum_kit_rnn.mag"))
```

When we wish to draw your attention to a particular part of a code block, the relevant lines or items are set in bold:

```
> drums_rnn_generate --helpfull

    USAGE: drums_rnn_generate [flags]
    ...

magenta.models.drums_rnn.drums_rnn_config_flags:
    ...

magenta.models.drums_rnn.drums_rnn_generate:
    ...
```

Any command-line input or output is written as follows:

```
> drums_rnn_generate --bundle_file=bundles/drum_kit_rnn.mag --output_dir
output
```

Bold: Indicates a new term, an important word, or words that you see on screen. For example, words in menus or dialog boxes appear in the text like this. Here is an example: "The main reason to stick with **bar** throughout this book is to follow Magenta's code convention, where bar is used more consistently than **measure**."

 Warnings or important notes appear like this.

Tips and tricks appear like this.

Code in Action

Visit the following link to check out videos of the code being run:
`http://bit.ly/2uHplI4`

Get in touch

Feedback from our readers is always welcome.

General feedback: If you have questions about any aspect of this book, mention the book title in the subject of your message and email us at `customercare@packtpub.com`.

Errata: Although we have taken every care to ensure the accuracy of our content, mistakes do happen. If you have found a mistake in this book, we would be grateful if you would report this to us. Please visit `www.packtpub.com/support/errata`, selecting your book, clicking on the Errata Submission Form link, and entering the details.

Piracy: If you come across any illegal copies of our works in any form on the internet, we would be grateful if you would provide us with the location address or website name. Please contact us at `copyright@packt.com` with a link to the material.

If you are interested in becoming an author: If there is a topic that you have expertise in and you are interested in either writing or contributing to a book, please visit `authors.packtpub.com`.

Reviews

Please leave a review. Once you have read and used this book, why not leave a review on the site that you purchased it from? Potential readers can then see and use your unbiased opinion to make purchase decisions, we at Packt can understand what you think about our products, and our authors can see your feedback on their book. Thank you!

For more information about Packt, please visit `packt.com`.

Section 1: Introduction to Artwork Generation

This section consists of an introduction to artwork generation and the use of machine learning in the field, with a comprehensive overview of Magenta and TensorFlow. We'll go through the different models used in music generation and explain why those models are important.

This section contains the following chapter:

- Chapter 1, *Introduction to Magenta and Generative Art*

Introduction to Magenta and Generative Art

1

In this chapter, you'll learn the basics of generative music and what already exists. You'll learn about the new techniques of artwork generation, such as machine learning, and how those techniques can be applied to produce music and art. Google's Magenta open source research platform will be introduced, along with Google's open source machine learning platform TensorFlow, along with an overview of its different parts and the installation of the required software for this book. We'll finish the installation by generating a simple MIDI file on the command line.

The following topics will be covered in this chapter:

- Overview of generative artwork
- New techniques with machine learning
- Magenta and TensorFlow in music generation
- Installing Magenta
- Installing the music software and synthesizers
- Installing the code editing software
- Generating a basic MIDI file

Technical requirements

In this chapter, we'll use the following tools:

- **Python**, **Conda**, and **pip**, to install and execute the Magenta environment
- **Magenta**, to test our setup by performing music generation
- **Magenta GPU (optional)**, CUDA drivers, and cuDNN drivers, to make Magenta run on the GPU
- **FluidSynth**, to listen to the generated music sample using a software synthesizer
- Other optional software we might use throughout this book, such as **Audacity** for audio editing, **MuseScore** for sheet music editing, and **Jupyter Notebook** for code editing.

It is recommended that you follow this book's source code when you read the chapters in this book. The source code also provides useful scripts and tips. Follow these steps to check out the code in your user directory (you can use another location if you want):

1. First, you need to install Git, which can be installed on any platform by downloading and executing the installer at git-scm.com/downloads. Then, follow the prompts and make sure you add the program to your PATH so that it is available on the command line.
2. Then, clone the source code repository by opening a new Terminal and executing the following command:

```
> git clone
https://github.com/PacktPublishing/hands-on-music-generation-with-m
agenta
> cd hands-on-music-generation-with-magenta
```

Each chapter has its own folder; Chapter01, Chapter02, and so on. For example, the code for this chapter is located at https://github.com/PacktPublishing/hands-on-music-generation-with-magenta/tree/master/Chapter01. The examples and code snippets will be located in this chapter's folder. For this chapter, you should open cd Chapter01 before you start.

We won't be using a lot of Git commands except git clone, which duplicates a code repository to your machine, but if you are unfamiliar with Git and want to learn more, a good place to start is the excellent Git Book (git-scm.com/book/en/v2), which is available in multiple languages.

Check out the following video to see the Code in Action:
`http://bit.ly/20847tW`

Overview of generative art

The term **generative art** has been coined with the advent of the computer, and since the very beginning of computer science, artists and scientists used technology as a tool to produce art. Interestingly, generative art predates computers, because generative systems can be derived by hand.

In this section, we'll provide an overview of generative music by showing you interesting examples from art history going back to the 18th century. This will help you understand the different types of generative music by looking at specific examples and prepare the groundwork for later chapters.

Pen and paper generative music

There's a lot of examples of generative art in the history of mankind. A popular example dates back to the 18th century, where a game called Musikalisches Würfelspiel (German for *musical dice game*) grew popular in Europe. The concept of the game was attributed to Mozart by Nikolaus Simrock in 1792, though it was never confirmed to be his creation.

The players of the game throw a dice and from the result, select one of the predefined 272 musical measures from it. Throwing the dice over and over again allows the players to compose a full minute (the musical genre that is generated by the game) that respects the rules of the genre because it was composed in such a way that the possible arrangements sound pretty.

In the following table and the image that follows, a small part of a musical dice game can be seen. In the table, the y-axis represents the dice throw outcome while the x-axis represents the measure of the score you are currently generating. The players will throw two dices 16 times:

1. On the first throw of two dices, we read the first column. A total of two will output the measure 96 (first row), a total of two will output the measure 32 (second row), and so on.

2. On the second throw of two dices, we read the second column. A total of two will output the measure 22 (first row), a total of three will output the measure 6 (second row), and so on.

After 16 throws, the game will have output 16 measures for the index:

	1	2	3	4	5	6	7	8	9	10	11	12	13	14	15	16
2	96	22	141	41	105	122	11	30	70	121	26	9	112	49	109	14
3	32	6	128	63	146	46	134	81	117	39	126	56	174	18	116	83
4	69	95	158	13	153	55	110	24	66	139	15	132	73	58	145	79
5	40	17	113	85	161	2	159	100	90	176	7	34	67	160	52	170
6	148	74	163	45	80	97	36	107	25	143	64	125	76	136	1	93
7	104	157	27	167	154	68	118	91	138	71	150	29	101	162	23	151
8	152	60	171	53	99	133	21	127	16	155	57	175	43	168	89	172
9	119	84	114	50	140	86	169	94	120	88	48	166	51	115	72	111
10	98	142	42	156	75	129	62	123	65	77	19	82	137	38	149	8
11	3	87	165	61	135	47	147	33	102	4	31	164	144	59	173	78
12	54	130	10	103	28	37	106	5	35	20	108	92	12	124	44	131

The preceding table shows a small part of the whole score, with each measure annotated with an index. For each of the generated 16 indexes, we take the corresponding measure in order, which constitutes our minuet (the minuet is the style that's generated by this game – basically, it's a music score with specific rules).

There are different types of generative properties:

- **Chance or randomness**, which the dice game is a good example of, where the outcome of the generated art is partially or totally defined by chance. Interestingly, adding randomness to a process in art is often seen as *humanizing* the process, since an underlying rigid algorithm might generate something that sounds *artificial*.

- **Algorithmic generation** (or rule-based generation), where the rules of the generation will define its outcome. Good examples of such generation include a cellular automaton, such as the popular Conway's Game of Life, a game where a grid of cells changes each iteration according to predefined rules: each cell might be on or off, and the neighboring cells are updated as a function of the grid's state and rules. The result of such generation is purely deterministic; it has no randomness or probability involved.
- **Stochastic-based generation**, where sequences are derived from the probability of elements. Examples of this include Markov chains, a stochastic model in which for each element of a sequence, the resulting probability of the said event is defined only on the present state of the system. Another good example of stochastic-based generation is machine learning generation, which we'll be looking at throughout this book.

We will use a simple definition of generative art for this book:

> *"Generative art is an artwork partially or completely created by an autonomous system"*.

By now, you should understand that we don't actually need a computer to generate art since the rules of a system can be derived by hand. But using a computer makes it possible to define complex rules and handle tons of data, as we'll see in the following chapters.

Computerized generative music

The first instance of generative art by computer dates back to 1957, where Markov chains were used to generate a score on an electronic computer, the ILLIAC I, by composers Lejaren Hiller and Leonard Issacson. Their paper, *Musical Composition with a High-Speed Digital Computer*, describes the techniques that were used in composing the music. The composition, titled *Illac Suite*, consists of four movements, each exploring a particular technique of music generation, from a rule-based generation of *cantus firmi* to stochastic generation with Markov chain.

Many famous examples of generative composition have followed since, such as Xenakis's *Atrées* in 1962, which explored the idea of stochastic composition; Ebcioglo's composition software named CHORAL, which contained handcrafted rules; and David Cope's software called EMI, which extended the concept to be able to learn from a corpus of scores.

As of today, generative music is everywhere. A lot of tools allow musicians to compose original music based on the generative techniques we described previously. A whole genre and musical community, called **algorave**, originated from those techniques. Stemming from the underground electronic music scene, musicians use generative algorithms and software to produce live dance music on stage, hence the name of the genre. Software such as *TidalCycles* and *Orca* allow the musician to define rules on the fly and let the system generate the music autonomously.

Looking back on those techniques, stochastic models such as Markov chains have been widely used in generative music. It stems from the fact that they are conceptually simple and easy to represent since the model is a transition probability table and can learn from a few examples. The problem with Markov models is that representing a long-term temporal structure is hard since most models will only consider n previous states, where n is small, to define the resulting probability. Let's take a look at what other types of models can be used to generate music.

 In a 2012 paper titled *Ten Questions Concerning Generative Computer Art*, the author talks about the possibility of machine creation, the formalization of human aesthetics, and randomness. More importantly, it defines the limitations of such systems. What can a generative system produce? Can machines only do what they are instructed to?

New techniques with machine learning

Machine learning is important for computer science because it allows complex functions to be modeled without them being explicitly written. Those models are automatically learned from examples, instead of being manually defined. This has a huge implication for arts in general since explicitly writing the rules of a painting or a musical score is inherently difficult.

In recent years, the advent of deep learning has propelled machine learning to new heights in terms of efficiency. Deep learning is especially important for our use case of music generation since using deep learning techniques doesn't require a preprocessing step of *feature extraction*, which is necessary for classical machine learning and hard to do on raw data such as image, text, and – you guessed it – audio. In other words, traditional machine learning algorithms do not work well for music generation. Therefore, all the networks in this book will be deep neural networks.

In this section, we'll learn what advances in deep learning allow for music generation and introduce the concepts we'll be using throughout this book. We'll also look at the different types of musical representations for those algorithms, which is important as it will serve as the groundwork for this book for data in general.

Advances in deep learning

We all know that deep learning has recently become a fast-growing domain in computer science. Not so long ago, no deep learning algorithms could outperform standard techniques. That was before 2012 when, for the first time, a deep learning algorithm, AlexNet, did better in an image classification competition by using a deep neural network trained on GPUs (see the *Further reading* section for the AlexNet paper, one of the most influential papers that was published in computer vision). Neural network techniques are more than 30 years old, but the recent reemergence can be explained by the availability of massive data, efficient computing power, and technical advances.

Most importantly, a deep learning technique is *general*, in the sense that, as opposed to the music generation techniques we've specified previously, a machine learning system is agnostic and can learn from an arbitrary corpus of music. The same system can be used in multiple musical genres, as we'll see during this book when we train an existing model on jazz music in Chapter 6, *Data Preparation for Training*.

Many techniques in deep learning were discovered a long time ago but only find meaningful usage today. Of the technical advances in the field that concern music generation, those are present in Magenta and will be explained later in this book:

- **Recurrent Neural Networks (RNNs)** are interesting for music generation because they allow us to operate over sequences of vectors for the input and output. When using classic neural networks or convolutional networks (which are used in image classification), you are limited to a fixed size input vector to produce a fixed size output vector, which would be very limiting for music processing, but works well for certain types of image processing. The other advantage of RNN is the possibility of producing a new state vector at each pass by combining a function with the previous state vector, which a powerful mean of describing complex behavior and long-term state. We'll be talking about RNNs in Chapter 2, *Generating Drum Sequences with Drums RNN*.

- **Long Short-Term Memory** (**LSTM**) is an RNN with slightly different properties. It solves the problem of vanishing gradients that is present in RNNs and makes it impossible for the network to learn long-term dependencies, even if it theoretically could. The approach of using LSTM in music generation has been presented by Douglas Eck and Jurgen Schmidhuber in 2002 in a paper called *Finding temporal structure in music: Blues improvisation with LSTM recurrent networks*. We'll be talking about LSTM in Chapter 3, *Generating Polyphonic Melodies*.

- **Variational autoencoders** (**VAEs**) are analogous to classical autoencoders, in the sense that their architecture is similar, consisting of an encoder (for the input to a hidden layer), a decoder (for a hidden layer to the output), and a loss function, with the model learning to reconstruct the original input with specific constraints. The usage of VAE in generative models is recent but has shown interesting results. We'll be talking about VAE in Chapter 4, *Latent Space Interpolation with Music VAE*.

- **Generative adversarial networks** (**GANs**) are a class of machine learning systems where two neural networks compete with each other in a game: a generative network generates candidates while a discriminating network evaluates them. We'll be talking about GANs in Chapter 5, *Audio Generation with NSynth and GANSynth*.

Recent deep learning advances have profoundly changed not only music generation but also genre classification, audio transcription, note detection, composition, and more. We won't be talking about these subjects here, but they all share common ground: musical representation.

Representation in music processes

These systems can work with different representations:

- **Symbolic representation**, such as the **MIDI** (**Musical Instrument Digital Interface** (**MIDI**), describes the music using a notation containing the musical notes and timing, but not the sound or timbre of the actual sound. In general, sheet music is a good example of this. A symbolic representation of music has no sound by itself; it has to be played by instruments.

- **Sub-symbolic representation**, such as a raw audio waveform or a spectrogram, describes the actual sound of the music.

Different processes will require a different representation. For example, most speech recognition and synthesis models work with spectrograms, while most of the examples we will see in this book uses MIDI to generate music scores. Processes that integrate both representations are rare, but an example of this could be a score transcription that takes an audio file and translate it into MIDI or other symbolic representations.

Representing music with MIDI

There are other symbolic representations than MIDI, such as MusicXML and AbcNotation, but MIDI is by far the most common representation. The MIDI specification also doubles down as a protocol since it is used to carry note messages that can be used in real-time performance as well as control messages.

Let's consider some parts of a MIDI message that will be useful for this book:

- **Channel [0-15]**: This indicates the track that the message is sent on
- **Note number [0-127]**: This indicates the pitch of the note
- **Velocity [0-127]**: This indicates the volume of the note

To represent a musical note in MIDI, you have to send two different message types with proper timing: a Note On event, followed by a Note Off event. This implicitly defines the **length** of the note, which is not present in the MIDI message. This is important because MIDI was defined with live performance in mind, so using two messages – one for a keypress and another for a key release – makes sense.

From a data perspective, we'll need either need to convert MIDI notes into a format that has the note length encoded in it or keep a note on and note off approach, depending on what we're trying to do. For each model in Magenta, we'll see how the MIDI notes are encoded.

The following image shows a MIDI representation of a generated drum file, shown as a plot of time and pitch. Each MIDI note is represented by a rectangle. Because of the nature of percussion data, all the notes have the same length ("note on" followed by "note off" messages), but in general, that could vary. A drum file, by essence, is polyphonic, meaning that multiple notes can be played at the same time. We'll be talking about monophony and polyphony in the upcoming chapters.

Note that the abscissa is expressed in seconds, but it is also common to note it with bars or measures. The MIDI channel is absent from this diagram:

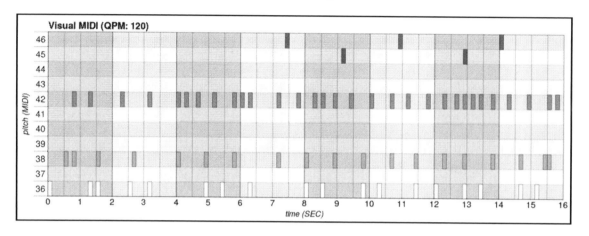

The script for plotting a generated MIDI file can be found in the GitHub code for this chapter in the `Chapter01/provided` folder. The script is called `midi2plot.py`.

In the case of music generation, the majority of current deep learning systems use symbolic notation. This is also the case with Magenta. There are a couple of reasons for this:

- It is easier to represent the essence of music in terms of composition and harmony with symbolic data.
- Processing those two types of representations by using a deep learning network is similar, so choosing between both boils down to whichever is faster and more convenient. A good example of this is that the WaveNet audio generation network also has a MIDI implementation, known as the MidiNet symbolic generation network.

We'll see that the MIDI format is not directly used by Magenta, but converted into and from `NoteSequence`, a **Protocol Buffers (Protobuf)** implementation of the musical structure that is then used by TensorFlow. This is hidden from the end user since the input and output data is always MIDI. The `NoteSequence` implementation is useful because it implements a data format that can be used by the models for training. For example, instead of using two messages to define a note's length, a `Note` in a `NoteSequence` has a length attribute. We'll be explaining the `NoteSequence` implementation as we go along.

Representing music as a waveform

An audio waveform is a graph displaying amplitude changes over time. Zoomed out, a waveform looks rather simple and smooth, but zoomed in, we can see tiny variations – it is those variations that represent the sound.

To illustrate how a waveform works, imagine a speaker cone that's is at rest when the amplitude is at 0. If the amplitude moves to a negative value of 1, for example, then the speaker moves backward a little bit, or forward in the case of a positive value. For each amplitude variation, the speaker will move, making the air move, thus making your eardrums move.

The bigger the amplitude is in the waveform, the more the speaker cone moves in terms of distance, and the louder the sound. This is expressed in **decibel (dB)**, a measure of sound pressure.

The faster the movement, the higher the pitch. This is expressed in **hertz (Hz)**.

In the following image, we can see the MIDI file from the previous section played by instruments to make a WAV recording. The instrument that's being used is a 1982 Roland TR-808 drum sample pack. You can visually match some instruments, such as double the Conga Mid (MIDI note 48) at around 4.5 seconds. In the upper right corner, you can see a zoom of the waveform at 100th of a second to show the actual amplitude change:

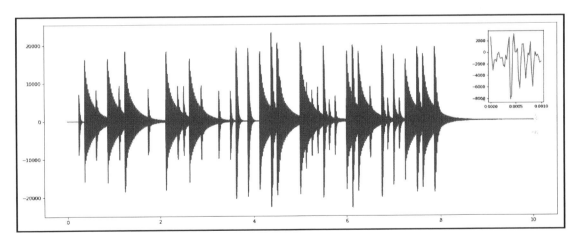

The script for plotting a WAV file can be found in the GitHub code for this chapter in the `Chapter01/provided` folder. The script is called `wav2plot.py`.

In machine learning, using a raw audio waveform used to be uncommon as a data source since the computational load is bigger than other transformed representations, both in terms of memory and processing. But recent advances in the field, such as WaveNet models, makes it on par with other methods of representing audio, such as spectrograms, which were historically more popular for machine learning algorithms, especially for speech recognition and synthesis.

Bear in mind that training on audio is really cost-intensive because raw audio is a dense medium. Basically, a waveform is a digital recreation of a dynamic voltage over time. Simply put, a process called **Pulse Code Modulation** (**PCM**) assigns a bit value to each sample at the sampling rate you are running. The sampling rate for recording purposes is pretty standard: 44,100 Hz, which is called the Nyquist Frequency. But you don't always need a 44,100 Hz sample rate; for example, 16,000 Hz is more than enough to cover human speech frequencies. At that frequency, the first second of audio is represented by 16,000 samples.

If you want to know more about PCM, the sampling theory for audio, and the Nyquist Frequency, check out the *Further reading* section at the end of this chapter.

This frequency was chosen for a very specific purpose. Thanks to the Nyquist theorem, it allows us to recreate the original audio without a loss of sounds that humans can hear.

 The human ear can hear sounds up to 20,000 Hz, so you need 40,000 Hz to represent it in a waveform since you need a negative value and a positive value to make a sound (see the explanation at the beginning of this subsection). Then, you can add 4,100 Hz for rounding errors on very low and very high frequencies to make 44,100 Hz.

This is a good example of a sampled (discrete) representation that can be reversed to its original continuous representation because the pitch spectrum the ear can hear is limited.

We'll look at audio representation in more detail in Chapter 5, *Audio Generation with NSynth and GANSynth*, since we are going to be using NSynth, a Wavenet model, to generate audio samples.

Representing music with a spectrogram

Historically, spectrograms have been a popular form of handling audio for machine learning, for two reasons – it is compact and extracting features from it is easier. To explain this, imagine the raw audio stream of the example from the previous section and cut it into chunks of 1/50th of a second (20 milliseconds) for processing. Now, you have chunks of 882 samples that are hard to represent; it is a mixed bag of amplitudes that don't really represent anything.

A spectrogram is the result of doing a Fourier transform on the audio stream. A Fourier transform will decompose a signal (a function of time) into its constituent frequencies. For an audio signal, this gives us the intensity of a frequency band, with a band being a small split of the whole spectrum, for example, 50 Hz. After applying a Fourier transform on our previous example and taking sample 1 of the 882 samples, we'll end up with the intensity for each frequency band:

- *[0 Hz - 50 Hz]: a_1*
- *[50 Hz - 100 Hz]: a_2*
- *...*
- *[22000 Hz - 22050 Hz:]: a_n*

You'll end up with intensity *[a_1, a_2, ..., a_n]* for each band of 50 Hz up to 22,050, which is the y-axis, with an assigned color spectrum for smaller to bigger intensities. Repeating that for each 20 ms on the x-axis until the whole audio is covered gives you a spectrogram. What is interesting in a spectrogram is that you can actually see the content of the music. If a C major chord is played, you'll see C, E, and G emerge in the spectrogram at their corresponding frequency.

The following spectrogram has been generated from the waveform of the previous section. From this, you can clearly see the frequencies that are being played by the TR 808 from the given MIDI file. You should be able to visually match the waveform from the previous section with the spectrogram:

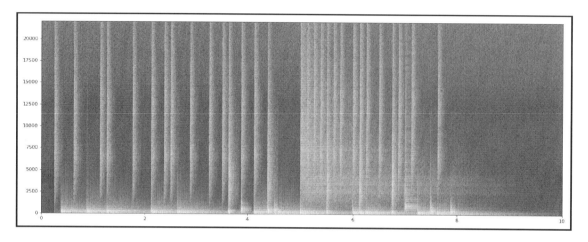

 The script for plotting the spectrogram of a WAV file can be in the GitHub code for this chapter in the `Chapter01/provided` folder. The script is called `wav2spectrogram.py`.

Spectrograms are mainly used in speech recognition. They are also used in speech synthesis: first, a model is trained on spectrograms aligned with text, and from there, the model will be able to produce a spectrogram that corresponds to a given text. The Griffin-Lim algorithm is used to recover an audio signal from a spectrogram.

We won't be using spectrograms in this book, but knowing how they work and what they are used for is important since they are used in many applications.

 Fun fact: musicians have been known to hide images in music that are visible when looking at the audio's spectrogram. A famous example is the Aphex Twin's *Windowlicker* album, where he embedded his grinning face on the second track.

So far, we have learned which deep learning technical advances are important in music generation and learned about music representation in those algorithms. These two topics are important because we'll be looking at them throughout this book.

In the next section, we'll introduce Magenta, where you'll see much of this section's content come into play.

Google's Magenta and TensorFlow in music generation

Since its launch, TensorFlow has been important for the data scientist community for being *An Open Source Machine Learning Framework for Everyone*. Magenta, which is based on TensorFlow, can be seen the same way: even if it's using state of the art machine learning techniques, it can still be used by anyone. Musicians and computer scientists alike can install it and generate new music in no time.

In this section, we'll look at the content of Magenta by introducing what it can and cannot do and refer to the chapters that explain the content in more depth.

Creating a music generation system

Magenta is a framework for art generation, but also for attention, storytelling, and the evaluation of generative music. As the book advances, we'll come to see and understand how those elements are crucial for pleasing music generation.

Evaluating and interpreting generative models is inherently hard, especially for audio. A common criterion in machine learning is the average log-likelihood, which calculates how much the generated samples deviate from the training data, which might give you the proximity of two elements, but not the musicality of the generated one.

Even if the progress in GANs is promising in such evaluations, we are often left with only our ears to evaluate. We can also imagine a Turing test for a music piece: a composition is played to an audience that has to decide whether the piece was generated by a computer.

We'll be using Magenta for two different purposes, assisting and autonomous music creation:

- **Assisting music systems** helps with the process of composing music. Examples of this would be the Magenta interface, `magenta_midi.py`, where the musician can enter a MIDI sequence and Magenta will answer with a generated sequence that's inspired by the provided one. These types of systems can be used alongside traditional systems to compose music and get new inspirations. We'll be talking about this in `Chapter 9`, *Making Magenta Interact with Music Applications*, where Magenta Studio can be integrated into a traditional music production tool.
- **Autonomous music systems** continuously produce music without the input of an operator. At the end of this book, you'll have all the tools you'll need to build an autonomous music generation system consisting of the various building blocks of Magenta.

Looking at Magenta's content

Remembering what we saw in the previous section, there are many ways of representing music: symbolic data, spectrogram data, and raw audio data. Magenta works mainly with symbolic data, meaning we'll mainly work on the underlying score in music instead of working directly with audio. Let's look into Magenta's content, model by model.

Differentiating models, configurations, and pre-trained models

In Magenta and in this book, the term **model** refers to a specific deep neural network that is specific for one task. For example, the Drums RNN model is an LSTM network with attention configuration, while the MusicVAE model is a variational autoencoder network. The Melody RNN model is also an LSTM network but is geared toward generating melodies instead of percussion patterns.

Each model has different **configurations** that will change how the data is encoded for the network, as well as how the network is configured. For example, the Drums RNN model has a `one_drum` configuration, which encodes the sequence to a single class, as well as a `drum_kit` configuration, which maps the sequence to nine drum instruments and also configures the attention length to 32.

Finally, each configuration comes with one or more **pre-trained models**. For example, Magenta provides a pre-trained Drums RNN `drum_kit` model, as well as multiple pre-trained MusicVAE `cat-drums_2bar_small` models.

We'll be using this terminology throughout this book. For the first few chapters, we'll be using the Magenta pre-trained models, since they are already quite powerful. After, we'll create our own configurations and train our own models.

Generating and stylizing images

Image generation and stylization can be achieved in Magenta with the *Sketch RNN* and *Style Transfer* models, respectively. Sketch-RNN is a **Sequence-to-Sequence (Seq2Seq)** variational autoencoder.

Seq2Seq models are used to convert sequences from one domain into another domain (for example, to translate a sentence in English to a sentence in French) that do not necessarily have the same length, which is not possible for a traditional model structure. The network will encode the input sequence into a vector, called a latent vector, from which a decoder will try to reproduce the input sequence as closely as possible.

Image processing is not part of this book, but we'll see the usage of latent space in `Chapter 4`, *Latent Space Interpolation with MusicVAE*, when we use the MusicVAE model. If you are interested in the SketchRNN model, see the *Further reading* section for more information.

Generating audio

Audio generation in Magenta is done with the *NSynth*, a WaveNet-based autoencoder, and *GANSynth* models. What's interesting about WaveNet is that it is a convolutional architecture, prevalent in image applications, but seldom used in music applications, in favor of recurrent networks. **Convolutional neural networks (CNNs)** are mainly defined by a convolution stage, in which a filter is slid through the image, computing a feature map of the image. Different filter matrices can be used to detect different features, such as edges or curves, which are useful for image classification.

We'll see the usage of these models in `Chapter 5`, *Audio Generation with NSynth and GANSynth*.

Generating, interpolating, and transforming score

Score generation is the main part of Magenta and can be split into different categories representing the different parts of a musical score:

- **Rhythms generation**: This can be done with the "Drums RNN" model, an RNN network that applies language modeling using an LSTM. Drum tracks are polyphonic by definition because multiple drums can be hit simultaneously. This model will be presented in Chapter 2, *Generating Drum Sequences with Drums RNN*.

- **Melody generation**: Also known as monophonic generation, this can be done with the "Melody RNN" and "Improv RNN" models, which also implement the use of attention, allowing the models to learn longer dependencies. These models will be presented in Chapter 3, *Generating Polyphonic Melodies*.

- **Polyphonic generation**: This can be done with the *Polyphony RNN* and *Performance RNN* models, where the latter also implements expressive timing (sometimes called groove, where the notes don't start and stop exactly in the grid, giving it a human fell) and dynamics (or velocity). These models will be presented in Chapter 3, *Generating Polyphonic Melodies*.

- **Interpolation**: This can be done with the MusicVAE model, a variational autoencoder that learns the latent space of a musical sequence and can interpolate between existing sequences. This model will be presented in Chapter 4, *Latent Space Interpolation with Music VAE*.

- **Transformation**: This can be done with the *GrooVAE* model, a variant of the MusicVAE model that will add groove to an existing drum performance. This model will be presented in Chapter 4, *Latent Space Interpolation with Music VAE*.

Installing Magenta and Magenta for GPU

Installing a machine learning framework is not an easy task and often a pretty big entry barrier, mainly because Python is an infamous language concerning dependency management. We'll try to make this easy by providing clear instructions and versions. We'll be covering installation instructions for Linux, Windows, and macOS since the commands and versions are mostly the same.

In this section, we'll be installing Magenta and Magenta for GPU, if you have the proper hardware. Installing Magenta for a GPU takes a bit more work but is necessary if you want to train a model, which we will do in Chapter 7, *Training Magenta Models*. If you are unsure about doing this, you can skip this section and come back to it later. We'll also provide a solution if you don't have a GPU but still want to do the chapter by using cloud-based solutions.

TensorFlow will be installed through Magenta's dependencies. We'll also look at optional but useful programs that can help you visualize and play audio content.

Choosing the right versions

At the time of writing, newer versions of Python and CUDA are available, but we are using the following versions because of incompatibilities with TensorFlow and TensorFlow GPU. We'll be using Magenta 1.1.7 since it is the stable version of Magenta at the time of writing. You can try using a newer version for the examples and roll back if it doesn't work:

- Magenta: 1.1.7
- TensorFlow: 1.15.0 (this version is installed automatically when installing Magenta)

This means that we need to use exactly the following versions for TensorFlow to work:

- Python: 3.6.x
- CUDA libraries: 10.0
- CudRNN: 7.6.x (the latest version is OK)

Let's look at how to install those versions.

Creating a Python environment with Conda

Throughout this book, we'll be using a Python environment, a standalone and separate installation of Python you can switch to when you are working with a specific piece of software, such as when you're working on this book or another piece of software. This also ensures that the system-wide installation remains safe.

There are many Python environment managers available, but we'll use Conda here, which we'll come installed with a standalone Python installation called **Miniconda**. You can think of Miniconda as a program with a packaged Python, some dependencies, and Conda.

To install Miniconda, go to `docs.conda.io/en/latest/miniconda.html`, download the installer for your platform, choose Python 3.7 as the Python version (this is NOT the Python version Magenta will run in), and either 32-bit or 64-bit (you probably have the latter).

For Windows, follow these steps:

1. Double-click the installer. Then, follow the prompts and leave the defaults as they are.
2. Add `conda` to PATH by going to `Control Panel > System > Advanced system settings > Environment Variables... > Path > Edit... > New` and add the `condabin` folder to the Miniconda installation folder (which should be `C:\Users\Packt\Miniconda3\condabin`).

> If you are facing issues installing Miniconda on Windows, you can also use **Anaconda**, which is the same software but packaged with more tools.
>
> First, download Anaconda from `www.anaconda.com/distribution`, double-click the installer, follow the prompts, and leave the defaults as they are.
>
> Then, launch **Anaconda Prompt** from the Start menu instead of the **Command Prompt**, which will launch a new command-line window with Conda initialized.

For macOS and Linux, open a Terminal where you downloaded the file as follow these steps:

1. Make the script executable for your user by replacing `<platform>` with the platform you downloaded:

   ```
   chmod u+x Miniconda3-latest-<platform>
   ```

   - Now, execute the script, which will install the software:

   ```
   ./Miniconda3-latest-<platform>
   ```

Now that Conda has been installed, let's check if it works properly:

1. Open a new Terminal and type in the following:

```
> conda info

         active environment : None
               shell level : 0
           user config file : C:\Users\Packt\.condarc
     populated config files :
             conda version : 4.7.5
       conda-build version : not installed
            python version : 3.7.3.final.0
          virtual packages : __cuda=10.1
          base environment : C:\Users\Packt\Miniconda3   (writable)
   [...]
           envs directories : C:\Users\Packt\Miniconda3\envs
                             C:\Users\Packt\.conda\envs
   C:\Users\Packt\AppData\Local\conda\conda\envs
                  platform : win-64
                user-agent : conda/4.7.5 requests/2.21.0 CPython/3.7.3
   Windows/10 Windows/10.0.18362
             administrator : False
                netrc file : None
              offline mode : False
```

Your output will look different, but the idea is the same.

2. Now, we need to create a new environment for this book. Let's call it "magenta":

```
> conda create --name magenta python=3.6
```

Notice that the Python version is 3.6, as we mentioned at the beginning of this section.

Your new environment with the correct version of Python and some dependencies has been created. You now have three different Python environments, each with a version of Python with its own dependencies :

- **None**: This is the system-wide installation of Python from the system (this might be absent on Windows), and you can switch to it with `conda deactivate`.
- **base**: This is the Miniconda Python installation of Python 3.7 we downloaded, and you can switch to it with `conda activate base`.
- **magenta**: This is our new Python 3.6 installation for this project, and you can switch to it with `conda activate magenta`.

Since we are still in the base environment, we need to activate the "magenta" environment.

3. Use the `activate` flag to change environments:

```
> conda activate magenta
```

From there, your Terminal should prefix the line with "(magenta)", meaning the commands you are executing are being executed in this specific environment.

4. Let's check our Python version:

```
> python --version
Python 3.6.9 :: Anaconda, Inc.
```

If you have something else here (you should have Python version 3.6.x and Anaconda packaging), stop and make sure you followed the installation instructions properly.

This is just a reminder that you **need Python 3.6.x**. An older version of Python won't be able to run the code in this book because we are using language features from 3.6, and a newer version won't run TensorFlow because it doesn't support 3.7 yet.

Installing prerequisite software

Now that we have a Python environment up and running, you'll need some prerequisite software that will be useful throughout this book. Let's get started:

1. First, we'll need to install `curl`, which is preinstalled on Windows and macOS, but not Linux (at least not in all distributions). On a Debian distribution, use the following command. On other distributions, use your package manager:

   ```
   > sudo apt install curl
   ```

2. Now, we need to install Visual MIDI, the MIDI visualization library we'll use to make the diagrams of our generated scores. While in the Magenta environment, run the following command:

   ```
   > pip install visual_midi
   ```

3. Finally, we'll install the tables modules, which will be useful later to read external datasets stored in H5 databases:

   ```
   > pip install tables
   ```

Installing Magenta

With our environment and the prerequisite software installed, we can now install Magenta version 1.1.7. You can use a more recent version of Magenta, but do this at your own risk: this book's code was written with version 1.1.7, and the Magenta source code has a tendency to change. Let's get started:

1. While in the Magenta environment, run the following command:

   ```
   > pip install magenta==1.1.7
   ```

   If you want to try a more recent version of Magenta, just remove the version information contained in the `pip` command. Then, it will install the latest version. If you have problems using a newer version, you can reinstall version 1.1.7 using the `pip install 'magenta==1.1.7' --force-reinstall` command.

2. Then, test the installation by importing Magenta into a Python shell and printing the version:

   ```
   > python -c "import magenta; print(magenta.__version__)"
   ```

Installing Magenta for GPU (optional)

Now that we have installed Magenta, we'll install Magenta for GPU, which is required for Magenta to execute on the GPU. This is optional if you don't have a GPU, are not planning to train any models, or want to use a cloud-based solution for training. Before continuing, we need to make sure our GPU is CUDA enabled with a compute capability greater than 3.0 by checking out NVIDIA's website: `developer.nvidia.com/cuda-gpus`.

On Windows, you need to download and install the Visual Studio Community IDE from `visualstudio.microsoft.com`, which should install all the required dependencies for us.

Then, for all platforms, follow these steps:

1. Download the **CUDA Toolkit** from `developer.nvidia.com/cuda-10.0-download-archive` and launch the installation wizard using any of the provided installation methods.

   During the CUDA driver's installation, you might get a message saying that "Your display drivers are more recent than the ones provided with this installation". This is normal since this CUDA version is not the latest. You can keep your current display drivers by selecting **CUDA drivers only**.

2. Now that CUDA has been installed, you might have to restart your computer to load the NVIDIA driver. You can test your installation by using the following command:

   ```
   > nvcc --version
   nvcc: NVIDIA (R) Cuda compiler driver
   Copyright (c) 2005-2018 NVIDIA Corporation
   Built on Sat_Aug_25_21:08:04_Central_Daylight_Time_2018
   Cuda compilation tools, release 10.0, V10.0.130
   ```

3. Now, we need to install the **cuDNN library**, which is a toolkit for executing deep learning commands on the GPU with the CUDA driver. You should be able to use the most recent cuDNN version from `developer.nvidia.com/rdp/cudnn-download` for CUDA 10.0. Choose `Download cuDNN v7.6.x (...), for CUDA 10.0`.
   Make sure you use the `cuDNN Library for Platform` link so that we have the full library archive to work with (do not download the `.deb` file, for example).

4. Once downloaded, we'll have to copy the files from the proper location; see the following commands for each platform:
   - **Linux:** `docs.nvidia.com/deeplearning/sdk/cudnn-install/index.html#installlinux-tar`
   - **macOS:** `docs.nvidia.com/deeplearning/sdk/cudnn-install/index.html#install-mac`
   - **Windows:** `docs.nvidia.com/deeplearning/sdk/cudnn-install/index.html#installwindows`

5. Now, we are ready to install Magenta for GPU:

```
> pip install magenta-gpu===1.1.7
```

Check out the tip in the *Generating a basic MIDI file* section to verify TensorFlow is working properly with your GPU.

Installing the music software and synthesizers

During the course of this book, we'll be handling MIDI and audio files. Handling the MIDI files requires specific software that you should install now since you'll need it for the entirety of this book.

Installing the FluidSynth software synthesizer

A software synthesizer is a piece of software that will play incoming MIDI notes or MIDI files with virtual instruments from sound banks (called SoundFont) or by synthesizing audio using waveforms. We will need a software synthesizer to play the notes that are generated by our models.

For this book, we'll be using FluidSynth, a powerful and cross-platform software synth available on the command line. We'll go through the installation procedure for each platform in this section.

Installing SoundFont

The SoundFont installation is the same for all platforms. We'll download and keep the SoundFont file in an easy-access location since we'll need it throughout this book. Follow these steps:

1. Download SoundFont at `ftp.debian.org/debian/pool/main/f/fluid-soundfont/fluid-soundfont_3.1.orig.tar.gz`.

2. Extract the `.tar.gz` file.

3. Copy the `FluidR3_GM.sf2` file to an easy-access location.

Installing FluidSynth

Unfortunately, for **Windows**, binaries are not maintained by the FluidSynth core team. Instead of building from the source, we'll need to fetch the binaries from a GitHub project (the versions might be a bit behind the release schedule, though). Follow these steps:

1. Download the zip at `github.com/JoshuaPrzyborowski/FluidSynth-Windows-Builds/archive/master.zip`.

2. Unzip the file and navigate to the `bin64` folder.

3. Copy the `fluidsynth-2.0.x` folder (containing the latest version of FluidSynth) to an easy-access location.

4. Copy the content of the `fluidsynth-required-dlls` file to `C:\Windows\System32`.

5. Add FluidSynth to `PATH` by going to `Control Panel > System > Advanced system settings > Environment Variables... > Path > Edit... > New` and add the `bin` folder from the copied folder from *step 3*.

For **Linux**, most distributions maintain a FluidSynth package. Here, we're providing the installation instruction for Debian-based distributions. Refer to your package manager for other distributions. In a Terminal, use the `sudo apt install fluidsynth` command to download FluidSynth.

For **MacOS X**, we'll be using Homebrew to install FluidSynth. Before starting, make sure you have the latest Homebrew version. In a Terminal, use the `brew install fluidsynth` command to download FluidSynth.

Testing your installation

Now, you can test your FluidSynth installation (do this by replacing `PATH_SF2` with the path to the SoundFont we installed previously):

- Linux: `fluidsynth -a pulseaudio -g 1 -n -i PATH_TO_SF2`
- macOS: `fluidsynth -a coreaudio -g 1 -n -i PATH_TO_SF2`
- Windows: `fluidsynth -g 1 -n -i PATH_TO_SF2`

You should see an output similar to the following, without any errors:

```
FluidSynth runtime version 2.0.3
Copyright (C) 2000-2019 Peter Hanappe and others.
Distributed under the LGPL license.
SoundFont(R) is a registered trademark of E-mu Systems, Inc
```

Using a hardware synthesizer (optional)

Instead of using a software synthesizer, you could use a hardware synthesizer to listen to your generated MIDI files. We'll look at this in more detail in Chapter 9, *Making Magenta Interact with Music Applications*, but you can already plug the synthesizer into your computer via USB; the device should register as a new input MIDI port. This port can be used by Magenta to send incoming MIDI notes.

Installing Audacity as a digital audio editor (optional)

We won't be handling audio until Chapter 5, *Audio Generation with NSynth and GANSynth*, so you can wait until that chapter to install Audacity. Audacity is an amazing open source cross-platform (Windows, Linux, macOS) software for editor audio clips. It doesn't have the functionality of a Digital Audio Workstation (see the *Installing a Digital Audio Workstation* section for more on this), but it is easy to use and powerful.

Audacity can be used to easily record audio, cut and split audio clips, add simple effects, do simple equalization, and export various formats:

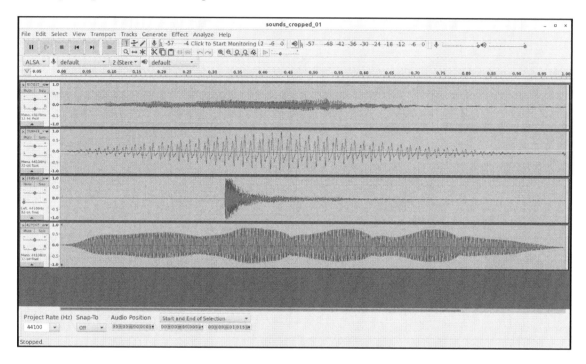

We'll be explaining how to use Audacity in `Chapter 5`, *Audio Generation with NSynth and GANSynth*.

Installing MuseScore for sheet music (optional)

Throughout this book, we'll be working with sheet music a lot, especially MIDI. We'll have command-line utilities to generate still images representing the score, but it is useful to see and edit the sheet music in a GUI, as well as listen to them with digital instruments. Take note that MuseScore cannot play live MIDI, so it is different from a software synthesizer. It also doesn't work well with expressive timing (where the notes do not fall on the beginning and end steps). We'll make note of when not to use MuseScore in the next chapter.

MuseScore is a good and free notation software available at `musescore.org` and works on all platforms. You can install it now if you want, or wait until later when you need it.

MuseScore also doubles down as a collaborative sheet music database at `musescore.com`, which we'll use throughout this book:

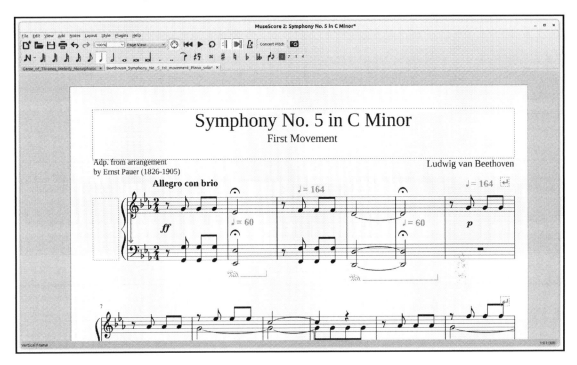

Installing a Digital Audio Workstation (optional)

Installing a DAW is not necessary for this book, except for `Chapter 9`, *Making Magenta Interact with Music Applications*. Such software comes in various forms and complexity and is important in music production in general since it can handle all the necessities of music production, such as audio and MIDI handling, composition, effects, mastering, VSTs, and so on.

Ardour (`ardour.org`) is the only open source and cross-platform DAW available and requires you to pay a small fee for a pre-built version of the software. Depending on your platform, you might want to try different DAWs. On Linux, you can go with Ardour. On macOS and Windows, you can use Ableton Live, a well-established DAW. We won't be recommending any specific software for this part, so you can go with whatever you are used to. In `Chapter 9`, *Making Magenta Interact with Music Applications*, we'll go into more detail by giving specific examples for specific DAWs, so you can wait until then to install a new one.

Installing the code editing software

In this section, we'll recommend optional software regarding code editing. While not mandatory, it might help considerably to use them, especially for newcomers, for whom plain code editing software can be daunting.

Installing Jupyter Notebook (optional)

Notebooks are a great way of sharing code that contains text, explanations, figures, and other rich content. It is used extensively in the data science community because it can store and display the result of long-running operations, while also providing a dynamic runtime to edit and execute the content in.

The code for this book is available on GitHub as plain Python code, but also in the form of Jupyter Notebooks. Each chapter will have its own notebook that serves as an example.

To install Jupyter and launch your first notebook, follow these steps:

1. While in the Magenta environment, execute the following command:

   ```
   > pip install jupyter
   ```

2. Now, we can start the Jupyter server by executing the following command (also while in the Magenta environment):

   ```
   > jupyter notebook
   ```

   The Jupyter interface will be shown in a web browser. The previous command should have launched your default browser. If not, use the URL in the output of the command to open it.

3. Once in the notebook UI, you should see your disk content. Navigate to the code for this book and load the notebook from `Chapter01/notebook.ipynb`.

4. Make sure the selected kernel is **Python 3**. This kernel corresponds to the Python interpreter that's been installed in your Magenta environment.

5. Run the code blocks using the **Run** button for each cell. This will make sure that Jupyter executes in a proper environment by printing the TensorFlow and Magenta versions.

This is what the notebook should look like:

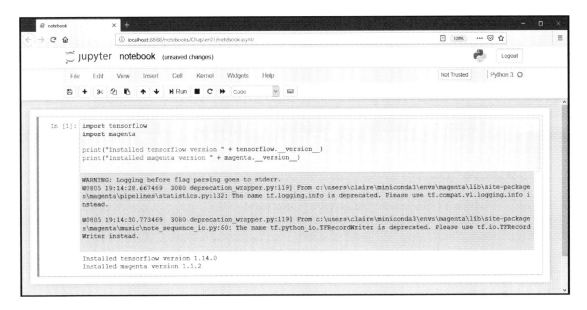

Installing and configuring an IDE (optional)

The usage of an **Integrated Development Environment** (**IDE**) is not necessary for this book since all the examples run from the command line. However, an IDE is a good tool to use since it provides autocompletion, integrated development tools, refactoring options, and more. It is also really useful for debugging since you can step into the code directly.

A good IDE for this book is JetBrains's PyCharm (`www.jetbrains.com/pycharm`), a Python IDE with a community (open source) edition that provides everything you need.

Whether you use PyCharm or another IDE, you'll need to change Python interpreter to the one we installed previously. This is the equivalent of activating our Magenta environment using Conda. In the project settings in the IDE, find the Python interpreter settings and change it to the installation path of our environment.

If you don't remember its location, use the following commands:

```
> conda activate magenta
> conda info
...
    active env location : C:\Users\Packt\Miniconda3\envs\magenta
...
```

On Windows, the Python interpreter is in the root folder, while on Linux or macOS, it is in the `bin` directory under it.

Generating a basic MIDI file

Magenta comes with multiple command-line scripts (installed in the `bin` folder of your Magenta environment). Basically, each model has its own console script for dataset preparation, model training, and generation. Let's take a look:

1. While in the Magenta environment, download the Drums RNN pre-trained model, `drum_kit_rnn`:

    ```
    > curl --output "drum_kit_rnn.mag"
    "http://download.magenta.tensorflow.org/models/drum_kit_rnn.mag"
    ```

2. Then, use the following command to generate your first few MIDI files:

    ```
    > drums_rnn_generate --bundle_file="drum_kit_rnn.mag"
    ```

    By default, the preceding command generates the files in `/tmp/drums_rnn/generated` (on Windows `C:\tmp\drums_rnn\generated`). You should see 10 new MIDI files, along with timestamps and a generation index.

    If you are using a GPU, you can verify if TensorFlow is using it properly by searching for "Created TensorFlow device ... -> **physical GPU** (name: ..., compute capability: ...)" in the output of the script. If it's not there, this means it is executing on your CPU.

    You can also check your GPU usage while Magenta is executing, which should go up if Magenta is using the GPU properly.

3. Finally, to listen to the generated MIDI, use your software synthesizer or MuseScore. For the software synth, refer to the following command, depending on your platform, and replace `PATH_TO_SF2` and `PATH_TO_MIDI` with the proper values:
    *   Linux: `fluidsynth -a pulseaudio -g 1 -n -i PATH_TO_SF2 PATH_TO_MIDI`
    *   macOS: `fluidsynth -a coreaudio -g 1 -n -i PATH_TO_SF2 PATH_TO_MIDI`
    *   Windows: `fluidsynth -g 1 -n -i PATH_TO_SF2 PATH_TO_MIDI`

Congratulations! You have generated your first musical score using a machine learning model! You'll learn how to generate much more throughout this book.

Summary

This chapter is important because it introduces the basic concepts of music generation with machine learning, all of which we'll build upon throughout this book.

In this chapter, we learned what generative music is and that its origins predate even the advent of computers. By looking at specific examples, we saw different types of generative music: random, algorithmic, and stochastic.

We also learned how machine learning is rapidly transforming how we generate music. By introducing music representation and various processes, we learned about MIDI, waveforms, and spectrograms, as well as various neural network architectures we'll get to look at throughout this book.

Finally, we saw an overview of what we can do with Magenta in terms of generating and processing image, audio, and score. By doing that, we introduced the primary models we'll be using throughout this book; that is, Drums RNN, Melody RNN, MusicVAE, NSynth, and others.

You also installed your development environment for this book and generated your first musical score. Now, we're ready to go!

The next chapter will delve deeper into some of the concepts we introduced in this chapter. We'll explain what an RNN is and why it is important for music generation. Then, we'll use the Drums RNN model on the command line and in Python while explaining its inputs and outputs. We'll finish by creating the first building block of our autonomous music generating system.

Questions

1. On what generative principle does the *musical dice game* rely upon?
2. What stochastic-based generation technique was used in the first computerized generative piece of music, *Illiac Suite*?
3. What is the name of the music genre where a live coder implements generative music on the scene?

4. What model structure is important for tracking temporally distant events in a musical score?

5. What is the difference between autonomous and assisting music systems?

6. What are examples of symbolic and sub-symbolic representations?

7. How is a note represented in MIDI?

8. What frequency range can be represented without loss at a sample rate of 96 kHz? Is it better for listening to audio?

9. In a spectrogram, a block of 1 second of intense color at 440 Hz is shown. What is being played?

10. What different parts of a musical score can be generated with Magenta?

Further reading

- **Ten Questions Concerning Generative Computer Art:** An interesting paper (2012) on generative computer art (users.monash.edu/~jonmc/research/Papers/TenQuestionsLJ-Preprint.pdf).

- **Pulse Code Modulation (PCM):** A short introduction to PCM (www.technologyuk.net/telecommunications/telecom-principles/pulse-code-modulation.shtml).

- **Making Music with Computers:** A good introduction to the sampling theory and the Nyquist frequency (legacy.earlham.edu/~tobeyfo/musictechnology/4_SamplingTheory.html).

- **SketchRNN model released in Magenta:** A blog post from the Magenta team on SketchRNN, with a link to the corresponding paper (magenta.tensorflow.org/sketch_rnn).

- **Creation by refinement: a creativity paradigm for gradient descent learning networks:** An early paper (1988) on generating content using a gradient-descent search (ieeexplore.ieee.org/document/23933).

- **A First Look at Music Composition using LSTM Recurrent Neural Networks:** An important paper (2002) on generating music using LSTM (www.semanticscholar.org/paper/A-First-Look-at-Music-Composition-using-LSTM-Neural-Eck-Schmidhuber/3b70fbcd6c0fdc7697c93d0c3fb845066cf34487).

- **ImageNet Classification with Deep Convolutional Neural Networks:** The AlexNet paper, one of the most influential papers that was published in computer vision (`papers.nips.cc/paper/4824-imagenet-classification-with-deep-convolutional-neural-networks.pdf`).

- **WaveNet: A Generative Model for Raw Audio:** A paper (2016) on WaveNet (`arxiv.org/abs/1609.03499`).

- **DeepBach: a Steerable Model for Bach Chorales Generation:** A paper (2016) on Bach-like polyphonic music generation (`arxiv.org/abs/1612.01010`).

- **SampleRNN: An Unconditional End-to-End Neural Audio Generation Model:** A paper (2017) on generating audio (`arxiv.org/abs/1612.07837`).

Section 2: Music Generation with Machine Learning

2

This section covers the use of Magenta in generating drum sequences and melodies, interpolating scores, and generating audio. We'll provide you with all the tools required to make a fully generative song.

This section contains the following chapters:

- Chapter 2, *Generating Drum Sequences with the Drums RNN*
- Chapter 3, *Generating Polyphonic Melodies*
- Chapter 4, *Latent Space Interpolation with MusicVAE*
- Chapter 5, *Audio Generation with NSynth and GANSynth*

2
Generating Drum Sequences with the Drums RNN

In this chapter, you'll learn what many consider the foundation of music—percussion. We'll show the importance of **Recurrent Neural Networks (RNNs)** for music generation. You'll then learn how to use the Drums RNN model using a pre-trained drum kit model, by calling it in the command-line window and directly in Python, to generate drum sequences. We'll introduce the different model parameters, including the model's MIDI encoding, and show how to interpret the output of the model.

The following topics will be covered in this chapter:

- The significance of RNNs in music generation
- Using the Drums RNN in the command line
- Using the Drums RNN in Python

Technical requirements

In this chapter, we'll use the following tools:

- The **command line** or **bash** to launch Magenta from the Terminal
- **Python** and its libraries to write music generation code using Magenta
- **Magenta** to generate music in MIDI
- **MuseScore** or **FluidSynth** to listen to the generated MIDI

In Magenta, we'll make the use of the **Drums RNN** model. We'll be explaining this model in depth, but if you feel like you need more information, the model's README in Magenta's source code (`github.com/tensorflow/magenta/tree/master/magenta/models/drums_rnn`) is a good place to start. You can also take a look at Magenta's code on GitHub, which is well documented. We also provide additional content in the last section, *Further reading*.

The code for this chapter is in this book's GitHub repository in the `Chapter02` folder, located at `github.com/PacktPublishing/hands-on-music-generation-with-magenta/tree/master/Chapter02`. For this chapter, you should run `cd Chapter02` in the command-line window before you start.

Check out the following video to see the Code in Action:
`http://bit.ly/37G0mmW`

The significance of RNNs in music generation

Specific neural network architectures are designed for specific problems. It doesn't mean that one architecture is better than another one—it just means it is better at a specific task.

In this section, we'll be looking at our specific problem, generating music, and see why RNNs are well suited for the task. We'll be building our knowledge of neural network architectures for music throughout this book, by introducing specific concepts in each chapter.

For music generation, we are looking at two specific problems that RNNs solve—operating on sequences in terms of input and output and keeping an internal state of past events. Let's have a look at those properties.

Musical score prediction is analogous to generating music. By predicting the next notes from an input sequence, you can iteratively generate a new sequence by choosing a prediction at each iteration. This process is described in the *Understanding the generation algorithm* section in this chapter.

Operating on a sequence of vectors

In many neural net architectures, **input size** and **output size** are fixed. Take a **Convolutional Neural Network (CNN)**, for example. This neural net can be used for image classification, with the input being an array of pixels representing the image and the output the prediction for each element of a set of classes (for example, "cat," "dog," and so on). Notice the input and output are of fixed size.

What is nice about RNNs is that input and output size can be of arbitrary lengths. For a music score prediction network, an input could be an arbitrary length sequence of notes, and the output could be a sequence of predicted notes from that input.

This is possible in an RNN because it works on a **sequence** of vectors. There are many ways of representing RNN types:

- **One-to-one**: This is where there's fixed input and output; an example is image classification.
- **One-to-many**: This is where there's fixed input to sequence output; an example is image captioning, where the network will generate a text based on the image content.
- **Many-to-one**: Here, there's sequence input to fixed output; an example is sentiment analysis, where the network will output a single word (sentiment) describing an input sentence.
- **Many-to-many**: Here, there's sequence input to sequence output; an example is language translation, where the network will output a full sentence in a language from a full sentence in another language.

A classic way of representing an RNN is shown in the following diagram. On the left side of the diagram, you have a compact representation of the network—the hidden layer outputs the feeds into itself. On the right side, you have the detailed representation of the same network—at each step, the hidden layer takes an input and the previous state and produces an output:

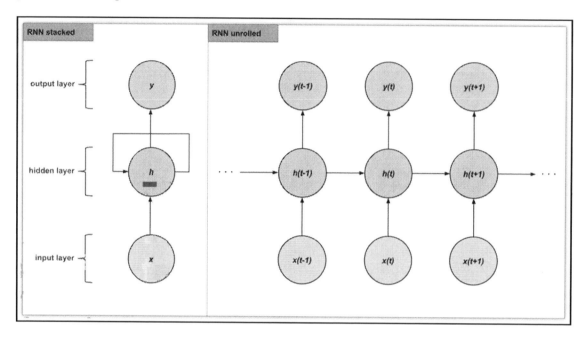

The bottom row of the diagram shows the input vectors, the middle row of the diagram shows the hidden layers, and the upper row of the diagram shows the output layer. This representation shows how well an RNN can represent many-to-many inputs and outputs for the following:

- A sequence of vectors for the input: { ..., x(t - 1), x(t), x(t + 1), ... }
- A sequence of vectors for the output: { ..., y(t - 1), y(t), y(t + 1), ... }

Remember the past to better predict the future

As we saw in the previous section, in RNNs, the input vector is combined with its state vector to produce the output, which is then used to update the state vector for the next step. This is different than feed-forward neural networks such as CNNs, where the network feeds information from the input to the output and only in that direction, meaning the output is a function of only its input, not previous events.

Let's look at how we define a simple RNN. We implement a single operation, the `step` operation, that takes an input vector, `x`, and returns an output vector, `y`. Each time the step operation is called, the RNN needs to update its state, the hidden vector, `h`.

What is important to note here, is that we can **stack** as many RNNs as we want by taking the output of an RNN and feeding it in the next RNN, just like in the previous diagram. For example, we could go `y1 = rnn1.step(x1)`, `y2 = rnn2.step(y1)`, and so on.

When training the RNN, during the forward pass, we need to update the state, calculate the output vector, and update the loss. But how do we update the state? Let's see the steps we need to follow:

1. First, we do the matrix multiplication of the hidden state matrix (`Whh`) with the previous hidden state (`hs[t-1]`), `np.dot(Whh, hs[t-1])`.
2. Then, we sum it with the matrix multiplication of the current input matrix (`Wxh`) and the input vector (`xs[t]`), `np.dot(Wxh, xs[t])`.
3. Finally, we use the `tanh` activation function on the resulting matrix to squash the activations between -1 and 1.

We do that at every step, meaning that, at every step of the training, the network has an **up-to-date** context in regards to the sequence it is handling.

To understand how an RNN handles sequential data, such as a note sequence, let's take the example of an RNN training on broken chords, which are chords broken down as a series of notes. We have the input data "A", "C", "E", and "G", which is encoded as a vector, for example *[1, 0, 0, 0]* for the first note (which corresponds to `x(t - 1)` in the previous diagram), *[0, 1, 0, 0]* for the second note (`x(t)` in the previous diagram), and so on.

During the first step, with the first input vector, the RNN outputs, for example, a confidence of the next note being 0.5 for "A", 1.8 for "C", -2.5 for "E", and 3.1 for "G". Because our training data tells us that the correct next note is "C", we want to increase the confidence score of 1.8, and decrease the other scores. Similarly, for each of the 4 steps (for the 4 input notes), we have a correct note to predict. Remember, at each step, the RNN uses both the hidden vector and the input vector to make a prediction. During backpropagation, the parameters are nudged in the proper direction by a small amount, and by repeating this enough times, we get predictions that match the training data.

During inference, if the network first receives an input of "C", it won't necessarily predict "E" because it hasn't seen "A" yet, which doesn't match the example chord that was used to train the model. The RNN prediction is based on its **recurrent connection**, which keeps track of the context, and doesn't rely on the input alone.

To sample from a trained RNN, we feed a note into the network, which outputs the distribution for the next note. By **sampling the distribution**, we get a probable next note that we can then feed back to the network. We can repeat the process until we have a long enough sequence. This generation process is described in more detail in the following section, *Understanding the generation algorithm*.

During backpropagation, we saw that we update the parameters going backward in the network. Imagine the network is learning a long sequence of notes: how far can the gradients be backpropagated in the network so that the link between a note far in the sequence and a note at the beginning still holds? Well, it turns out that this is a difficult problem for vanilla RNNs. One answer to that is **Long-Short Term Memory** (LSTM) cell, which uses a different mechanism for keeping the current state.

Using the right terminology for RNNs

Now that we understand RNNs, we can say that most RNNs are using LSTM cells. Those RNNs are sometimes called **LSTM networks**, but more often than not, they are just called RNNs. Unfortunately, the two terms are often used interchangeably. In Magenta, all of the RNNs are LSTMs but aren't named as such. This is the case of the Drums RNN model we're looking at in this chapter and all of the models we're going to use in the next chapters.

We'll be explaining LSTMs in `Chapter 3`, *Generating Polyphonic Melodies*. For now, just remember that what we saw in the previous section still holds, but the hidden state update is more complex than what we described.

Using the Drums RNN on the command line

Now that we understand how RNNs make for powerful tools of music generation, we'll use the Drums RNN model to do just that. The pre-trained models in Magenta are a good way of starting music generation straightaway. For the Drums RNN model, we'll be using the `drum_kit` pre-trained bundle, which was trained on thousands of percussion MIDI files.

This section will provide insight into the usage of Magenta on the command line. We'll be primarily using Python code to call Magenta, but using the command line has some advantages:

- It is simple to use and useful for quick use cases.
- It doesn't require writing any code or having any programming knowledge.
- It encapsulates parameters in helpful commands and flags.

In this section, we'll use the Drums RNN model in the command line and learn to configure the generation though flags. We'll explain how the generation algorithm works and look at its parameters and output.

Magenta's command-line utilities

Magenta comes with multiple command-line utilities. These command-line utilities are Python scripts that can be called directly from the command line as console entry points and are installed in your Conda environment when you install Magenta (look in the `bin` folder of your Magenta environment or the `scripts` folder if using Windows). The complete list of command-line utilities is located in Magenta's source code, in `setup.py`, under `CONSOLE_SCRIPTS`.

> You can always checkout Magenta's source code and have a look at it. It might seem intimidating at first, but the source code is well documented and provides invaluable insight into the inner workings of the software. Using Git, execute `git clone` `https://github.com/tensorflow/magenta` in a Terminal and then open the repository in your favorite IDE. Another advantage of having the source code is to have a look at certain files that are not packaged with the app.

For the Drums RNN model that we are going to use, we have three command-line utilities (like much of the models):

- `drums_rnn_create_dataset` will help to create a dataset for the training command. We'll be looking into this command in Chapter 6, *Data Preparation for Training*.
- `drums_rnn_generate` will be used in this chapter to generate a musical score.
- `drums_rnn_train` will train the model on an input dataset. We'll be looking into this command in Chapter 7, *Training Magenta Models*.

Generating a simple drum sequence

In the previous chapter, we generated a simple MIDI file to test our installation. We'll take that example and change it a bit.

Before starting, go back on a terminal to the main book's folder and then change directory to Chapter02. Make sure you are in your Magenta environment. If not, use conda activate magenta to do so:

1. First, we download the Drums RNN bundle file, drum_kit_rnn.mag, in the bundles folder. You only need to do this once:

   ```
   > curl --output bundles/drum_kit_rnn.mag
   http://download.magenta.tensorflow.org/models/drum_kit_rnn.mag
   ```

   A bundle file is a file containing the model checkpoint and metadata. This is a pre-trained model that contains the weights from the training phase, which will be used to initialize the RNN network. We'll be seeing this format in detail in Chapter 7, *Training Magenta Models*.

2. Then, we can use the bundle to generate MIDI files in the output directory with --output-dir:

   ```
   > drums_rnn_generate --bundle_file=bundles/drum_kit_rnn.mag --output_dir output
   ```

3. Open one of the generated files in the output folder in MuseScore or Visual MIDI. For the latter, you need to convert the MIDI file into a plot rendered in an HTML file, which you can then open in a browser. To convert the MIDI file into a plot, use the following command:

   ```
   # Replace GENERATED by the name of the file
   > visual_midi "output/GENERATED.mid"
   ```

4. Then, open the output/GENERATED.html HTML file, which contains the plot:

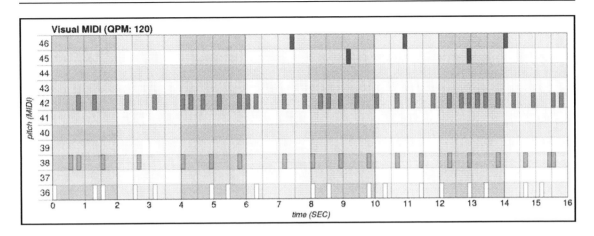

5. To listen to the generated MIDI, use your software synthesizer or MuseScore. For the software synthesizer, refer to the following command depending on your platform and replace PATH_TO_SF2 and PATH_TO_MIDI with the proper values:
    - **Linux:** `fluidsynth -a pulseaudio -g 1 -n -i PATH_TO_SF2 PATH_TO_MIDI`
    - **macOS:** `fluidsynth -a coreaudio -g 1 -n -i PATH_TO_SF2 PATH_TO_MIDI`
    - **Windows:** `fluidsynth -g 1 -n -i PATH_TO_SF2 PATH_TO_MIDI`

Understanding the model's parameters

From the screenshot in the last section, you can already see that the model used some default configurations to generate the score: the number of steps to generate, the tempo, and so on. Now, let's see what other flags are possible. To see what kind of flags the model takes, use the `--helpfull` flag:

```
> drums_rnn_generate --helpfull

    USAGE: drums_rnn_generate [flags]
    ...

magenta.models.drums_rnn.drums_rnn_config_flags:
    ...

magenta.models.drums_rnn.drums_rnn_generate:
    ...
```

You will see a lot of possible flags showing. The sections that are of interest for us are `drums_rnn_config_flags` and `drums_rnn_generate`, which are flags specific for the Drums RNN model.

The following subsections will explain the most important ones. Because most also apply to other models, you'll be able to apply what you learn to the next chapters as well. We'll explain other model-specific flags of the later chapters as we go.

Changing the output size

A simple flag to change the number of generated samples is `--num_outputs`:

```
--num_outputs: The number of drum tracks to generate. One MIDI file will be
created for each. (default: '10')
```

You can also use the `--num_steps` flag to change the size of the generated samples:

```
--num_steps: The total number of steps the generated drum tracks should be,
priming drum track length + generated steps. Each step is a 16th of a bar.
(default: '128')
```

The last example we generated was 128 steps long because we generated it using the default value. By looking at the previous screenshot, you can count the vertical bar lines, which counts to 8 bars. This is because, with 128 steps at 16 steps per bar, you get *128/16 = 8* bars. If you want a 1 bar generation, you'll be asking for 16 steps, for example. You can see a single step as a single note slot, in the sense that generators will generate one note per step maximum. It is a convenient way of dividing time.

We'll be using the term **bar** in this book, which is more popular in British English, but readers might be used to the word **measure**, which is more popular in American English. There are some differences in their usage, and depending on the context, one or the other might be used more often. However, both words mainly have the same significance.

The main reason to stick with bar throughout this book is to follow Magenta's code convention, where bar is used more consistently than measure.

We can show the steps by zooming on the last two bars of the previous example:

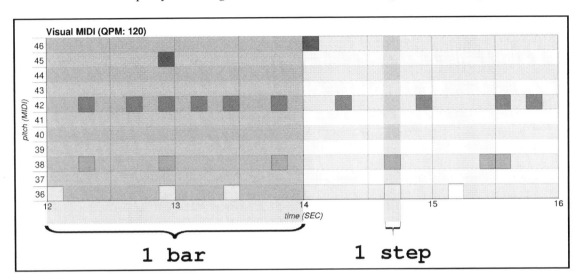

You can see in this diagram that there are 2 bars, each of 2 seconds (see the next section for information on the tempo), with a different background for each bar. You can also see that there are 16 steps per bar; we've marked one of those steps with a different background. A step can contain multiple notes if the model is polyphonic, like the Drums RNN model. Depending on the model, a note can spawn multiple steps, which is not the case here. For this model, the note will always start and stop exactly on the step start and end since the model outputs quantized sequences.

Changing the tempo

The tempo is the speed at which the score is played. Be aware that it won't change the number of notes or the generation length—it will only put the information in the generated MIDI so that the MIDI player will later be able to play it at the right speed.

The tempo in Magenta is expressed in **Quarter-notes Per Minute (QPM)**. A **quarter** is a bar separated into four—if you have 16 steps in a bar, then a quarter contains 4 steps. So, if your tempo is 120 QPM, then you have *120 quarters/60 seconds* = 2 quarters per second. That means you play 1 bar per 2 seconds (see the previous diagram for an example of that).

QPM is a measure of tempo similar but not to be confused with **BPM** (**Beats Per Minute**) since, in the latter, the meaning of a beat might change for some time signature. Also, the concept of a beat might change depending on the listener. QPM is well defined and used in the MIDI and MusicXML format.

To change the tempo, use the --qpm flag:

```
--qpm: The quarters per minute to play generated output at. If a primer
MIDI is given, the qpm from that will override this flag. (default: '120')
```

In the following diagram, we've generated a drum file at 150 QPM using --qpm 150:

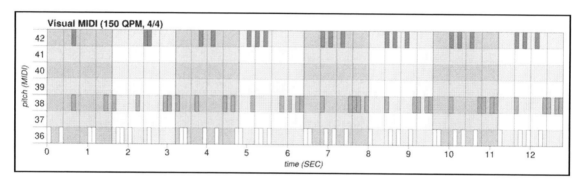

You can see the bars are not aligned with 2, 4, and more seconds anymore. This is because, at 120 QPM, a bar is exactly 2 seconds long, but it is now slightly less. Our generated sample still has --num_steps 128 but now has a duration of 12.8 seconds (and still 8 bars) because we still have the same amounts of steps—they are just played faster.

To find the duration in seconds of a sequence for a specific QPM such as 150, we first calculate the length of a step in seconds, by taking the number of seconds in a minute (60), dividing by the QPM (150), and dividing by the number of steps per quarter (4). This gives us 0.1 seconds per step. For 128 steps, the sequence is 12.8 seconds long.

Changing the model type

The `--config` flag changes the configuration of the model. With each configuration in Magenta comes a pre-trained model. In this chapter, we are using the `drum_kit_rnn.mag` pre-trained model (or bundle) for the `drum_kit` configuration. The chosen pre-trained model must match the configuration it was trained with:

```
--config: Which config to use. Must be one of 'one_drum' or 'drum_kit'.
(default: 'drum_kit')
```

It won't be useful for us now, but it will come in handy in `Chapter 3`, *Generating Polyphonic Melodies*. This also changes the mapping of the drums, where the resulting encoded vector is different in both cases. We'll be talking about vector encoding in the next section when we look at the Python code.

Priming the model with Led Zeppelin

A primer sequence can be given to the model to **prepare** it before the generation. This is used extensively with Magenta and is really useful if you want the model to generate something that is inspired by your primer. You can either prime the model with a hardcoded sequence or directly from a MIDI file. The priming sequence is fed to the model before the generation starts.

The string representation of the `--primer_drums`flag reads as follows: you enter a list of tuples, each tuple corresponding to a step, with each tuple containing the MIDI notes being played at the same time. In this example, on the first step, both MIDI notes, 36 and 42, are played at the same time, followed by 3 steps of silence, then MIDI note 42 is played alone in its own step:

```
--primer_drums: A string representation of a Python list of tuples
containing drum pitch values. For example:
"[(36,42),(),(),(),(42,),(),(),()]". If specified, this drum track will be
used as the priming drum track. If a priming drum track is not specified,
drum tracks will be generated from scratch. (default: ''
```

As you might remember from the previous chapter, a MIDI note also have velocity information, which is not given here. This is not necessary since the Drums RNN doesn't support velocity. Each generated note will have a default value of 100 for velocity (on a maximum value of 127).

Some models in Magenta support velocity as we'll see in the next chapters. Since the velocities have to be encoded in the input vectors that are fed to the network during training, it is a design choice to include them or not. We'll also talk about encoding in the next chapters.

To give a primer corresponding to a bar, you'll have to provide 16 tuples, because there are 16 steps per bar. The previous primer is half a bar long.

You can also provide the path to a MIDI file with the `--primer_midi` flag:

```
--primer_midi: The path to a MIDI file containing a drum track that will
be used as a priming drum track. If a primer drum track is not specified,
drum tracks will be generated from scratch. (default: '')
```

A primer MIDI file gives the tempo and will override your `--qpm` flag if you also provide it.

When initializing the model with a primer, you also get the primer in the resulting output sequence. That means `--num_steps` needs to be bigger than the primer's length or else Magenta won't have space left to generate. For example, this command will output an error because the number of steps is not high enough:

```
> drums_rnn_generate --bundle_file=bundles/drum_kit_rnn.mag --
output_dir=output --primer_drums="[(36,),(36,),(36,),(36,)]" --num_steps=4
```

This results in the following output:

```
CRITICAL - Priming sequence is longer than the total number of steps
requested: Priming sequence length: 0.625, Generation length requested:
0.62
```

Let's generate something based on a small drum part of Jon Bonham's (Led Zeppelin) *When The Levee Breaks* track. Here's a two-bar primer:

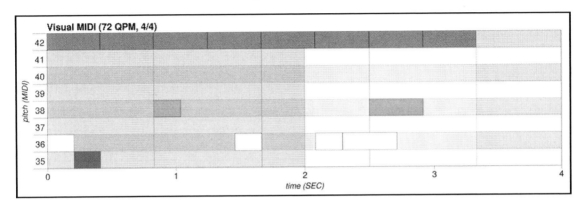

Then, we generate some MIDI files by setting the primer, the temperature, and the proper number of steps. Remember, the number of steps is the total number of steps, primer included:

```
drums_rnn_generate --bundle_file bundles/drum_kit_rnn.mag --output_dir
output --num_steps 46 --primer_midi
primers/When_The_Levee_Breaks_Led_Zeppelin.mid --temperature 1.1
```

We get an interesting sequence shown in the following diagram:

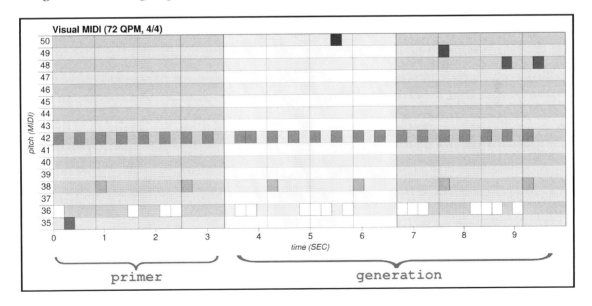

You can still find the primer in the first 3 seconds or so, then we notice that the model kept the musical structure of the track, but improvised over it, adding a few kick drums, hit hats, and snares here and there. We'll be looking at the MIDI mapping of percussion sequences, including the mapping of each pitch to their corresponding instrument, in the next section, *Mapping MIDI notes to the real world*.

Now, we verify whether Magenta knows how to count: you have 16 steps of primer, 1 step of silence, then 29 steps of generation for a total of 46, which is what we asked for. The step of silence comes from the way Magenta calculates the start of the generation. We'll see in the Python code how to handle that in a better way.

We also notice that the length of the notes in the primer are different in the generated score. You can see the same primer notes are present, but not with the same duration. This is because Magenta will **quantize the primer before feeding it to the model** and will generate quantized sequences. This depends on the model. **Quantization** is the process of moving the note's beginning and end so that they fall directly on some subdivisions of bars. In this case, Magenta moved the notes' end so that they fall on the closest step.

Configuring the generation algorithm

The `--temperature` flag is important because it changes how random the generated sequence is:

```
--temperature: The randomness of the generated drum tracks. 1.0 uses the
unaltered softmax probabilities, greater than 1.0 makes tracks more random,
less than 1.0 makes tracks less random. (default: '1.0')
```

Let's try to generate a drum track with more randomness using `--temperature 1.5`:

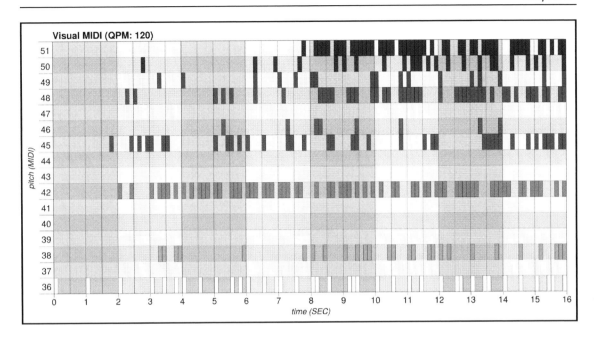

This is pretty wild! Remember a temperature of 1.5 is high, so you might have a more coherent sample with a more conservative value, like 1.1, for example.

Now, to generate a track with less randomness, use `--temperature 0.9`:

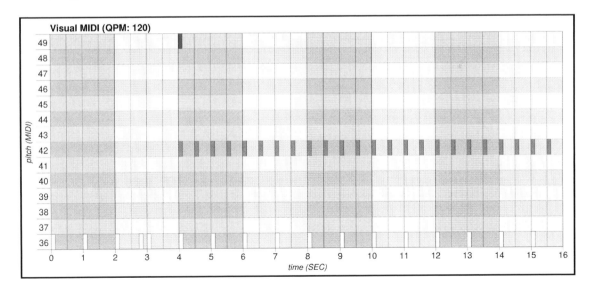

You can clearly see the generation is more conservative here. Choosing the temperature is up to taste and depends on what you are trying to achieve. Try different temperature values and see what fits best with the music you are trying to generate. Also, some models might sound better with wilder temperature values than others.

Other Magenta and TensorFlow flags

There are other flags that we haven't talked about, such as the configuration of the hyperparameters of the model with `--hparams`, but we'll be looking into this when we train our own model in `Chapter 7`, *Training Magenta Models*.

Understanding the generation algorithm

In the previous sections, we introduced how the generation algorithm works—by predicting at each generation step what the next note in the sequence is, we can iteratively generate a full score. The resulting prediction depends on what the model has learned during the training phase. This section will delve deeper into the generation algorithm by showing it in action on an example being executed step by step.

We'll also be explaining the parameters that modify the generation's execution:

```
--beam_size: The beam size to use for beam search when generating drum
tracks. (default: '1')
--branch_factor: The branch factor to use for beam search when generating
drum tracks. (default: '1')
--steps_per_iteration: The number of steps to take per beam search
iteration. (default: '1')
```

Generating the sequence branches and steps

Let's use this command to launch the generation:

```
drums_rnn_generate --bundle_file=bundles/drum_kit_rnn.mag --
output_dir=output --temperature 1.1 --beam_size 1 --branch_factor 2 --
steps_per_iteration 1 --num_steps 64
```

Magenta will do the following operations:

1. It converts the primer sequence into a format that the model understands (this is called **encoding**—check the *Encoding percussion events as classes* section).
2. It uses that encoded primer to initialize the model state.
3. It loops until all of the steps (--num_steps 64) have been generated:
    1. It loops to generate *N* branches (--branch_factor 2):
        1. It generates *X* steps (--steps_per_iterations 1) by running the model with its current state using the **temperature** (--temperature 1.1). This returns the predicted sequence as well as the resulting **softmax probabilities**. The softmax probabilities are the actual probability scores for each class (the encoded notes) at the final layer of the network.
        2. It calculates the **negative log-likelihood** of the resulting sequence, which is a scoring evaluation of the entire sequence from the softmax probabilities.
        3. It updates the model state for the next iteration.
    2. It prunes the generated branches to best *K* branches (--beam_size 1) by using the calculated score.

This diagram shows the generation process with a final sequence of **36, 38,** and **42:**

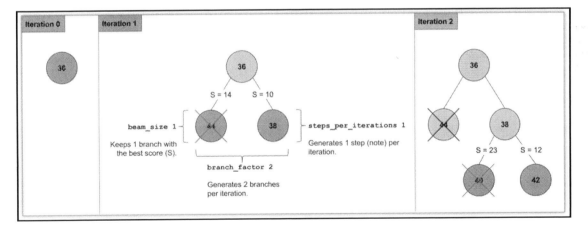

In the diagram, the **S** value denotes the calculated score of the entire sequence (see *steps 3.1.2* and *3.2*). The beam search algorithm shown here is linear in complexity on the output sequence length (which is the depth of the tree), so it is pretty fast. The default value of `--beam_size 1` is useful since the algorithm becomes a best-first search algorithm, where you don't actually do a breadth-first search since you are keeping only the best candidate.

Making sense of the randomness

When we launch a generation that uses the beam search, Magenta shows the resulting log-likelihood of the whole sequence:

```
Beam search yields sequence with log-likelihood: -16.006279
```

What happens with `--temperature 1.25` instead of 1.1? The log-likelihood will be smaller (further from zero) since the generation is more random:

```
Beam search yields sequence with log-likelihood: -57.161125
```

What if we generate only 1 branch with `--branch_factor 1` but keep the same temperature at 1.25? The log-likelihood will be smaller:

```
Beam search yields sequence with log-likelihood: -140.033295
```

Why is the log-likelihood smaller? Because we've reduced the branch factor, the algorithm will generate fewer branches per iteration, meaning, at each iteration, it will have fewer branches to choose its best from, resulting in a globally more random sequence.

Let's now use what we've learned about the Drums RNN model and create a small Python application using those concepts.

Using the Drums RNN in Python

In the previous section, we've seen how much we can already do on the command line with the Drums RNN model. In this section, you'll get to create a small application that will use that model to generate music in Python.

Using Magenta in Python is a bit difficult because of the following reasons:

- It requires you to write code and understand Magenta's architecture.
- It requires more boilerplate code and is less straightforward.

But it also has advantages that we think are important:

- You have more freedom in the usage of the models.
- You can create new models and modify existing ones.
- You can go beyond generating single sequences.

The last point is important for us because we'll be building a small music application that generates music autonomously. Calling Magenta's scripts on the command line is convenient, but you cannot build an app using only this. You'll be starting this in the last section of this chapter, *Creating a music generation application*, and building on it in the next chapters.

Let's dive into the code by recreating what we've done on the command line and then building from there.

Generating a drum sequence using Python

We are going to generate a MIDI file from a primer in Python, much like we've done in the previous section.

 You can follow this example in the `chapter_02_example_01.py` file in the source code of this chapter. There are more comments and content in the source code, so you should go check it out.

1. Let's start by downloading the bundle. There are a lot of useful tools in the `magenta.music` package, and we'll be using it in many examples:

```
import os
import magenta.music as mm

mm.notebook_utils.download_bundle("drum_kit_rnn.mag", "bundles")
bundle = mm.sequence_generator_bundle.read_bundle_file(
  os.path.join("bundles", "drum_kit_rnn.mag"))
```

2. We then use the drums generator to initialize the generator class with the drum_kit configuration. We are importing the Drums RNN models from its own package, and we'll do the same for each model:

```
from magenta.models.drums_rnn import drums_rnn_sequence_generator

generator_map = drums_rnn_sequence_generator.get_generator_map()
generator = generator_map["drum_kit"](checkpoint=None,
bundle=bundle)
generator.initialize()
```

3. By declaring the tempo, we can also calculate the length of a bar in seconds. We need this because the generation start and end is given in seconds to Magenta.

    We first calculate the seconds per step, which is equal to the number of seconds in a minute, divided by the quarter per minute (the tempo), divided by the number of steps per quarter. This last value is dependent on the generator, but it is mostly equal to 4:

```
from magenta.music import constants

qpm = 120
seconds_per_step = 60.0 / qpm / generator.steps_per_quarter
```

4. Then, we calculate the seconds per bar, which is equal to the number of steps per bar multiplied by the seconds per step we previously calculated. The number of steps per bar changes depending on the time signature, but for now, we'll just put the default value, which is 16, for 4/4 music sampled at 4 steps per quarter note:

```
num_steps_per_bar = constants.DEFAULT_STEPS_PER_BAR
seconds_per_bar = num_steps_per_bar * seconds_per_step

print("Seconds per step: " + str(seconds_per_step))
print("Seconds per bar: " + str(seconds_per_bar))
```

5. We are now ready to initialize our primer sequence. We'll use a small jazz drum sequence of 1 bar for the primer (you can check it out in this book's source code in the Chapter02 folder, primers/Jazz_Drum_Basic_1_bar.mid), so we'll need a list of 16 steps. We'll be explaining the primer definition in the next section.

We convert that primer drum track into a primer sequence using the QPM we've already defined:

```
primer_drums = mm.DrumTrack(
  [frozenset(pitches) for pitches in
    [(38, 51),     (), (36,),      (),
     (38, 44, 51), (), (36,),      (),
     (),           (), (38,),      (),
     (38, 44),     (), (36, 51), (),]])
primer_sequence = primer_drums.to_sequence(qpm=qpm)
```

6. We can calculate the time of the primer in seconds, which is only the seconds per bar value since the primer is 1 bar:

```
primer_start_time = 0
primer_end_time = primer_start_time + seconds_per_bar
```

7. We now calculate the start and end time of the generator section. First, we define the number of generation bars, which is 3, then we start the generation at the end of the primer and extend it for a three-bars duration in seconds:

```
num_bars = 3
generation_start_time = primer_end_time
generation_end_time = generation_start_time + (seconds_per_bar *
num_bars)

print("Primer start and end: [" + str(primer_start_time) + ", "
 + str(primer_end_time) + "]")
print("Generation start and end: [" + str(generation_start_time) +
", "
 + str(generation_end_time) + "]")
```

8. We can now configure our generator options with the start and end times. The generation options also take the temperature, which we'll set to 1.1 for a bit of randomness. The generator interface is common for all models:

```
from magenta.protobuf import generator_pb2

generator_options = generator_pb2.GeneratorOptions()
generator_options.args['temperature'].float_value = 1.1
generator_options.generate_sections.add(
  start_time=generation_start_time,
  end_time=generation_end_time)
```

9. It is time to generate! You can now call the generate method on the generator with the primer sequence as input. The return value of this method is a NoteSequence instance:

```
sequence = generator.generate(primer_sequence, generator_options)
```

10. There are many utilities to then convert the resulting NoteSequence instance into other formats such as PrettyMidi. We'll now convert the result, and write the file and the plot to disk:

```
from visual_midi import Plotter

# Write the resulting midi file to the output directory
midi_file = os.path.join("output", "out.mid")
mm.midi_io.note_sequence_to_midi_file(sequence, midi_file)
print("Generated midi file: " + str(os.path.abspath(midi_file)))

# Write the resulting plot file to the output directory
from visual_midi import Plotter
plot_file = os.path.join("output", "out.html")
print("Generated plot file: " + str(os.path.abspath(plot_file)))
pretty_midi = mm.midi_io.note_sequence_to_pretty_midi(sequence)
plotter = Plotter()
plotter.show(pretty_midi, plot_file)
```

11. Let's open the output/out.html file:

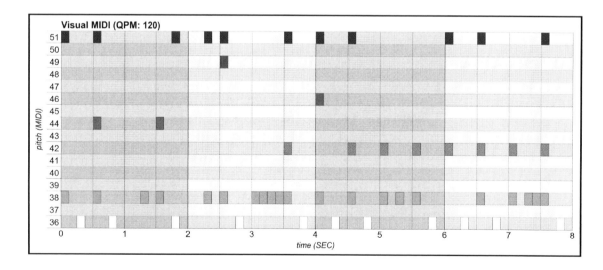

Notice that your primer at the beginning should be the same (because it is hardcoded), but your 3 generated bars should be different than these.

12. To listen to the generated MIDI, use your software synthesizer or MuseScore. For the software synth, refer to the following command depending on your platform and replace PATH_TO_SF2 and PATH_TO_MIDI with the proper values:

    - **Linux**: `fluidsynth -a pulseaudio -g 1 -n -i PATH_TO_SF2 PATH_TO_MIDI`
    - **macOS**: `fluidsynth -a coreaudio -g 1 -n -i PATH_TO_SF2 PATH_TO_MIDI`
    - **Windows**: `fluidsynth -g 1 -n -i PATH_TO_SF2 PATH_TO_MIDI`

Packaging checkpoints as bundle files

In the last example, we saw the usage of a bundle. In Magenta, a bundle is a convenient way of packaging a **TensorFlow checkpoint** and metadata information into a single file. A checkpoint is used in TensorFlow to save the model state that occurs during training, making it easy to reload the model's state at a later time.

Another nice usage of a bundle is that it defines a **common interface** for multiple generators. You can check the `generator.proto` file in the Magenta's source code, in the `magenta/protobuf` folder, which defines that interface, including the generator `id` and `description`, as well as generator options such as `generate_sections` that we'll be using to provide the generation length in many examples.

This common interface covers many models, including all of the models of Chapter 2 and Chapter 3. Unfortunately, bundles aren't used in Chapter 4 for the MusicVAE models, but we'll see more of them in `Chapter 7`, *Training Magenta Models*.

Encoding MIDI using Protobuf in NoteSequence

In the last example, we saw the usage of a class named `NoteSequence`, which is an important part of Magenta, since every model working on the score will use it to represent a sequence of MIDI notes. `NoteSequence` and `GeneratorOptions` are Protobuf (Protocol Buffers), a language-neutral, platform-neutral extensible mechanism for serializing structured data. In Magenta's source code, in the `magenta/protobuf/music.proto` file, you can see the message definition of `NoteSequence`.

The definition of `NoteSequence` is based on a MIDI message content, so you have the following:

- A list of `TimeSignature` changes: By default, 4/4 is assumed per MIDI standard.
- A list of `KeySignature` changes: By default, C Major is assumed per MIDI standard.
- A list of `Tempo` changes: By default, 120 QPM is assumed per MIDI standard.
- A list of `Note` changes.

There's also much more including annotations, quantization information, pitch bend, and control changes, but we won't be looking into that in this book.

The `Note` list is one we'll be mainly using, with the `pitch` (which is the MIDI note, based on the MIDI tuning standard), `start_time`, and `end_time` properties, representing a note.

Converting into and from `NoteSequence` is important. In the previous example, we've used the following functions:

- `magenta.music.midi_io.note_sequence_to_midi_file`: This is for converting from a note sequence into a MIDI file. You can also convert into `PrettyMIDI`, a useful format to edit MIDI in memory.
- `magenta.music.midi_io.midi_file_to_note_sequence`: This is for converting from a MIDI file into a note sequence; this would have been useful in our previous example. Instead of hardcoding the primer in the Python code, we could have used
  `midi_file_to_note_sequence("primers/Jazz_Drum_Basic_1_bar.mid")`.

Another important point about `NoteSequence` is that it doesn't explicitly define a start and end; it just assumes it starts at the start of the first note and ends at the end of the last note. In other words, a sequence starting or ending with silence cannot be defined.

In the following diagram, the sequence is expected to be of 2 bars, which is 32 steps, but stops at the 31st step, meaning the last note end time is 3.875 seconds, not 4 seconds:

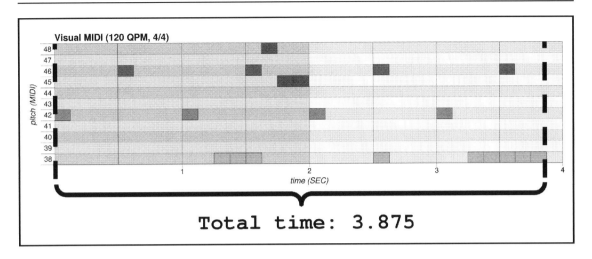

Total time: 3.875

Concatenating this sequence with another might yield unexpected resulting sequence length. Fortunately, methods that handle note sequences have options to make this work properly.

Mapping MIDI notes to the real world

In the previous example, we've shown the following 1-bar primer but we haven't explained what those pitches correspond to:

```
[(38, 51),       (), (36),       (),
 (38, 44, 51), (), (36),       (),
 (),            (), (38),       (),
 (38, 44),     (), (36, 51), (),]
```

We won't be going into detail in the MIDI specification since it is pretty big (you can check it out at www.midi.org/specifications), but we'll look at the parts that concern this book. Two specifications are interesting to us:

- The **MIDI specification** that defines the low-level protocol of communication and encoding between the different instruments
  - The **General MIDI specification (GM)** that defines a higher-level protocol, defining requirements for instruments to be compliant and specifying instrument sounds

January 2019 marks the first major update of the MIDI specification since its standardization in 1983 with the release of MIDI 2.0 specification. That's after more than 25 years of usage by millions of devices and users.

MIDI 2.0 introduces higher resolution values with 16 bits of precision instead of 7 and the addition of the MIDI Capability Inquiry, enabling better integration between tools. The new version of MIDI is completely backward compatible with the old version.

The instrument sounds definition is interesting for us and we'll be looking into the **GM 1 Sound Set** specification, which defines the sound that should be played for each MIDI note. In GM 1 Sound Set, each MIDI Program Change (PC#) corresponds to a specific instrument in the synthesizer. For example, PC# 1 is **Acoustic Grand Piano** and PC# 42 is **Viola**. Remember, those sounds are defined by the synthesizer that implements the GM 1 specification and might change from synth to synth.

The percussion keymap is a bit different. On MIDI Channel 10, each MIDI note number (pitch) corresponds to a specific drum sound. Our previous example can be read as follows:

- **36**: Bass Drum 1
- **38**: Acoustic Snare
- **44**: Pedal Hi-Hat
- **51**: Ride Cymbal 1

You can always refer to the full table later at `www.midi.org/specifications-old/item/gm-level-1-sound-set`.

Encoding percussion events as classes

The last section explained percussion mapping in terms of MIDI mapping. But how do we encode the percussion for the Drums RNN model? To encode the MIDI mapping to a vector, we'll use what is called **one-hot encoding**, which basically maps every possible input events to classes then to a binary vector.

For that to happen, we need to reduce the number of drum classes first, from all of the possible drums in MIDI (46 different drums is way too much) to a more manageable 9 classes. You can see the mapping in the `DEFAULT_DRUM_TYPE_PITCHES` property of the `magenta.music.drums_encoder_decoder` module. We then bit flip in a vector at the index defined by summing two to the power of the class index for each class in the set.

For example, our set of pitches, *{51, 38}*, for the first step maps to classes *{8, 1}*. This value will bit flip index 258 in the vector, because $2^8 + 2^1 = 258$. The vector is of the size 2^9 for each step, plus some binary counters and flags we won't talk about here.

This diagram shows the encoding part of the first step of the primer example as described:

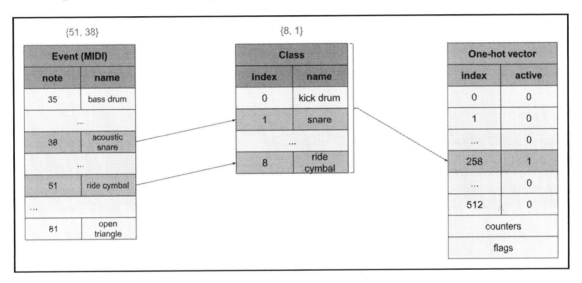

In that specific encoding, some information is lost because there are less class then MIDI notes. This means that, for example, if both MIDI notes, 35 and 36, map to the same class index 0, then the difference between either 35 or 36 is lost. In that specific case, 36 is chosen arbitrarily (you can actually see that from the previous example in the section, *Priming the model with Led Zeppelin*, the MIDI note 35 is lost).

This encoding is used for training when converting from the dataset into the sequences, and during generation, if a primer is used to initialize the model. When using a primer, the primer is encoded to produce input for the model. The model state is then initialized with that input.

The reverse of that operation is also important for a generation: when the model makes a new generation, it needs to be decoded to find the sequence it represents.

There are different ways of encoding the events, and others are used in Magenta. This is the encoding for the "drum_kit" configuration for this model, which is `LookbackEventSequenceEncoderDecoder`, implementing the encoding of repeated events using binary counters. The encoding of the `one_drum` configuration is different and simpler; you can check it out in `OneHotEventSequenceEncoderDecoder`.

The one-hot encoding of the drum classes is implemented in the `MultiDrumOneHotEncoding` class, which is used in other models as well, such as the MusicVAE model we'll see in Chapter 4. When instantiated with no drum pitches, it will use the reduced drum encoding of 9 classes that we saw in this section, which is expressive enough to capture many instruments, while keeping the model at a manageable size.

We'll be seeing more on the subject of encoding in the following chapters.

Sending MIDI files to other applications

While generating MIDI files and writing them on disk is nice, dynamically sending the MIDI notes to another piece of software would be more useful, so that our Python Magenta application could interact directly with other music software. We will dedicate a whole chapter to this topic since there is a lot to talk about.

If you want to know more about this topic right now, you can go see Chapter 9, *Making Magenta Interact with Music Applications*, and come back here later.

Summary

In this chapter, we introduced an RNN and the role it plays in music generation, by showing that operating on a sequence and remembering the past are mandatory properties for music generation.

We also generated a MIDI file using the Drums RNN model on the command line. We've covered most of its parameters and learned how to configure the model's output. By looking at the generation algorithm, we explained how it worked and how the different flags can change its execution.

By using the Drums RNN model in Python, we've shown how we can build a versatile application. By doing that, we learned about the MIDI specification, how Magenta encodes `NoteSequence` using Protobuf, and how to encode a sequence as a one-hot vector. We've also introduced the idea of sending the generated MIDI to other applications, a topic we'll cover in Chapter 9, *Making Magenta Interact with Music Applications*.

In the next chapter, we'll be using other models to generate melody. We'll also continue writing Python code by finishing our learning of RNNs.

Questions

1. If you want to generate a musical score, what do you train your model to do?
2. What are the properties that are interesting in RNNs concerning music prediction?
3. Given an RNN hidden layer with the notation $h(t + 2)$, what two inputs is the hidden layer getting?
4. Given the following parameters for the generation, `--num_steps 32` and `--qpm 80`, how long will the generated MIDI be in seconds? How many bars will it be?
5. What happens if you increase `--branch_factor` and increase `--temperature` during the generation phase?
6. How many nodes will the beam search algorithm go through at the last iteration for a generation of 3 steps with the `--branch_factor 4` and `--beam_size 2` parameters?
7. What is the Protobuf Message class that is used in Magenta to represent a sequence of MIDI notes? (NoteSequence)
8. Using the one-hot encoding described in the encoding section, what is the encoded vector for a step playing the MIDI notes, *{36, 40, 42}*?
9. Using the same encoding, what are the decoded MIDI notes from an encoded vector with index 131 at 1?

Further reading

- **The Unreasonable Effectiveness of Recurrent Neural Networks**: An excellent article on RNNs (`karpathy.github.io/2015/05/21/rnn-effectiveness/`)
- **Understanding softmax and the negative log-likelihood**: Complimentary information on log-likelihood (`ljvmiranda921.github.io/notebook/2017/08/13/softmax-and-the-negative-log-likelihood/`)
- **Finding Structure in Time**: An original paper (1990) on RNNs (`crl.ucsd.edu/~elman/Papers/fsit.pdf`)
- **Gradient-Based Learning Applied to Document Recognition**: An original paper (1998) on CNNs (`yann.lecun.com/exdb/publis/pdf/lecun-98.pdf`)
- **The Neural Network Zoo**: An amazing list of neural network architectures that you can refer to throughout this book (`asimovinstitute.org/neural-network-zoo/`)

3
Generating Polyphonic Melodies

Building on the last chapter where we created drum sequences, we can now proceed to create the heart of music—its melody. In this chapter, you'll learn the importance of **Long Short-Term Memory (LSTM)** networks in generating longer sequences. We'll see how to use a monophonic Magenta model, the Melody RNN—an LSTM network with a loopback and attention configuration. You'll also learn to use two polyphonic models, the Polyphony RNN and Performance RNN, both LSTM networks using a specific encoding, with the latter having support for note velocity and expressive timing.

The following topics will be covered in this chapter:

- LSTM for long-term dependencies
- Generating melodies with the Melody RNN
- Generating polyphony with the Polyphony RNN and Performance RNN

Technical requirements

In this chapter, we'll use the following tools:

- The **command line** or **bash** to launch Magenta from the Terminal
- **Python** and its libraries to write music generation code using Magenta
- **Magenta** to generate music in MIDI
- **MuseScore** or **FluidSynth** to listen to the generated MIDI

In Magenta, we'll make the use of the **Melody RNN, the Polyphony RNN**, and **Performance RNN** models. We'll be explaining those models in depth, but if you feel like you need more information, the model's README in Magenta's source code (`github.com/tensorflow/magenta/tree/master/magenta/models`) is a good place to start. You can also take a look at Magenta's code, which is well documented. We also provide additional content in the last section, *Further reading*.

The code for this chapter is in this book's GitHub repository in the `Chapter03` folder, located at `github.com/PacktPublishing/hands-on-music-generation-with-magenta/tree/master/Chapter03`. The examples and code snippets will presume you are located in the chapter folder. For this chapter, you should do `cd Chapter03` before you start.

Check out the following video to see the Code in Action:
`http://bit.ly/314KEzq`

LSTM for long-term dependencies

In the previous chapter, we learned how **Recurrent Neural Networks (RNNs)** are essential for music generation because they make it possible to operate on a sequence of vectors and remember past events. This second part is really important in music generation since past events play an important role in defining the global musical structure. Let's consider the example of a broken minor ninth chord of "A," "C," "E," "G," "B." To predict the last note, "B," the network has to remember four events back to know that this is probably a minor ninth chord being played.

Unfortunately, as the gap between the relevant information and the point where it is needed grows, RNNs become unable to learn the dependency. In theory, the network could be able to do it, but in practice, it is really difficult. Two common problems with vanilla RNNs are the vanishing gradient problem and the exploding gradient problem, which we'll get to see in this section.

Fortunately, LSTM networks, introduced in 1997, solve that problem. They are a special type of RNN where each neuron has a memory cell with special gates. As introduced in the previous chapter, the Drums RNN model is an LSTM network as are all of the models in this chapter. Now, let's have a look at how LSTMs work.

Looking at LSTM memory cells

LSTM networks have been popular since their invention and for a good reason: they were designed specifically to handle the long-term dependency problem we've been talking about. In Magenta, the RNN models are LSTM networks.

Let's have a quick refresher with the RNN diagram from the previous chapter. We'll take the same diagram but zoom in on one of the cells and add a bit of detail:

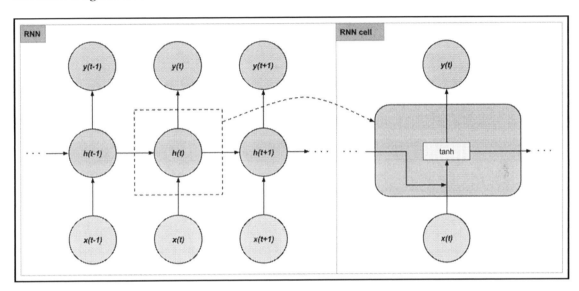

We see here that the repeated module is pretty simple: it takes the output from the previous layer, concatenates it with the current input, and uses an activation function (such as tanh, sigmoid, or ReLU) layer to produce both the layer's output and the next layer's input. We also remember that long-term information has to travel through all of the cells and layers in a sequential matter, meaning that information has to be multiplied at each step. This is where the vanishing gradient problem arrives: the values getting multiplied many times by small numbers tend to vanish.

Let's now see how an LSTM memory cell is designed:

LSTM memory cell

y(t)

c(t-1) forget gate layer input gate layer output gate layer *c(t+1)*

h(t-1) *h(t+1)*

x(t)

The first thing to notice here is the added horizontal line, annotated { ..., *c(t-1)*, *c(t)* , *c(t+1)*, ... }, that carries the cell state information forward. The cell state can be modified by three gates—**forget**, **input**, and **output**. We won't go into details on how those gates work since this is outside the scope of this book, but we'll be looking at an example of how it works for our use case.

 Check out the last section, *Further reading*, for references containing more information on LSTM.

Let's take our example of a broken minor ninth chord to illustrate how the gate layers work. The network is training and has received so far "A", "C", "E", "G", "B", which is its current state. Now the LSTM sees a new note, "C", and what happens? First, let's have a look at the **forget gate layer**. The LSTM will look at *h(t-1)*, the previous layer output, and *x(t)*, the current input, which is "C", and output a number for each element in the previous cell state, *c(t-1)*. The state is then multiplied by that output, varying from 0 to 1, meaning a value closer to 0 will result in a state losing this value, and a value closer to 1 will result in a state keeping this value. Because the input is a "C", and in our state, we already saw a full chord, the network might learn to forget previous information because we are starting a new chord.

Next, the **input gate layer** will look at *h(t-1)* and *x(t)* and decide what additions are going to be made to the state. Using this, the forget gate output gets updated, producing *c(t)*. The cell state now has new content, meaning our input "C" is now added in the cell state, which will be useful for later layers to detect, for example, a potential start of a C major chord. At this point, the network might also learn other chords, depending on the training data. A properly trained network will learn about the different musical chords based on its training and will output predictions accordingly during inference.

Finally, the **output gate layer** will produce the output, *h(t)*, by looking at the new state *c(t)*, *h(t-1)*, and *x(t)*. At this point, the state is already updated and doesn't need further updates. Since our model just saw a "C", it might want to output an "E" to constitute a C Major chord.

This is a simplified explanation of LSTM but it serves the purpose of understanding how it works for our use case.

Looking at the code, you can see where the LSTM memory cell is used. In the `events_rnn_graph.py` module, the `make_rnn_cell` function uses `tf.contrib.rnn.BasicLSTMCell`. You can see that Magenta uses TensorFlow as a backing engine, as LSTM is not defined in Magenta.

Exploring alternative networks

To summarize the last section, we have RNNs, which are capable of handling sequences and looking at past events, and LSTM, a specific memory cell implementation for an RNN. Often, a network might be called only RNN but actually uses LSTM memory cells.

While LSTMs are a huge step forward for keeping long-term information, there are possible improvements. Another type of similar memory cell, **Gated Recurrent Units (GRU)**, has gained popularity in recent years for its simpler design. Because of that, GRUs are also less expressive, which is a trade-off to look out for.

A problem with LSTMs is that they use more resources to run because the memory cell takes more memory and more computation to operate. A popular idea for further improvement is the introduction of **attention**, where the RNN can look at a subset of past outputs, making it possible to look at past events without using too much cell memory. We'll be looking at attention in the *Having attention for specific steps* section.

Generating melodies with the Melody RNN

In this section, we'll be building on our previous chapter's knowledge by using our Python code to generate music with a new model, the Melody RNN. This section will show how to generate monophony and the next section will show how to handle polyphony.

Monophony is the simplest form of musical texture, where the notes, a **melody**, are played by a single instrument, one by one. Sometimes, a melody can be played by multiple instruments, or multiple singers, at a different octave (for example, in a choir), but are still considered monophonic because the backing score is.

Polyphony, on the other hand, consists of two or more melody lines played together. For example, a piano score played with two hands is polyphonic since there are two separate melodies to be played together.

An instrument can be monophonic or polyphonic. For example, a monophonic synthesizer will be able to play only one note at a time (so if you press two notes, only one will come out), and a polyphonic synthesizer or a classic piano will be able to play multiple notes at the same time.

Here is a small monophonic example from the piano score of *Fur Elisa* from Beethoven, at bar #37:

You notice there's only one melody and the notes are played one by one. And here is a small polyphonic example from the same score, at bar #25:

In this example, you have two melodies played at the same time, typically using both hands on the piano.

Does polyphony sound familiar? It might, because percussion scores are polyphonic in essence, since multiple melodies (kick drum, hit hats, snare, and so on) are played together to form a complete rhythm. What we're going to see in the next section about polyphony is a bit different though, since we'll need a way to represent a note that spans longer than a single step's length, unlike the previous chapter.

Let's start by writing some code to generate melodies.

Generating a song for Fur Elisa

For this example, we'll be using a small primer from the piano score of *Fur Elisa* to generate melodies based on it. The primer looks like this:

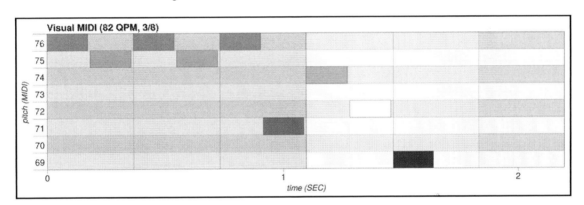

Notice the time signature is 3/8. We'll be looking into this in a later section, *Losing track of time*.

Since you already know how to generate a sequence, we'll only provide what has changed from the previous code; you can reuse what you've written from the previous chapter. We'll be encapsulating the code in a `generate` function, making it easy to call with different models and configurations.

You can follow this example in the `chapter_03_example_01.py` file in the source code of this chapter. There are more comments and content in the source code, so you should go check it out.

You can find the `generate` function in that file. We'll be making more versions of this method as we go. The primer for this example is located at `primers/Fur_Elisa_Beethoveen_Monophonic.mid`.

We'll go through the important changes in the `generate` function by explaining the new content step by step. The new function signature is as follows:

```
from magenta.music import DEFAULT_QUARTERS_PER_MINUTE
from magenta.protobuf.music_pb2 import NoteSequence

def generate(bundle_name: str,
             sequence_generator,
             generator_id: str,
             primer_filename: str = None,
             qpm: float = DEFAULT_QUARTERS_PER_MINUTE,
             total_length_steps: int = 64,
             temperature: float = 1.0,
             beam_size: int = 1,
             branch_factor: int = 1,
             steps_per_iteration: int = 1) -> NoteSequence:
```

At the beginning of the function, we can keep the same code we previously had, changing the references to the Drums RNN bundle, generator, and configuration to the respective parameters—`bundle_name`, `sequence_generator`, and `generator_id`:

1. First, we'll handle the `primer_filename` parameter by using the MIDI file to note sequence function we previously saw, using an empty sequence if no primer is provided:

```
import magenta.music as mm

if primer_filename:
  primer_sequence = mm.midi_io.midi_file_to_note_sequence(
    os.path.join("primers", primer_filename))
else:
  primer_sequence = NoteSequence()
```

2. Then, we'll handle the `qpm` parameter. If a primer sequence has a tempo, we'll use it. If not, we'll use the provided `qpm` parameter:

```
if primer_sequence.tempos:
  if len(primer_sequence.tempos) > 1:
    raise Exception("No support for multiple tempos")
qpm = primer_sequence.tempos[0].qpm
```

This introduces the `tempos` attribute on the `NoteSequence` message, which contains a list of tempo changes. As in MIDI, a score can have multiple tempos, each of them starting and stopping at a specific time. We won't be handling multiple tempos for the sake of simplicity and because Magenta doesn't handle them.

3. We then change how we calculate the primer length. This used to be a fixed value, but now we take the end of the last note, given by `total_time`, a sequence attribute, and round it up to the closest step beginning. We then calculate the sequence length in seconds from that value:

```
primer_sequence_length_steps = math.ceil(primer_sequence.total_time
                                          / seconds_per_step)
primer_sequence_length_time = (primer_sequence_length_steps
                               * seconds_per_step)
```

The resulting primer end time will be of `primer_sequence_length_time`. Remember Magenta handles sequences in seconds, so we always have to calculate timing in seconds.

4. We also change how the generation length is calculated by subtracting the primer length by the provided `total_length_steps` value:

```
generation_length_steps = total_length_steps -
primer_sequence_length_steps
generation_length_time = generation_length_steps * seconds_per_step
```

We've been using bars to calculate the primer and generation length in the previous chapter, and now, we are using steps to do the same thing. Both approaches are useful in different circumstances and we wanted to show both.

More often than not, using steps is easier to calculate because you don't need to worry about time signatures, which makes the number of steps per bar change.

Using bars, on the other hand, makes it easier to make loops that start and stop with proper timing as we did in the previous chapter's exercises.

5. We can also add `beam_size`, `branch_factor`, and `steps_per_iteration` to the generator options, as follows:

```
generator_options.args['beam_size'].int_value = beam_size
generator_options.args['branch_factor'].int_value = branch_factor
generator_options.args['steps_per_iteration'].int_value =
steps_per_iteration
```

6. Finally, we'll save the MIDI and plot to disk so that we can listen to the sequence and show it. It is the same code you saw previously with a bit more information in the filename, with the `<generator_name>_<generator_id>_<date_time>.<format>` pattern:

```
# Writes the resulting midi file to the output directory
date_and_time = time.strftime('%Y-%m-%d_%H%M%S')
generator_name = str(generator.__class__).split(".")[2]
midi_filename = "%s_%s_%s.mid" % (generator_name,
                                  generator_id,
                                  date_and_time)
midi_path = os.path.join("output", midi_filename)
mm.midi_io.note_sequence_to_midi_file(sequence, midi_path)
print("Generated midi file: " + str(os.path.abspath(midi_path)))

# Writes the resulting plot file to the output directory
date_and_time = time.strftime('%Y-%m-%d_%H%M%S')
generator_name = str(generator.__class__).split(".")[2]
plot_filename = "%s_%s_%s.html" % (generator_name,
                                   generator_id,
                                   date_and_time)
plot_path = os.path.join("output", plot_filename)
pretty_midi = mm.midi_io.note_sequence_to_pretty_midi(sequence)
plotter = Plotter()
plotter.save(pretty_midi, plot_path)
print("Generated plot file: " + str(os.path.abspath(plot_path)))
```

7. We can now call our brand new `generate` method! Let's do a simple example with the Melody RNN model:

```
from magenta.models.melody_rnn import melody_rnn_sequence_generator

generate(
    "basic_rnn.mag",
    melody_rnn_sequence_generator,
    "basic_rnn",
    primer_filename="Fur_Elisa_Beethoveen_Polyphonic.mid",
    total_length_steps=64)
```

So, we've used the `basic_rnn.mag` pre-trained bundle with the `basic_rnn` configuration and `melody_rnn_sequence_generator`. We've asked for 64 steps, which is 4 bars in 4/4 time. But didn't we say the primer has a 3/8 time signature? Yes, but the generated sequence will be in 4/4 time, so we have to make our calculations based on that. We'll be discussing this in a later section, *Losing track of time*.

Calling the method will generate two files in the `output` directory, a MIDI `.mid` file and a plot `.html` file.

8. To listen to the generated MIDI, use your software synthesizer or MuseScore. For the software synth, refer to the following command depending on your platform and replace `PATH_TO_SF2` and `PATH_TO_MIDI` with the proper values:

- Linux: `fluidsynth -a pulseaudio -g 1 -n -i PATH_TO_SF2 PATH_TO_MIDI`
- macOS: `fluidsynth -a coreaudio -g 1 -n -i PATH_TO_SF2 PATH_TO_MIDI`
- Windows: `fluidsynth -g 1 -n -i PATH_TO_SF2 PATH_TO_MIDI`

9. Opening the plot file, we get something like this:

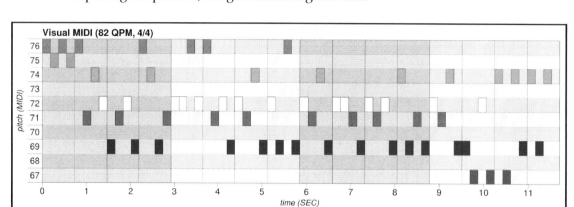

If you listen to it, you'll hear that the generated sample is in the same key as the primer and with similar notes, but the global structure of the primer is lost. That is because the `basic_rnn` configuration doesn't learn musical structure as well as the lookback configuration since the encoded vector doesn't contain step positions and repeating musical steps.

Let's see how we can fix that by looking at the `attention_rnn` and `lookback_rnn` configurations, which are both LSTMs with specific encodings.

Understanding the lookback configuration

To see the lookback configuration in action, we'll first generate a new sequence using the following parameters:

```
generator.generate(
  "lookback_rnn.mag",
  melody_rnn_sequence_generator,
  "lookback_rnn",
  primer_filename="Fur_Elisa_Beethoveen_Monophonic.mid",
  total_length_steps=64,
  temperature=1.1)
```

You can see we're using the same `melody_rnn_sequence_generator` function but changing the configuration and bundle files. Let's look at the generated sample for the **lookback** configuration:

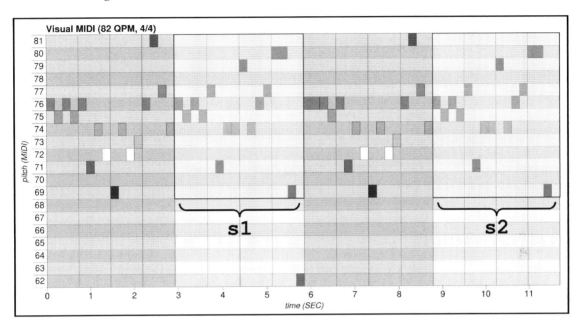

You can see here that bar 1 and bar 3 have a repeating musical structure annotated with **s1** and **s2** in the diagram, with bar 0 and bar 2 also having a similar structure.

If repeating musical structures rings a bell, this is because we've already seen that concept—the Drums RNN uses a lookback encoder, namely, `LookbackEventSequenceEncoderDecoder`, the same as we are using here. In the section on encoding in the previous chapter, we saw that the drum notes are encoded into a one-hot vector for the input of the RNN. We have the same thing here, but instead, it's the melody that gets encoded as a one-hot vector.

Let's take the diagram we had in `Chapter 2`, *Generating Drum Sequences with Drums RNN*, and add more details:

LookbackEventSequenceEncoderDecoder			
		Input vector	**Example vector**
		index range	value
1. event of current step	....	[0, 15]	[..., 0, 0, 0, 0, 1]
2. event of the next step for first lookback	....	[16, 31]	[..., 0, 0, 1, 1, 0]
3. event of the next step for second lookback	....	[32, 47]	[..., 0, 1, 0, 0, 0]
4. step position in bar binary counter	....	[48, 52]	[0, 0, 0, 1, 1]
5. repeating lookback flags	....	[53, 54]	[0, 0]

We provide a small example vector for the sake of the example. The index range for the one-hot encoding is 16, which means we can encode 16 classes only. Remember that the encoding for the drum classes had a length of 512. The `basic_rnn` configuration of the Melody RNN model encodes the melody to 36 classes by mapping only a portion of the pitches. If we want the full pitch range of 127, we should use the `mono_rnn` configuration. The total length of the vector is 55 since we have 3 times a one-hot encoding of 16 classes, plus a binary counter of 5 bits, plus 2 lookback flags.

Let's break it down into five parts and explain the vector's composition:

1. First, we encode the **event of the current step**, which is the part we've already explained in the previous chapter. In the example vector, the event class 1 is encoded, meaning the lowest pitch is played at the current step.

2. Then, we encode the **event of the next step for the first lookback**. So, what is a lookback? When the encoder-decoder gets initialized, it takes by default the lookback distances of *[default steps per bar, default steps per bar * 2]*, namely, [16, 32], which corresponds to the last two bars in the 4/4 time signature. Now, we are looking at the first lookback, which is 16 steps, or 1 bar, before the current step. The encoded event is the next step of that first lookback. In the example vector, the event class 6 is encoded, meaning the corresponding pitch was played 15 steps ago.

3. Then, we encode the **event of the next step for the second lookback**, which is 31 steps, or 2 bars minus one step, before the current step. In the example vector, the event class 8 is encoded, meaning the corresponding pitch was played 31 steps ago.

4. Then, we encode the **step position in the bar binary counter**. The 5-bit vector can encode values from 0 to 15, which is the range of steps we have in 4/4 music. This helps the model to learn musical structure by keeping track of its position inside a bar. In the example vector, the position in the bar is the third step.

5. Finally, we encode the **repeating lookback flags**, which encodes whether the current step is repeating the first lookback or second lookback. It helps to learn whether the event is new content or a repetition of previous content. In the example vector, there are no repetitions.

Magenta's source code is well documented and you can see this code in the `encoder_decoder.py` file in the `magenta.music` module. The class we are looking at is `LookbackEventSequenceEncoderDecoder` and the method is `events_to_input`.

Also, if you are wondering how the models are configured, you can go find the configuration module. For the Melody RNN, search for the `melody_rnn_model.py` file; you'll find, in this module, the configurations we are talking about in this section.

This is important information to feed the model because it enables it to keep the musical structure of the sequence. The model also uses custom labels to reduce the complexity of the information the model has to learn to represent. Since music often has repeating structures on one bar and two bars, the model will use custom labels as appropriate, for example, `repeat-1-bar-ago` and `repeat-2-bar-ago`. This makes it easier for the model to repeat such phrases without having to store them in its memory cell.

Understanding the attention mask

Now that we understand the lookback configuration, let's have a look at the attention configuration. We'll start by generating a sequence using the following:

```
generator.generate(
    "attention_rnn.mag",
    melody_rnn_sequence_generator,
    "attention_rnn",
    primer_filename="Fur_Elisa_Beethoveen_Monophonic.mid",
    total_length_steps=128,
    temperature=1.1)
```

We're generating a longer sequence of 128 steps to try and see the longer dependencies in the musical structure. Let's look at the generated sample for the **attention** configuration:

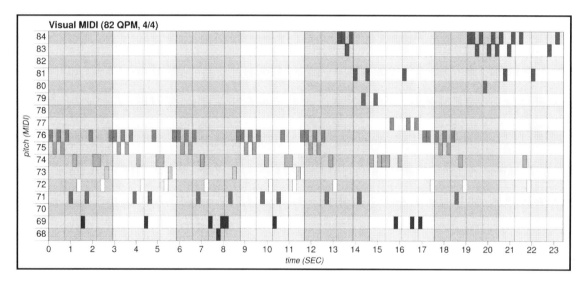

You can see here that, during the eight-bar generation, the model was able to keep track of the musical structure for six bars before wandering off. As previously stated in this chapter's first section, *Looking at an LSTM memory cell*, attention models are relatively new but powerful tools to remember long-term structures.

In Magenta, attention is implemented by looking at the previous *n* steps using an attention mechanism. The exact way the attention mechanism works is outside the scope of this book, but we'll show an example to have an idea of how it works.

First, an *n* length vector is calculated using the previous *n* steps and the current cell state. This gives us how much attention each step should receive. By normalizing it, we get the **attention mask**. For example, it could be *[0.2, 0.8, 0.5]* for *n* equals 3, with the first element (0.2) corresponding to the attention the previous step gets, the second element (0.8) the attention for the step before that, and so on.

Then, we take the three previous steps' output and apply the attention mask on them. The output of a step, for example *[0.0, 1.0, 1.0, 0.0]*, represents to the encoding of one step. Take a look at this example:

- **Step 1**: *[0.0, 1.0, 1.0, 0.0]* becomes *[0.0, 0.2, 0.2, 0.0]* by applying 0.2 (the first element of the attention mask) to each value.
- **Step 2**: *[0.0, 0.0, 1.0, 0.0]* becomes *[0.0, 0.0, 0.8, 0.0]* by applying 0.8 (the second element of the attention mask) to each value.
- **Step 3**: *[0.5, 0.0, 0.0, 0.0]* becomes *[0.25, 0.0, 0.0, 0.0]* by applying 0.5 (the third element of the attention mask) to each value.

Finally, we sum the resulting vectors and get *[0.25, 0.2, 1.0, 0.0]*, which corresponds to the *n* previous outputs, each contributing in a different proportion. That resulting vector is then combined with the RNN output for that current step and applied to the input of the next step.

By using attention, we can directly inject information of the previous outputs into the current step's calculation, without having to store all of the information about the cell's state. This is a powerful mechanism that has usage in many network types.

In Magenta, you can see when attention is used by searching for the `attn_length` argument in the model configuration. If that argument is provided, when the RNN cell is instantiated, an attention wrapper is used. You can see the code in `events_rnn_graph.py` in `make_rnn_cell`:

```
# Add attention wrapper to first layer.
cell = tf.contrib.rnn.AttentionCellWrapper(cell, attn_length,
                                      state_is_tuple=True)
```

The length of the attention will define the number of steps (*n*) of the previous outputs the attention will take into account during training. You can see that the Drums RNN, the Melody RNN, and Improv RNN have attention configurations.

To change the attention configuration during training to 64 steps, for example, use the `attn_length=64` hyperparameter.

Losing track of time

By now, you will have noticed that we lost the initial primer time signature of 3/8. To understand what 3/8 means, let's go back to what we've learned. First, let's remember we have 4 steps per quarter note because this is mainly the sample rate in Magenta. Then, we have the following:

- In **4/4 time**, you have 4 steps per quarter notes times 4 quarter notes in a bar (numerator), which equals 16 steps per bar.
- In **3/4 time**, you have 4 steps per quarter notes times 3 quarter notes in a bar (numerator), which equals 12 steps per bar.
- In **3/8 time**, you have 2 steps per eight notes times 3 eight notes in a bar (numerator), which equals 6 steps per bar. This is because an eight note means it is half the time of a quarter note, so we have 2 steps per eight notes.

Why are we looking into this? We are doing so because time signature doesn't change how many steps or notes we have in a score, but it does change its structure. Because the Melody RNN model supposes a certain structure, it won't be able to adapt to a new one. In our case, the model assumes 4/4 time for two reasons:

- The binary counter representing the position in the bar is defined for 4/4 time because it counts from 0 to 15 for one bar (instead of 0 to 5 in 3/8 time).
- The default lookback in the model is configured to [16, 32] steps, which are the number of steps to lookback in 4/4 time for 1 and 2 bars respectively (instead of 6 and 12 in 3/8 time).

Those are the reasons why this model won't understand our primer's time signature, and finds structures and repetitions on 4/4 time instead of 3/8 time. You might also notice the generate sequence doesn't have a time signature, which, by default, we assume is 4/4.

A time signature is important for the global musical structure of a musical piece and for quantization. Different time signatures will change the way the notes are rounded to the closest steps since it makes the number of steps change.

You can always get the time signature by using `sequence.time_signatures` on a `NoteSequence` instance. This returns a list in Protobuf, on which you can use the `add` method, which adds and returns a new `TimeSignature` element.

Magenta supports any time signature, but all of the models in Magenta were trained in 4/4 time. To generate sequences in another time signature, we'll have to build a proper dataset, create a new configuration, and train the model. Refer to `Chapter 6`, *Data Preparation for Training*, and `Chapter 7`, *Training Magenta Models*, for information on how to do that.

Generating polyphony with the Polyphony RNN and Performance RNN

Now that we've talked in depth about melodies, their representation, encoding, and configuration, we can talk about polyphony. We'll use two models, the Polyphony RNN and Performance RNN, to generate polyphonic music. We'll also look into the encoding of such a musical structure since it is different than monophonic encoding.

Let's start by reminding ourselves that we've used a primer from Beethoven's *Fur Elise* composition in the last example. We'll now use the polyphonic version of it, which looks like this:

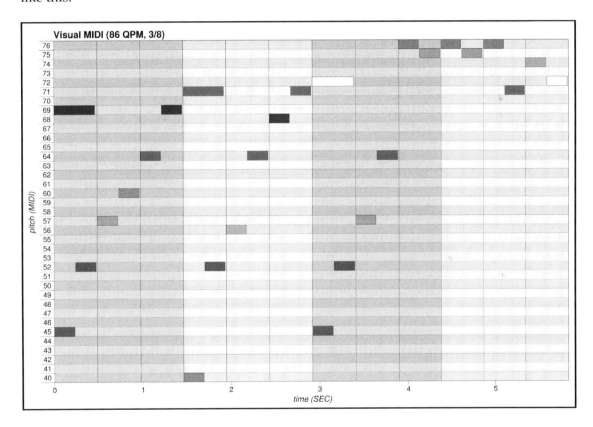

You can see that indeed the primer is polyphonic since multiple notes are being played at the same time. You should know that using a polyphonic primer in a monophonic model will result in an error. You can verify that by calling our generate method from the previous section using the following parameters:

```
generate(
  "basic_rnn.mag",
  melody_rnn_sequence_generator,
  "basic_rnn",
  primer_filename="Fur_Elisa_Beethoveen_Polyphonic.mid",
  total_length_steps=32,
  temperature=0.9)
```

You'll get the following error because there are too many extracted melodies:

```
Traceback (most recent call last):
  File "/home/Packt/hands-on-music-generation-with-
magenta/Chapter03/01.py", line 263, in <module>
    tf.app.run(app)
...
  File "/home/Packt/miniconda3/envs/magenta/lib/python3.5/site-
packages/magenta/models/melody_rnn/melody_rnn_sequence_generator.py", line
91, in _generate
    assert len(extracted_melodies) <= 1
AssertionError
```

Differentiating conditioning and injection

Let's now take the code we've already written, our generate function, and add some content so that we can call it with the Polyphony RNN model:

You can follow this example in the chapter_03_example_02.py file in the source code of this chapter. There are more comments and content in the source code, so you should go check it out.

You can find the generate method in that file. We'll be making more versions of this method as we go. The primer for this example is located at primers/Fur_Elisa_Beethoveen_Polyphonic.mid.

1. First, we'll add two new parameters that are specific to this model, `condition_on_primer` **and** `inject_primer_during_generation`. You can modify the generate method signature as follow:

```
from magenta.music import DEFAULT_QUARTERS_PER_MINUTE
from magenta.protobuf.music_pb2 import NoteSequence

def generate(bundle_name: str,
             sequence_generator,
             generator_id: str,
             qpm: float = DEFAULT_QUARTERS_PER_MINUTE,
             primer_filename: str = None,
             condition_on_primer: bool = False,
             inject_primer_during_generation: bool = False,
             total_length_steps: int = 64,
             temperature: float = 1.0,
             beam_size: int = 1,
             branch_factor: int = 1,
             steps_per_iteration: int = 1) -> NoteSequence:
```

2. And then add the parameters to the generator options:

```
generator_options.args['condition_on_primer'].bool_value = (
    condition_on_primer)
generator_options.args['no_inject_primer_during_generation'].bool_v
alue = (
    not inject_primer_during_generation)
```

Be careful with `inject_primer_during_generation`; it is inverted in the arguments map.

3. We can now launch some generations:

```
generate(
  "polyphony_rnn.mag",
  polyphony_sequence_generator,
  "polyphony",
  condition_on_primer=True,
  inject_primer_during_generation=False,
  temperature=0.9,
  primer_filename="Fur_Elisa_Beethoveen_Polyphonic.mid")

generate(
  "polyphony_rnn.mag",
  polyphony_sequence_generator,
  "polyphony",
  condition_on_primer=False,
  inject_primer_during_generation=True,
```

```
                    temperature=0.9,
                    primer_filename="Fur_Elisa_Beethoveen_Polyphonic.mid")
```

What we've done here is activated only one of the new parameters at a time to see its impact on the generated sequence.

The `condition_on_primer` parameter is used to provide the primer sequence to the RNN before it begins its generation. This needs to be activated for the primer to be taken into account. It is useful to start a sequence with, on a certain key. You can see it in action in this generation:

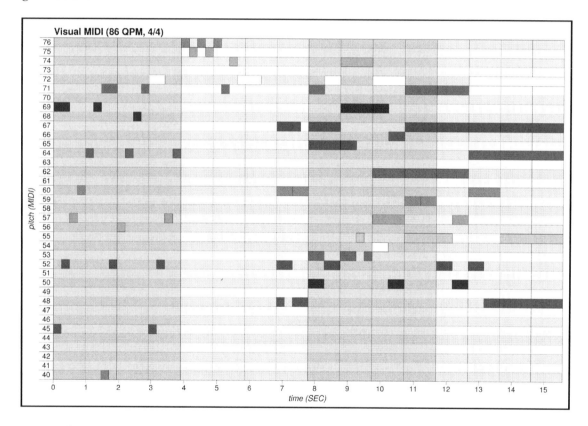

Notice the generated sequence is in key.

The `inject_primer_during_generation` parameter will inject the primer in the generator's output, which means we'll basically have the full primer in the output. You can see it in action in this generation:

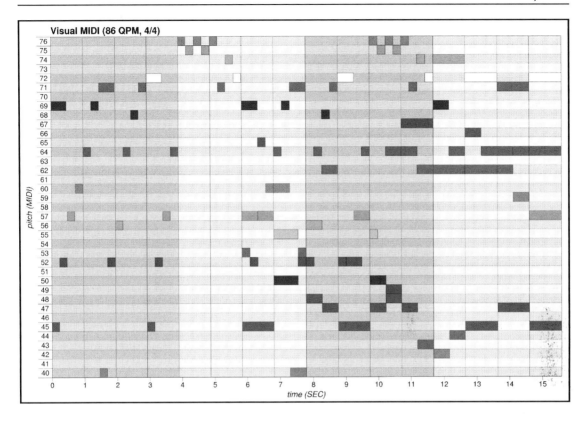

Notice the generated sequence has the full primer in it. You should try different values to see their impact on the generated sequence.

Explaining the polyphonic encoding

Now that we saw a generated polyphonic sequence, let's look at how this type of sequence gets generated. First, let's look at the `PolyphonyRnnModel` model in the module, `polyphony_model.py`. We first notice that the model doesn't define anything new, which means the generation's code is the same as the previous chapter, defined in the *Understanding the generation algorithm* section.

What is different is the way the model encodes its one-hot vector using `PolyphonyOneHotEncoding`. Now, multiple notes can be played at the same time and a single note can spawn multiple steps.

In the Drums RNN encoding, multiples notes could be struck at the same time because it encoded a combination of multiple notes to a specific event, but it couldn't encode a note that spawned multiple steps since a note didn't have a specific marker for start and stop. The Melody RNN encoding is similar in that matter.

Let's take the first four steps of our previously generated example to see how that polyphonic encoding works:

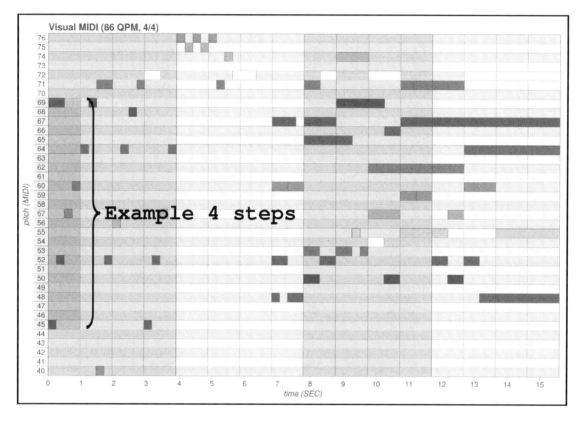

Here, we see 5 notes of pitches, *{69, 45, 52, 57, 60}*, over 4 steps, with the first note, 69, spanning two steps. The Polyphony RNN uses five different event classes to encode this. For the classes without pitch, used to represent the structure of the sequence, you have START, END, and STEP_END. For the classes with a pitch, used to represent a note, you have NEW_NOTE and CONTINUED_NOTE.

Let's try to encode our sequence:

```
START
NEW_NOTE 69
NEW_NOTE 45
STEP_END
CONTINUED_NOTE 69
NEW_NOTE 52
STEP_END
NEW_NOTE 57
STEP_END
NEW_NOTE 60
STEP_END
END
```

What is interesting here is to notice the note continuation on the second step. Also, note endings are not explicitly specified; a note will end if, at CONTINUED_NOTE, the event is not present in the following step. This is different to the encoding presented in the next section.

This sequence gets generated by multiple passes of an RNN generation. This is different than what we saw for a monophonic generation since, previously, it would take the RNN one step to generate one sequence step. Now, we need approximately 5 RNN steps to generate one sequence step. You can see that in the console output. For this example, we have the following:

```
[polyphony_sequence_generator.py:171] Need to generate 40 more steps
for this sequence, will try asking for 200 RNN steps
```

Performance music with the Performance RNN

Now that we have a grip on the Polyphony RNN, we'll be looking into the Performance RNN, a powerful model with more options and pre-trained models than the Polyphony RNN. First, let's have a look at the different pre-trained bundles. Remember that a pre-trained bundle is associated with a specific configuration. This time, you can go see the different configurations in the performance_model.py module.

In the Performance RNN, a different encoding than the Polyphony RNN is used, with new event classes such as NOTE_ON and NOTE_OFF. That might sound familiar because this is also how MIDI encodes its information.

Let's first look at a couple of configuration to start:

- The `performance` configuration supports expressive timing, where the notes won't fall exactly on steps beginning and end, giving it a more "human" feel or "groove" (we'll be also looking into groove in the following chapter, *Latent Space Interpolation with Music VAE*). An event class, `TIME_SHIFT`, is used to represent that, which defines an advance in time.
- The `performance_with_dynamics` configuration supports note velocity, where the notes aren't all played with the same force. An event class, `VELOCITY`, is used to represent that.

Those two additions are important in generating expressive sequences that are closer to what a human player would do.

Now, let's look at two more configurations:

- The `density_conditioned_performance_with_dynamics` configuration supports density conditioning, where the quantity of generated notes can be modified.
- The `pitch_conditioned_performance_with_dynamics` configuration supports pitch conditioning, where the pitch distribution of the generated sequence can be controlled.

These configurations do not change the encoding but control how the generation is executed.

For the first configuration, we need to remember our previous example with the Polyphony RNN, where multiple RNN steps were needed to generate one sequence step. Changing the generation option, `notes_per_second`, will change the number of RNN steps for each sequence step, reducing or augmenting the generation density.

For the second configuration, a histogram can be provided with the relative density of each pitch in an octave using the generator option, `pitch_class_histogram`. The histogram is a list of 12 values (there are 12 notes per octave) with a value of frequency for each pitch, corresponding to *[C, C#, D, D#, E, F, F#, G, G#, A, A#, B]*. For an F Major scale, with F happening twice as much, you would have: *[1, 0, 1, 0, 1, 2, 0, 1, 0, 1, 0, 1]*.

 You can see this example in action in the `chapter_03_example_03.py` file in the source code of this chapter. We won't be looking at the code here since it is similar to the previous two examples.

To learn expressive timing and dynamics, these models have been trained on real piano performances from the Yamaha e-Piano Competition (you can find them at `www.piano-e-competition.com/midiinstructions.asp`).

Generating expressive timing like a human

Here is an example of a generation with the Performance RNN, with the pre-trained model, `density_conditioned_performance_with_dynamics`, with a parameter of `notes_per_second=8`. We're showing only the generated part, which is four bars after the primer:

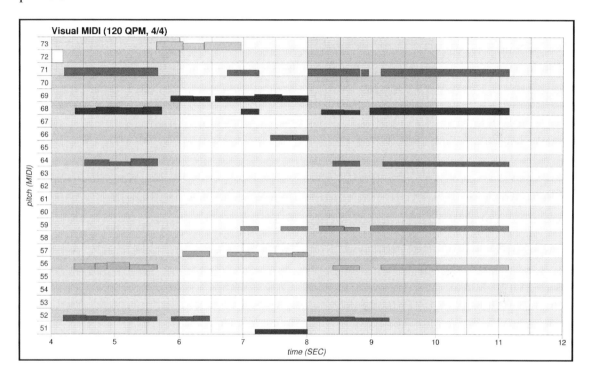

You will notice a couple of things here:

- First, the notes do not all have the same height. This is because we can ask Visual MIDI to scale the note height according to their velocity. The bigger the note, the louder it is. Remember, velocity in MIDI is from 0 to 127. For example, the first note of pitch 71 has a velocity of 77.
- Second, the notes do not fall directly on bar subdivisions—they start and end a bit off, just before or after the steps boundaries. This is possible because the model uses a `TIME_SHIFT` event and was trained on a dataset that was played by human players, which contained such a groove. This is very interesting and different than what we were previously doing: we are not generating sheet music anymore; we are generating a performance.

Generating a quantized score or generating a groovy performance, both have their specific usage, so you'll need to decide which suits best your goals. Because of the performance nature of the generated sequence, opening the file in music notation software such as MuseScore might look a bit messy.

Summary

In this chapter, we looked at generating melodies, using both monophonic and polyphonic models.

We first started by looking at LSTM cells and their usage in RNNs to keep information for a long period of time, using forget, input, and output gates.

Then, we generated melodies with the Melody RNN, using multiple pre-trained models such as basic, lookback, and attention. We saw that the basic model cannot learn repeating structure, because its input vector encoding do not contain such information. We then looked at the lookback encoding, where step position in bar and repeating structure are encoded into the input vector, making it possible for the model to learn such information. We finally saw the attention model, where the attention mechanism makes it possible to look at multiple previous steps, using an attention mask that gives a weight to each step.

Finally, we generated polyphony using the Polyphony RNN and the Performance RNN. In the former model, we learned how polyphony can be encoded in a vector, using start and continue events. In the latter model, we learned another polyphony encoding, using note on and note off events, similar to what MIDI uses. In the Performance RNN, we also learned about expressive generation, both in terms of timing and velocity changes.

As we now know, expressive timing is what gives the music a human feel, where the notes do not fall on predefined times. This is what we sometimes call groove, and we'll be looking more into this subject in the next chapter, *Latent Space Interpolation with Music VAE*. We'll also be looking at score interpolation, which makes it possible to gradually transition from one score to another.

Questions

1. What are the main problems RNN suffers from when learning, and what are the solutions brought by LSTMs?

2. What is a simpler alternative to LSTM memory cells? What are their advantages and disadvantages?

3. You want to configure the lookback encoder-decoder from the Melody RNN to learn structures with a 3/4 time signature. How big is the binary step counter? How are the lookback distances configured for 3 lookback distances?

4. You have the resulting vector, *[0.10, 0.50, 0.00, 0.25]*, from the applied attention mask of *[0.1, 0.5]*, with $n = 2$, and the previous step 1 of *[1, 0, 0, 0]* and step 2 of *[0, 1, 0, x]*. What is the value of x?

5. You have the following the Polyphony RNN encoding: *{ (START), (NEW_NOTE, 67), (NEW_NOTE, 64), (NEW_NOTE, 60), (STEP_END), (CONTINUED_NOTE, 67), (CONTINUED_NOTE, 64), (CONTINUED_NOTE, 60), (STEP_END), (CONTINUED_NOTE, 67), (CONTINUED_NOTE, 64), (CONTINUED_NOTE, 60), (STEP_END), (CONTINUED_NOTE, 67), (CONTINUED_NOTE, 64), (CONTINUED_NOTE, 60), (STEP_END), (END) }*. What is being played?

6. What event would be used to end a note of pitch 56 in the Polyphony RNN encoding? And in the Performance RNN?

7. What are two components of a generated score that would give them a more human fell? What model and arguments would you use to achieve that?

8. When using the `notes_per_seconds` parameter in the `density_conditioned_performance_with_dynamics` model, what is the impact on the generation algorithm?

Further reading

- **Learning Long-Term Dependencies with Gradient Descent is Difficult**: A paper (1994) describing the difficulties of RNN to learn long-term dependencies in practice (`ai.dinfo.unifi.it/paolo//ps/tnn-94-gradient.pdf`)

- **Long Short-Term Memory**: An original paper (1997) on LSTM (`www.bioinf.jku.at/publications/older/2604.pdf`)

- **Understanding LSTM Networks**: An excellent article explaining in detail LSTM memory cells, which contains more information than this chapter (`colah.github.io/posts/2015-08-Understanding-LSTMs/`)

- **Illustrated Guide to LSTM's and GRU's: A step by step explanation**: an excellent in-depth article about LSTM and GRU (`towardsdatascience.com/illustrated-guide-to-lstms-and-gru-s-a-step-by-step-explanation-44e9eb85bf21`)

- **Understanding LSTM and its diagrams**: Another excellent article on LSTMs (`medium.com/mlreview/understanding-lstm-and-its-diagrams-37e2f46f1714#.swstv6z61`)

- **Generating Long-Term Structure in Songs and Stories**: An excellent blog post from Magenta's developers looking into the lookback and attention models of the Melody RNN (`magenta.tensorflow.org/2016/07/15/lookback-rnn-attention-rnn/`)

- **Attention Is All You Need**: A paper (2017) on the usage and performance of the attention mechanism (`arxiv.org/abs/1706.03762`)

4
Latent Space Interpolation with MusicVAE

In this chapter, we'll learn about the importance of continuous latent space of **Variational Autoencoders (VAEs)** and its importance in music generation compared to standard **Autoencoders (AEs)**. We'll use the MusicVAE model, a hierarchical recurrent VAE, from Magenta to sample sequences and then interpolate between them, effectively morphing smoothly from one to another. We'll then see how to add groove, or humanization, to an existing sequence using the GrooVAE model. We'll finish by looking at the TensorFlow code used to build the VAE model.

The following topics will be covered in this chapter:

- Continuous latent space in VAEs
- Score transformation with MusicVAE and GrooVAE
- Understanding TensorFlow code

Technical requirements

In this chapter, we'll use the following tools:

- A **command line** or **bash** to launch Magenta from the Terminal
- **Python** and its libraries to write music generation code using Magenta
- **Magenta** to generate music in MIDI
- **MuseScore** or **FluidSynth** to listen to the generated MIDI

In Magenta, we'll make the use of the **MusicVAE** and **GrooVAE** models. We'll be explaining these models in depth, but if you feel like you need more information, the model's README in Magenta's source code (`github.com/tensorflow/magenta/tree/master/magenta/models`) is a good place to start. You can also take a look at Magenta's code, which is well documented. We also provide additional content in the last section, *Further reading*.

The code for this chapter is in this book's code GitHub in the `Chapter04` folder, located at `github.com/PacktPublishing/hands-on-music-generation-with-magenta/tree/master/Chapter04`. The examples and code snippets will suppose you are located in this chapter's folder. For this chapter, you should go to `cd Chapter04` before you start.

Check out the following video to see the Code in Action: `http://bit.ly/3176ylN`

Continuous latent space in VAEs

In `Chapter 2`, *Generating Drum Sequences with the Drums RNN*, we saw how we can use an RNN (LSTM) and a beam search to iteratively generate a sequence, by taking an input and then predicting, note by note, which next note is the most probable. That enabled us to use a primer as a basis for the generation, using it to set a starting melody or a certain key.

Using that technique is useful, but it has its limitations. What if we wanted to start with a primer and explore variations around it, and not just in a random way, but in a desired **specific direction**? For example, we could have a two-bars melody for a bass line, and we would like to hear how it sounds when played more as an arpeggio. Another example would be transitioning smoothly between two melodies. This is where the RNN models we previously saw fall short and where VAEs comes into play.

Before getting into the specifics of VAEs and how they are implemented in MusicVAE, let's first introduce standard AEs.

The latent space in standard AEs

An AE network is a pair of two connected networks, an **encoder** and a **decoder**, where the encoder produces an **embedding** from an input that the decoder will try to replicate. The embedding is a dense representation of the input, where useless features have been dropped, but is still representative enough so that the decoder can try and reproduce the input.

What's the use of the encoder and decoder pair if the decoder merely tries to reproduce the input? Its main use is **dimensionality reduction**, where the input can be represented in a lower spatial resolution (with fewer dimensions) while still keeping its meaning. This forces the network to discover significant features to be encoded in the hidden layer nodes.

In the following diagram, we illustrate a VAE network, which is separated into three main parts—the hidden layer nodes (latent space or latent variables) in the middle, the encoder on the left, and the decoder on the right:

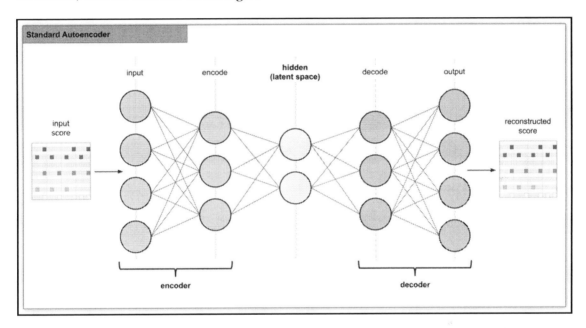

Regarding the network training, the loss function, called **reconstruction loss**, is defined such as the network is penalized for creating outputs different from the input.

Generation is possible by instantiating the latent variables, which produces the embeddings, and then decoding that to produce a new output. Unfortunately, the learned latent space of the AE might not be continuous, which is a major shortcoming of that architecture, making its real-world usages limited. A latent space that is not continuous means that sampling a point at random might result in a vector that the decoder cannot make sense of. This is because the encoder hasn't learned how to handle that specific point and cannot generalize from its other learning.

In the following diagram, the black point marked by **?** falls in such a space, meaning the encoder won't be able to reconstruct the input from it. This is an example visualization of samples of the latent space (for three classes), with the axis representing the first two dimensions of the latent space and the colors representing three classes, which shows the formation of distinct clusters:

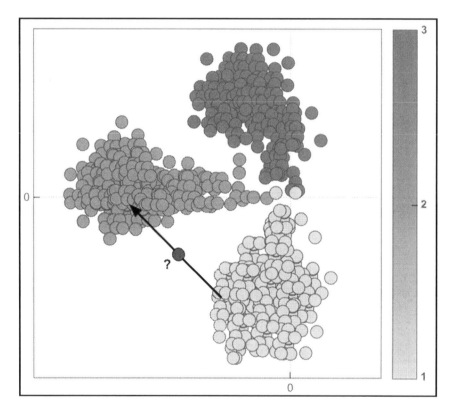

This is fine if you are just replicating an input, but what if you want to sample from the latent space or interpolate between two inputs? In the diagram, you can see that the black data point (denoted with a question mark) falls in a region the decoder won't be able to make sense of. This is why the discontinuous latent space from AEs is a problem for our use case.

Now, let's see how a VAE solves that problem.

Using VAEs in generating music

There is one property in VAEs that makes them useful for generating music (or any generation) is that their latent space is **continuous**. To achieve that, the encoder doesn't output a vector, but rather two vectors: a vector of means called **μ** (mu) and a vector of standard deviations called **σ** (sigma). Therefore, latent variables, often called **z** by convention, follow a probability distribution of $P(z)$, often a Gaussian distribution.

In other words, the mean of the vector controls where the encoding of the input should be located and the standard deviation controls the size of the area around it, making the latent space continuous. Reusing the previous example, an example plot of the latent space, with the x and y axes representing its first two dimensions, for three classes represented by three colors, you can see the clusters now cover an area instead of being discrete:

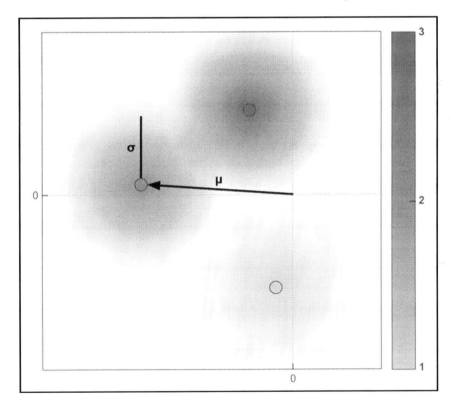

Here is the VAE network, where you can see the change in the hidden layer with µ and σ:

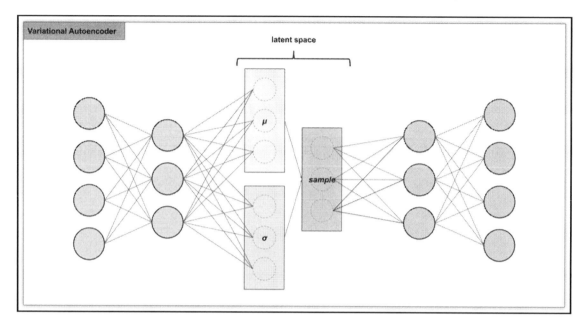

This network architecture is very powerful for generating music and is often considered in a class of model called generative models. One property of that type of model is that the generation is stochastic, meaning that for a given input (and the same values of mean and standard deviation), the sampling will make the encoding vary a little for each pass.

This model has multiple properties that are really interesting for music generation, such as the following:

- **Expression**: A musical sequence can be mapped to the latent space and reconstructed from it.
- **Realism**: Any point of the latent space represents a realistic example.
- **Smoothness**: Samples from nearby points are similar.

We'll be explaining more on VAE in this chapter, but this minimal introduction is important to understand the code we're about to write.

Score transformation with MusicVAE and GrooVAE

In the previous chapters, we've learned to generate various parts of a score. We've generated percussion and monophonic and polyphonic melodies and learned about expressive timing. This section builds on that foundation and shows how to manipulate the generated scores and transform them. In our example, we'll sample two small scores from the latent space, we'll then interpolate between the two samples (progressively going from the first sample to the second sample), and finally, we'll add some groove (or **humanization**, see the following information box for more information) on the resulting score.

For our example, we'll work on percussion since adding groove in MusicVAE only works on drums. We'll be using different configurations and pre-trained models in MusicVAE to perform the following steps. Remember, there are more pre-trained models in Magenta than we can present here (see the first section, *Technical requirements*, for a link to the README that contains all of them):

- **Sample:** By using the `cat-drums_2bar_small` configuration and pre-trained model, we sample two different scores of two bars each. We could do the same thing for the melody by using the `cat-mel_2bar_big` configuration.
- **Interpolate**: By using the same configuration, we can interpolate between the two generated scores. What interpolation means is that it will progressively change the score, going from the first sample to the second. By asking a different number of outputs, we can decide how gradually we go between the two samples.
- **Groove:** By using the `groovae_2bar_humanize` configuration, we can then humanize the previous 16-bars sequence by adding groove.

Here is a diagram explaining the different steps of our example:

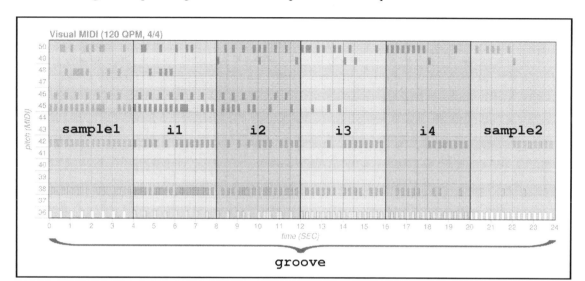

First, we'll be sampling `sample1` and `sample2` (2 bars each). Then, we'll ask the interpolation for 4 output sequences ("i1", "i2", "i3", and "i4") of 2 bars each. The resulting 6 output sequences of 12 bars will contain the 2 input sequences in both ends, plus the score progression of 6 sequences in between. Finally, we'll add groove to the whole sequence.

 If you remember from the last chapter, in the *Performance music with the Performance RNN* section, we introduced what **groove** or **humanization** is and how to generate sequences that feel less robotic. This boils down to two things: expressive timing and dynamics. The former changes the timing of the notes so that they don't fall exactly on step boundaries, while the latter changes the force at which each note is played (its velocity) to emulate a human playing an instrument.

We'll be explaining more on these configurations as we go along. If you want to try out the examples for the melody instead of the percussion, follow the example by changing the mentions of `cat-drums_2bar_small` to `cat-mel_2bar_big`. We'll also be looking at other models, including the melody model, later in this chapter.

Initializing the model

Before sampling, interpolating, and grooving, we need to initialize the model that we're going to use. The first thing you'll notice is that MusicVAE doesn't have a similar interface to the previous chapters; it has its own interface and model definition. This means the code we've written up to now cannot be reused, except for some things such as MIDI and plot files handling.

 You can follow this example in the `chapter_04_example_01.py` file in the source code of this chapter. There are more comments and content in the source code, so you should go check it out.

The pre-trained MusicVAE models are not packaged in bundles (the `.mag` files) unlike in the previous chapters. A model and a configuration now correspond to a **checkpoint**, which is slightly less expressive than bundles. We've already briefly explained what a checkpoint is and we'll be looking into this in detail in Chapter 7, *Training Magenta Models*. Just remember for now that checkpoints are used in TensorFlow to save the model state that occurs during training, making it easy to reload the model's state at a later time:

1. Let's first make a `download_checkpoint` method that downloads a checkpoint corresponding to a model:

```python
import os
import tensorflow as tf
from six.moves import urllib

def download_checkpoint(model_name: str,
                        checkpoint_name: str,
                        target_dir: str):
  tf.gfile.MakeDirs(target_dir)
  checkpoint_target = os.path.join(target_dir, checkpoint_name)
  if not os.path.exists(checkpoint_target):
    response = urllib.request.urlopen(
      f"https://storage.googleapis.com/magentadata/models/"
      f"{model_name}/checkpoints/{checkpoint_name}")
    data = response.read()
    local_file = open(checkpoint_target, 'wb')
    local_file.write(data)
    local_file.close()
```

You don't have to worry too much about the details of this method; basically, it downloads the checkpoint from online storage. It is analogous to the `download_bundle` method from `magenta.music.notebook_utils`, which we've been using in the previous chapters.

2. We can now write a `get_model` method that instantiates the MusicVAE model using the checkpoint:

```
from magenta.models.music_vae import TrainedModel, configs

def get_model(name: str):
  checkpoint = name + ".tar"
  download_checkpoint("music_vae", checkpoint, "bundles")
  return TrainedModel(
    # Removes the .lohl in some training checkpoints
    # which shares the same config
    configs.CONFIG_MAP[name.split(".")[0] if "." in name else name]
    # The batch size changes the number of sequences
    # to be run together
    batch_size=8,
    checkpoint_dir_or_path=os.path.join("bundles", checkpoint))
```

In this method, we first download the checkpoint for the given model name with our `download_checkpoint` method. Then, we instantiate the `TrainedModel` class from `magenta.models.music_vae` with the checkpoint, `batch_size=8`. This value defines how many sequences the model will process at the same time.

Having a batch size that's too big will result in wasted overhead; a batch size too small will result in multiple passes, probably making the whole code run slower. Unlike during training, the batch size doesn't need to be big. In this example, the sample uses two sequences, the interpolation two sequences, and the humanizing code six sequences, so if we wanted to nitpick, we could change `batch_size` to match each call.

For the first argument of `TrainedModel`, we pass an instance of `Config`. Each model corresponds to a configuration in the `models/music_vae/configs.py` file. If you look at the content of that file, you'll probably recognize some content we already saw. For example, let's take the configuration named `cat-drums_2bar_small` from `CONFIG_MAP`, which is the configuration we'll be using for sampling.

Now, follow the reference of the `data_converter` attribute, you'll end up in a class named `DrumsConverter` in `models.music_vae.data`. In the `__init__` method, you can see classes and methods we've already covered in `Chapter 2`, *Generating Drum Sequences with the Drums RNN* for the DrumsRNN models, such as the `MultiDrumOneHotEncoding` class that we explained in the section, *Encoding percussion events as classes*.

The MusicVAE code builds on the content we previously saw, adding a new layer that enables the conversion of note sequences to Tensforflow tensors. We'll be looking into the TensorFlow code in more detail in the *Understanding TensorFlow 2.0 code* section.

Sampling the latent space

Now that we can download and initialize our MusicVAE models, we can sample (analogous to generate) sequences. Remembering what we've learned from the previous section on VAEs, we know that we can sample any point in the latent space, by instantiating the latent variables corresponding to our probability distribution and then decoding the embeddings.

Until now, we've been using the term **generate** when speaking of creating a new sequence. That term refers to the generation algorithm we described in `Chapter 2`, *Generating Drum Sequences with the Drums RNN*, and that was also used in `Chapter 3`, *Generating Polyphonic Melodies*.

We're now using the term **sample** when speaking of creating a new sequence. This refers to the act of sampling (because we're effectively sampling a probability distribution) the latent space and differs from the generation algorithm we previously described.

Writing the sampling code

Let's now write the first method for our example, the `sample` method:

1. First, let's define the method, which takes a model name as an input and returns a list of two generated `NoteSequence` objects:

```
from typing import List
from magenta.protobuf.music_pb2 import NoteSequence

from utils import save_midi, save_plot

def sample(model_name: str,
```

```
                num_steps_per_sample: int) -> List[NoteSequence]:
    model = get_model(model_name)

    # Uses the model to sample 2 sequences
    sample_sequences = model.sample(n=2, length=num_steps_per_sample)

    # Saves the midi and the plot in the sample folder
    save_midi(sample_sequences, "sample", model_name)
    save_plot(sample_sequences, "sample", model_name)

    return sample_sequences
```

In this method, we first instantiate the model using our previous `get_model` method. We then call the `sample` method, asking for n=2 sequences that the method will return. We are keeping the default temperature (which is 1.0, for all models), but we can change it using the `temperature` parameter. Finally, we save the MIDI files and the plot files using the `save_midi` and `save_plot` methods respectively, from the previous chapter, present in the `utils.py` file.

2. Let's call the sample method we created:

```
num_bar_per_sample = 2
num_steps_per_sample = num_bar_per_sample * DEFAULT_STEPS_PER_BAR
generated_sample_sequences = sample("cat-drums_2bar_small.lokl",
                                    num_steps_per_sample)
```

You might have noticed that the pre-trained model, `cat-drums_2bar_small.lokl`, has `.lokl` suffixed. There's also a `.hikl` model, which refers to the KL divergence during training. We'll be explaining that in the next section, *Refining the loss function with KL divergence*.

In the previous snippet, `num_bar_per_sample` and `num_steps_per_sample` define the number of bars and steps respectively for each sample. The configuration we are using, `cat-drums_2bar_small`, is a small 9 classes drum kit configuration, similar to the one we saw in `Chapter 2`. For our example, we'll use 32 steps (2 bars).

3. Let's open the `output/sample/music_vae_00_TIMESTAMP.html` file, changing `TIMESTAMP` for the printed value in the console. Here is the first generated sample we are going to work with:

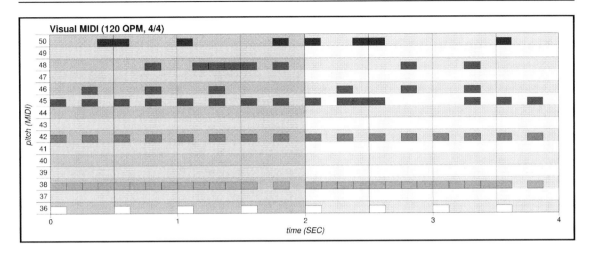

Notice we've activated the velocity output in Visual MIDI, meaning the notes don't quite fill the whole vertical space because the default velocity in Magenta is 100 (remember MIDI values go from 0 to 127). Because we'll be adding groove later, we need to see the notes' velocity.

4. Let's open the `output/sample/music_vae_01_TIMESTAMP.html` file, changing `TIMESTAMP` for the printed value in the console. Here is the second sample:

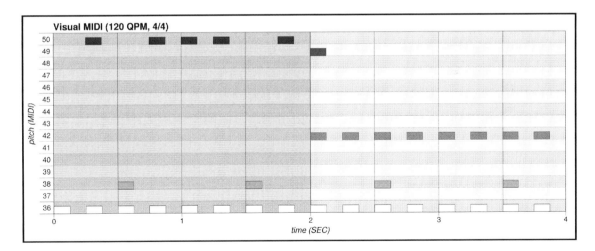

5. To listen to the generated MIDI, use your software synthesizer or MuseScore. For the software synthesizer, refer to the following command depending on your platform and replace `PATH_TO_SF2` and `PATH_TO_MIDI` with the proper values:

- Linux: `fluidsynth -a pulseaudio -g 1 -n -i PATH_TO_SF2 PATH_TO_MIDI`

- macOS: `fluidsynth -a coreaudio -g 1 -n -i PATH_TO_SF2 PATH_TO_MIDI`

- Windows: `fluidsynth -g 1 -n -i PATH_TO_SF2 PATH_TO_MIDI`

We now have two 2 bar samples to work with; we'll be interpolating between them in the next section.

Refining the loss function with KL divergence

You might have noticed in the previous code snippet that the `cat-drums_2bar_small.lokl` checkpoint we are using is suffixed with `lokl`. This is because this configuration has two different trained checkpoints: `lokl` and `hikl`. The first one has been trained for more realistic sampling, while the second one has been trained for better reconstruction and interpolation. We've used the first one in the previous code for sampling, and we'll use the second one in the next section for interpolation.

But what do `lokl` and `hikl` mean exactly? These refer to **low** or **high Kulback-Leibler (KL)** divergence. The KL divergence measures how much two probability distributions diverge from each other. Reusing our previous example, we can show that we want to minimize the KL divergence to achieve smoothness during interpolation:

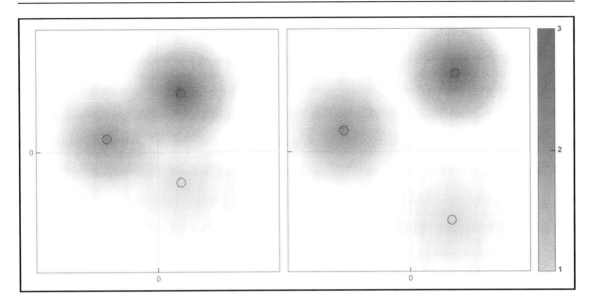

This is an example visualization of samples of the latent space (for 3 classes), with the axis representing the first 2 dimensions of the latent space, and the colors representing 3 classes. On the left, we have encodings that are fairly close to one another, enabling smooth interpolation. On the right, we have clusters that are further apart, which means the interpolation will be harder but might result in a better sampling because the clusters are more distinct.

The KL loss function sums all the KL divergences with the standard normal. Alone, the KL loss results in a random cluster centered around the prior (a round blob around 0), which is not really useful by itself. By **combining** the reconstruction loss function and the KL loss function, we achieve clusters of similar encodings that are densely packed around the latent space origin.

You can look at the implementation of the model loss function in Magenta's code in the MusicVAE class, in the magenta.models.music_vae package, in the _compute_model_loss function.

During training, the KL divergence is tuned using the hyperparameters, free_bits and max_beta. By increasing the effect of the KL loss (which means decreasing free_bits or increasing max_beta), you'll have a model that produces better random samples but is worse at reconstruction.

Sampling from the same area of the latent space

What is interesting for sampling is that we can reuse the same z variable for each of the generated sequences in the same batch. That is useful for generating sequences from the same area of the latent space. For example, to generate 2 sequences of 64 steps (4 bars) using the same z variable for both, we would be using the following code:

```
sample_sequences = model.sample(n=2, length=64, same_z=True)
```

Sampling from the command line

You can also call the model sampling from the command line. The example from this section can be called using the following command line:

```
> curl --output "checkpoints/cat-drums_2bar_small.lokl.tar"
"https://storage.googleapis.com/magentadata/models/music_vae/checkpoints/ca
t-drums_2bar_small.lokl.tar"
> music_vae_generate --config="cat-drums_2bar_small" --
checkpoint_file="checkpoints/cat-drums_2bar_small.lokl.tar" --mode="sample"
--num_outputs="2" --output_dir="output/sample"
```

Interpolating between two samples

We now have 2 generated samples and we want to interpolate between the two of them, with 4 intermediate sequences in between, resulting in a continuous 6 sequences of 2 bars each, for a 12 bars total sequence.

Getting the sequence length right

For our example, we used length=32 when calling the sample method on the model, so the return of the method are sequences of 2 bars each. You should know that the sequence length is important in MusicVAE since each model works on different sequence lengths—cat-drums_2bar_small works on 2 bar sequences, while hierdec-mel_16bar works on 16 bar sequences.

When sampling, Magenta won't complain, because it can generate a longer sequence and then truncate it. But during interpolation, you'll end up with an exception like this, meaning that you haven't asked for the proper number of steps:

```
Traceback (most recent call last):
...
   File "/home/Packt/miniconda3/envs/magenta/lib/python3.5/site-
packages/magenta/models/music_vae/trained_model.py", line 224, in encode
     (len(extracted_tensors.inputs), note_sequence))
magenta.models.music_vae.trained_model.MultipleExtractedExamplesError:
Multiple (2) examples extracted from NoteSequence: ticks_per_quarter: 220
```

Exceptions in MusicVAE are especially cryptic and the encoder is quite finicky, so we'll try listing the common mistakes and their associated exception.

Writing the interpolation code

Let's now write the second method for our example, the `interpolate` method:

1. First, let's define the method, which takes a list of two `NoteSequence` objects as an input and returns a 16 bar interpolated sequence:

```
import magenta.music as mm

def interpolate(model_name: str,
                sample_sequences: List[NoteSequence],
                num_steps_per_sample: int,
                num_output: int,
                total_bars: int) -> NoteSequence:
  model = get_model(model_name)

  # Use the model to interpolate between the 2 input sequences
  interpolate_sequences = model.interpolate(
      start_sequence=sample_sequences[0],
      end_sequence=sample_sequences[1],
      num_steps=num_output,
      length=num_steps_per_sample)

  save_midi(interpolate_sequences, "interpolate", model_name)
  save_plot(interpolate_sequences, "interpolate", model_name)

  # Concatenates the resulting sequences into one single sequence
  interpolate_sequence = mm.sequences_lib.concatenate_sequences(
      interpolate_sequences, [4] * num_output)

  save_midi(interpolate_sequence, "merge", model_name)
```

```
        save_plot(interpolate_sequence, "merge", model_name,
                plot_max_length_bar=total_bars,
                bar_fill_alphas=[0.50, 0.50, 0.05, 0.05])

    return interpolate_sequence
```

We first instantiate the model, then we call the `interpolate` method with the first and last sample using the parameters, `start_sequence` and `end_sequence` respectively, the number of output sequences of 6 using the `num_steps` parameter (be careful it has nothing to do with the sequence length in steps) and the `length` parameter of 2 bars (in steps). The interpolation result is a list of six `NoteSequence` objects, each of 2 bars.

We then concatenate the elements of the list to form a single `NoteSequence` object of 12 bars using `concatenate_sequences` from `magenta.music.sequence_lib`. The second argument (`[4] * num_output`) is a list containing the time in seconds of each element of the first argument. We should remember that this is necessary because `NoteSequence` doesn't define a start and an end, so a 2 bars sequence ending with silence concatenated with another sequence of 2 bars won't result in a 4 bars sequence.

When calling the `interpolate` method, a `NoExtractedExamplesError` exception could occur if the input sequences are not quantized or an input sequence is empty, for example. Remember you also have to ask for the proper length or you'll receive `MultipleExtractedExamplesError`.

2. We can then call the `interpolate` method:

```
num_output = 6
total_bars = num_output * num_bar_per_sample
generated_interpolate_sequence = \
interpolate("cat-drums_2bar_small.hikl",
            generated_sample_sequences,
            num_steps_per_sample,
            num_output,
            total_bars)
```

3. Let's open the `output/merge/music_vae_00_TIMESTAMP.html` file, changing `TIMESTAMP` for the printed value in the console. Corresponding to our samples, we have this interpolated sequence:

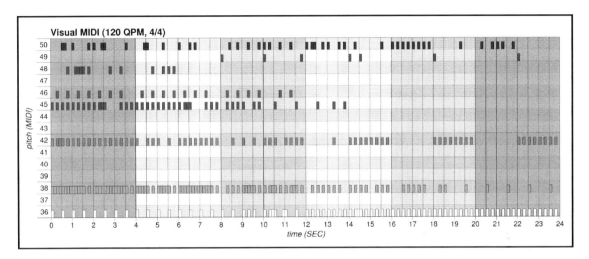

We've marked every 2 bars with a different background alpha. You can locate the first sample we've generated in the previous section between 0 and 4 seconds, with a darker background. Then, 4 new interpolated chunks can be located between 4 and 20 seconds. Finally, you can see the second input sample on the right between 20 and 24 seconds.

4. To listen to the generated MIDI, use your software synthesizer or MuseScore. For the software synth, refer to the following command depending on your platform and replace `PATH_TO_SF2` and `PATH_TO_MIDI` with the proper values:

   - Linux: `fluidsynth -a pulseaudio -g 1 -n -i PATH_TO_SF2 PATH_TO_MIDI`
   - macOS: `fluidsynth -a coreaudio -g 1 -n -i PATH_TO_SF2 PATH_TO_MIDI`
   - Windows: `fluidsynth -g 1 -n -i PATH_TO_SF2 PATH_TO_MIDI`

Interpolating between two sequences is a hard problem, but MusicVAE does it well and the result in our example is quite impressive. You should try other generations with different lengths and listen to them.

Interpolating from the command line

You can also call the interpolation from the command line. The example from this section can be called using the following command line (you'll need to download the checkpoint by yourself):

```
> curl --output "checkpoints/cat-drums_2bar_small.hikl.tar"
"https://storage.googleapis.com/magentadata/models/music_vae/checkpoints/ca
t-drums_2bar_small.hikl.tar"
> music_vae_generate --config="cat-drums_2bar_small" --
checkpoint_file="checkpoints/cat-drums_2bar_small.hikl.tar" --
mode="interpolate" --num_outputs="6" --output_dir="output/interpolate" --
input_midi_1="output/sample/SAMPLE_1.mid" --
input_midi_2="output/sample/SAMPLE_2.mid"
```

By changing the `SAMPLE_1.mid` and `SAMPLE_2.mid` file names for a previous sampled file from the previous sampling section, you'll be able to interpolate between the two sequences.

Humanizing the sequence

Finally, we'll be adding humanization (or **groove**) to the generated sequence. The groove models are part of GrooVAE (pronounced *groovay*) and are present in MusicVAE's code.

Writing the humanizing code

Let's now write the last method of our example, the `groove` method:

1. First, let's define the method, which takes `NoteSequence` as input and returns a humanized sequence:

```python
def groove(model_name: str,
           interpolate_sequence: NoteSequence,
           num_steps_per_sample: int,
           num_output: int,
           total_bars: int) -> NoteSequence:
    model = get_model(model_name)

    # Split the sequences in chunks of 4 seconds
    split_interpolate_sequences =
    mm.sequences_lib.split_note_sequence(
        interpolate_sequence, 4)

    # Uses the model to encode the list of sequences
```

```
encoding, mu, sigma = model.encode(
    note_sequences=split_interpolate_sequences)

# Uses the model to decode the encoding
groove_sequences = model.decode(
    z=encoding, length=num_steps_per_sample)

groove_sequence = mm.sequences_lib.concatenate_sequences(
    groove_sequences, [4] * num_output)

save_midi(groove_sequence, "groove", model_name)
save_plot(groove_sequence, "groove", model_name,
        plot_max_length_bar=total_bars, show_velocity=True,
        bar_fill_alphas=[0.50, 0.50, 0.05, 0.05])

return groove_sequence
```

First, we download the model. Then, we split the sequence in chunks of 4 seconds, because we need chunks of 2 bars for the model to handle. We then call the `encode` function, followed by the `decode` function. Unfortunately, there isn't a `groove` method on the model yet.

The `encode` method takes a list of sequence that it will encode, returning the `encoding` vector (also called z or latent vector), mu and `sigma`. We won't be using mu and `sigma` here but we left them for clarity. The resulting shape of the encoding array is *(6, 256)*, where 6 is the number of split sequences, and 256 is the encoding size that is defined in the model, explained in a later section, *Building the hidden layer*.

As for the `interpolate` method, the call to the `encode` method might throw an exception if the sequences are not properly formed.

Then, the `decode` method takes the previous `encoding` value and the number of steps per sample and tries to reproduce the input, resulting in a list of 6 humanized sequences of 2 bars each.

Finally, we concatenate the sequences like in the interpolate code snippet.

2. Let's try calling the `groove` method:

```
generated_groove_sequence = groove("groovae_2bar_humanize",
                                    generated_interpolate_sequence,
                                    num_steps_per_sample,
                                    num_output,
                                    total_bars)
```

The returned sequence, `generated_groove_sequence`, is our final sequence for this example.

3. Let's open the `output/groove/music_vae_00_TIMESTAMP.html` file, changing `TIMESTAMP` for the printed value in the console. Corresponding to our interpolated sequence, we have this humanized sequence:

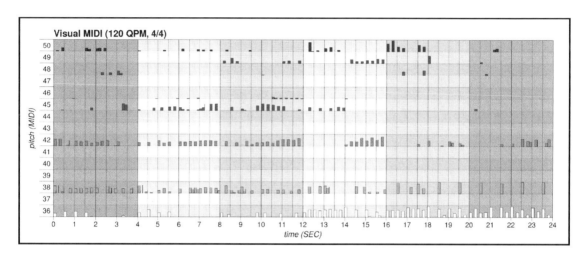

Let's look at the resulting plot file. First, the notes' velocities are dynamic now, for example, with notes being played louder to mark the end or the start of a beat like a real drummer would do. You can see an example of that on the bass drum between the 20 and 24 seconds mark. Then, notice that the notes are played with expressive timing, meaning the notes do not fall exactly on steps beginning and end. Finally, some notes are not being played anymore, while others have been added to the resulting score.

4. To listen to the generated MIDI, use your software synthesizer but **NOT MuseScore** since it will have a hard time with the expressive timing and you might hear a different score than what you actually have. For the software synth, refer to the following command depending on your platform and replace `PATH_TO_SF2` and `PATH_TO_MIDI` with the proper values:

   - Linux: `fluidsynth -a pulseaudio -g 1 -n -i PATH_TO_SF2 PATH_TO_MIDI`
   - macOS: `fluidsynth -a coreaudio -g 1 -n -i PATH_TO_SF2 PATH_TO_MIDI`
   - Windows: `fluidsynth -g 1 -n -i PATH_TO_SF2 PATH_TO_MIDI`

To learn more about groove and humanization, you can refer to the last section, *Further reading*, for more information on the topic, which is thoroughly explained in the GrooVAE blog post and GrooVAE paper.

Humanizing from the command line

Unfortunately, the humanization methods cannot be called from the command line for now. We will see other ways of humanizing a sequence in Chapter 9, *Making Magenta Interact with Music Applications*.

More interpolation on melodies

In the previous sections, we've been doing sampling and interpolation on drum sequences. By changing the code a bit, we can also do the same thing on melodies. Unfortunately, you won't be able to humanize the sequence since the GrooVAE model was trained on percussion data:

> You can follow this example in the chapter_04_example_02.py file in the source code of this chapter. There are more comments and content in the source code, so you should go check it out.

1. To make that happen, we change the calling code and keep the sample and interpolate methods as they are. We'll generate a sightly longer sequence with 10 interpolations instead of 6. Here is the code (warning: the checkpoint size is 1.6 GB):

```
num_output = 10
num_steps_per_sample = num_bar_per_sample * DEFAULT_STEPS_PER_BAR
total_bars = num_output * num_bar_per_sample

generated_sample_sequences = sample("cat-mel_2bar_big",
                                    num_steps_per_sample)
interpolate("cat-mel_2bar_big",
            generated_sample_sequences,
            num_steps_per_sample,
            num_output,
            total_bars)
```

You'll notice we're using the cat-mel_2bar_big configuration for both the sampling and the interpolation.

2. Let's open the generated `output/merge/cat-mel_2bar_big_00_TIMESTAMP.html` file by replacing `TIMESTAMP` with the proper value. A generated output looks like this:

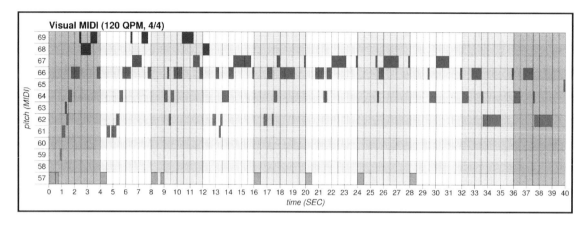

3. To listen to the generated MIDI, use your software synthesizer or MuseScore. For the software synth, refer to the following command depending on your platform and replace `PATH_TO_SF2` and `PATH_TO_MIDI` with the proper values:

- Linux: `fluidsynth -a pulseaudio -g 1 -n -i PATH_TO_SF2 PATH_TO_MIDI`
- macOS: `fluidsynth -a coreaudio -g 1 -n -i PATH_TO_SF2 PATH_TO_MIDI`
- Windows: `fluidsynth -g 1 -n -i PATH_TO_SF2 PATH_TO_MIDI`

Sampling the whole band

In the previous sections, we've been sampling and interpolating for drums and melodies. Now, we'll sample a trio of percussion, melody, and bass at the same time using one of the bigger models. This is perhaps one of the most impressive models because it can generate rather long sequences of 16 bars at once, using multiple instruments that work well together:

You can follow this example in the `chapter_04_example_03.py` file in the source code of this chapter. There are more comments and content in the source code, so you should go check it out.

1. For that example, we use our `sample` method with the `hierdec-trio_16bar` pre-trained model name as an argument (warning: the checkpoint size is 2.6GB):

```
sample("hierdec-trio_16bar", num_steps_per_sample)
```

2. Let's open the generated `output/sample/hierdec-trio_16bar_00_TIMESTAMP.html` file by replacing `TIMESTAMP` with the proper value. A generated output looks like this:

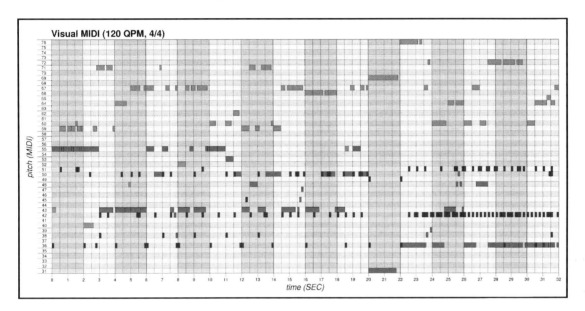

By using the `coloring=Coloring.INSTRUMENT` parameter in Visual MIDI, we can color each instrument with a separate color. It is hard to read because the bass line is on the same pitch as the drum line, but you can see the three instruments in the diagram.

3. To listen to the generated MIDI, use your software synthesizer or MuseScore. For the software synth, refer to the following command depending on your platform and replace `PATH_TO_SF2` and `PATH_TO_MIDI` with the proper values:
    - Linux: `fluidsynth -a pulseaudio -g 1 -n -i PATH_TO_SF2 PATH_TO_MIDI`
    - macOS: `fluidsynth -a coreaudio -g 1 -n -i PATH_TO_SF2 PATH_TO_MIDI`
    - Windows: `fluidsynth -g 1 -n -i PATH_TO_SF2 PATH_TO_MIDI`

You can hear that the generated MIDI has three instruments, and your synthesizer should assign a different instrument sound for each track (normally, a piano, a bass, and a drum). This is the only pre-trained model in Magenta that can generate multiple instruments at the same time, see the first section, *Technical requirements*, for a link to the README, which lists all of the available pre-trained models.

What is interesting in that model is that the long term structure of the 16 bars sequence is kept using a special type of decoder called `HierarchicalLstmDecoder`. That architecture adds another layer between the latent code and the decoder, called a **conductor**, which is an RNN that outputs a new embedding for each bar of the output. The decoder layer then proceeds to decode each bar.

To learn more about the hierarchical encoder and decoder architecture, you can refer to the last section, *Further reading*, for more information on the topic, which is thoroughly explained in the MusicVAE blog post and MusicVAE paper.

An overview of other pre-trained models

We already saw many pre-trained models present in MusicVAE and there are some more that are interesting but cannot be covered in depth here. Remember you can find the full list of them in the README, see the first section, *Technical requirements*, for the link to it.

Here's an overview of some of them we find interesting:

- The `nade-drums_2bar_full` model is a drums pre-trained model similar to the one from our example, but using the 61 classes from General MIDI instead of 9 classes. The model is bigger though. You can see which classes are encoded and what they correspond to in the `data.py` file in the `magenta.models.music_vae` module.

- The `groovae_2bar_tap_fixed_velocity` pre-trained model converts a "tap" pattern into a full-fledged drum rhythm while keeping the same groove. A "tap" sequence is a sequence that you could be taking from another rhythm, or even by tapping on your desk with your finger. In other words, it is a single note sequence, with groove, that can be transformed into a drum pattern. Usage of this would be to record a bass line from a real instrument, then "tap" the rhythm (or convert it from the audio), and then feed it to the network to sample a drum pattern that fits the same groove as the bass line.

- The `groovae_2bar_add_closed_hh` pre-trained model adds or replaces hi-hat on an existing groove.

Understanding TensorFlow code

In this section, we'll take a quick look at the TensorFlow code to understand a bit more how the sampling, interpolating, and humanizing code works. This will also make references to the first section of this chapter, *Continuous latent space in VAEs*, so that we make sense of both the theory and the hands-on practice we've had.

But first, let's do an overview of the model's initialization code. For this section, we'll take the `cat-drums_2bar_small` configuration as an example and the same model initialization code we've been using for this chapter, meaning `batch_size` of 8.

Building the VAE graph

We'll start by looking at the `TrainedModel` constructor in the `models.music_vae.trained_model` module. By taking the configuration values, `z_size`, `enc_rnn_size`, and `dec_rnn_size`, from the config map we've already introduced in a previous section, *Initializing the model*, we can find relevant information about the encoder's RNN, the hidden layer, and the decoder's RNN.

Notice the encoder is `BidirectionalLstmEncoder` and the decoder is `CategoricalLstmDecoder`, both from the `magenta.models.music_vae.lstm_models` module.

Building an encoder with BidirectionalLstmEncoder

Let's first have a look at the encoder's RNN, which is initialized in the `BidirectionalLstmEncoder` class of the `magenta.models.music_vae.lstm_models` module, in the `build` method, where the encoding layer gets initialized as follows:

```
lstm_utils.rnn_cell(
    [layer_size],
    hparams.dropout_keep_prob,
    hparams.residual_encoder,
    is_training)
```

You can see in the `rnn_cell` method from the
`magenta.models.music_vae.lstm_utils` module that the layer is `LSTMBlockCell`
(from the `tensorflow.contrib.rnn` module) with 512 units and a dropout wrapper:

```
cell = rnn.LSTMBlockCell(rnn_cell_size[i])
cell = rnn.DropoutWrapper(cell, input_keep_prob=dropout_keep_prob)
```

In the `DrumsConverter` class from the `magenta.models.music_vae.data` module
(instantiated in the `configs.py` file), you can see that we use the same
`MutltiDrumOneHotEncoding` class that we explained in `Chapter 2`:

```
self._oh_encoder_decoder = mm.MultiDrumOneHotEncoding(
    drum_type_pitches=[(i,) for i in range(num_classes)])
```

The melody configurations will use the `OneHotMelodyConverter` class.

Building a decoder with CategoricalLstmDecoder

Then, let's look at the decoder's RNN initialization in the `BaseLstmDecoder` class of the
`magenta.models.music_vae.lstm_models` module, in the `build` method, where the
decoding layer get initialized as follows:

```
self._output_layer = layers_core.Dense(
    output_depth, name='output_projection')
self._dec_cell = lstm_utils.rnn_cell(
    hparams.dec_rnn_size, hparams.dropout_keep_prob,
    hparams.residual_decoder, is_training)
```

Here, `output_depth` will be 512. The output layer is initialized as a dense layer, followed
by 2 layers of `LSTMBlockCell` of 256 units each.

You can also find the information on the encoder and decoder of your current configuration
in the console during execution:

```
INFO:tensorflow:Building MusicVAE model with BidirectionalLstmEncoder,
CategoricalLstmDecoder:
INFO:tensorflow:Encoder Cells (bidirectional): units: [512]
INFO:tensorflow:Decoder Cells: units: [256, 256]
```

Building the hidden layer

Finally, the hidden layer initialization is in the `MusicVAE` class of the `magenta.models.music_vae.base_model` module, in the `encode` method:

```
mu = tf.layers.dense(
    encoder_output,
    z_size,
    name='encoder/mu',
    kernel_initializer=tf.random_normal_initializer(stddev=0.001))
sigma = tf.layers.dense(
    encoder_output,
    z_size,
    activation=tf.nn.softplus,
    name='encoder/sigma',
    kernel_initializer=tf.random_normal_initializer(stddev=0.001))

return ds.MultivariateNormalDiag(loc=mu, scale_diag=sigma)
```

Both the `mu` and `sigma` layers are densely connected to the previous `encoder_output` value with a shape of *(8, 256)*, where 8 corresponds to `batch_size` and 256 corresponds to `z_size`. The method returns `MultivariateNormalDiag`, which is a normal distribution with `mu` and `sigma` as parameters:

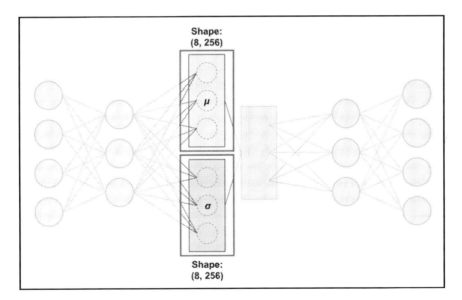

Looking at the sample method

Let's now look at the `sample` method content, located in the `TrainedModel` class of the `models.music_vae.trained_model` module. The core of the method is as follows:

```
for _ in range(int(np.ceil(n / batch_size))):
  if self._z_input is not None and not same_z:
    feed_dict[self._z_input] = (
        np.random.randn(batch_size, z_size).astype(np.float32))
  outputs.append(self._sess.run(self._outputs, feed_dict))
samples = np.vstack(outputs)[:n]
```

The method will split the number of required samples, n, in batches of maximum `batch_size`, then sample `z_input` from the standard normal distribution of size *(8, 256)* using `randn`, and finally run the model using those values. Remember, z is the embedding, so essentially what we are doing here is instantiating the latent variables and then decoding them.

Remembering what we saw in the previous section, *Sampling from the same area of the latent space*, we know that z might be sampled only once if we are reusing the same z variable.

The samples are then converted back to sequences by calling the one-hot decoding of the samples:

```
self._config.data_converter.to_items(samples)
```

Looking at the interpolate method

The interpolate method, located in the `TrainedModel` class, is pretty short:

```
_, mu, _ = self.encode([start_sequence, end_sequence], assert_same_length)
z = np.array([_slerp(mu[0], mu[1], t)
              for t in np.linspace(0, 1, num_steps)])
return self.decode(
    length=length,
    z=z,
    temperature=temperature)
```

What we are doing here is encoding the start and end sequence and getting back only the `mu` value from the encodings, using it to instantiate z, then decoding z for the resulting list of interpolated sequences.

But what is that _slerp method that instantiates z? Well, "slerp" stands for "spherical linear interpolation", and it calculates the direction between the first sequence and the second sequence so that the interpolation can move in the latent space in the proper direction.

We won't worry too much about the implementation details of the slerp method; we'll just remember the diagram from the section, *The latent space in standard autoencoders*, which showed how moving in a specific direction in the latent space would resulting in a transition from one sequence to another. By decoding at regular intervals along that direction, we end up with sequences that progressively goes from one to another.

Looking at the groove method

Finally, let's have a look at our groove method. As a reminder, the groove method is not present in Magenta so we had to write it ourselves:

```
encoding, _, _ = model.encode(split_interpolate_sequences)
groove_sequences = model.decode(encoding, num_steps_per_sample)
```

Apart from variable naming, this code snippet is almost identical to the interpolate method, but instead of using the μ value to instantiate the latent variables to move in a direction, we're just encoding the sequences and then decoding them with the model.

Summary

In this chapter, we looked at sampling, interpolating, and humanizing scores using a variational autoencoder with the MusicVAE and GrooVAE models.

We first explained what is latent space in AE and how dimensionality reduction is used in an encoder and decoder pair to force the network to learn important features during the training phase. We also learned about VAEs and their continuous latent space, making it possible to sample any point in the space as well as interpolate smoothly between two points, both very useful tools in music generation.

Then, we wrote code to sample and transform a sequence. We learned how to initialize a model from a pre-trained checkpoint, sample the latent space, interpolate between two sequences, and humanize a sequence. Along the way, we've learned important information on VAEs, such as the definition of the loss function and the KL divergence.

Finally, we looked at TensorFlow code to understand how the VAE graph is built. We showed the building code for the encoder, the decoder, and the hidden layer and explained the layers configurations and shapes. We also looked at the sample, interpolate, and groove methods, by explaining their implementations.

This chapter marks the end of the content aimed at models generating symbolic data. With the previous chapters, we've had a deep look at the most important models for generating and handling MIDI. The next chapter, *Audio Generation with NSynth and GANSynth*, will look at generating sub-symbolic content, such as audio.

Questions

1. What is the main use of the encoder and decoder pair in AE and what is a major shortcoming of such design?
2. How is the loss function defined in AE?
3. What is the main improvement in VAE on AE, and how is that achieved?
4. What is KL divergence and what is its impact on the loss function?
5. What is the code to sample z with a batch size of 4 and z size of 512?
6. What is the usage of the **slerp** method during interpolation?

Further reading

- **MusicVAE: Creating a palette for musical scores with machine learning**: Magenta's team blog post on MusicVAE, explaining in more detail what we've seen in this chapter (magenta.tensorflow.org/music-vae)
- **A Hierarchical Latent Vector Model for Learning Long-Term Structure in Music**: Magenta's team paper on MusicVAE, a very approachable and interesting read (arxiv.org/abs/1803.05428)
- **GrooVAE: Generating and Controlling Expressive Drum Performances**: Magenta's team blog post on GrooveVAE, explaining in more detail what we've seen in this chapter (magenta.tensorflow.org/groovae)
- **Learning to Groove with Inverse Sequence Transformations**: Magenta's team paper on GrooVAE, very approachable and interesting read (arxiv.org/abs/1905.06118)

- **Groove MIDI Dataset**: The dataset used for the GrooVAE training, composed of 13.6 hours of aligned MIDI and synthesized audio (magenta.tensorflow.org/datasets/groove)

- **Using Artificial Intelligence to Augment Human Intelligence**: An interesting read on AI interfaces enabled by latent space type models (distill.pub/2017/aia/)

- **Intuitively Understanding Variational Autoencoders**: An intuitive introduction to VAE, very clear (www.topbots.com/intuitively-understanding-variational-autoencoders/)

- **Tutorial - What is a variational autoencoder?**: A more in-depth overview of VAEs (jaan.io/what-is-variational-autoencoder-vae-tutorial)

- **Autoencoders — Guide and Code in TensorFlow 2.0**: Hands-on code for AE and VAE in TensorFlow 2.0 (medium.com/red-buffer/autoencoders-guide-and-code-in-tensorflow-2-0-a4101571ce56)

- **Kullback-Leibler Divergence Explained**: The KL divergence explained from a statistical viewpoint (www.countbayesie.com/blog/2017/5/9/kullback-leibler-divergence-explained)

- **An Introduction to Variational Autoencoders**: Good and complete paper on VAEs (arxiv.org/pdf/1906.02691.pdf)

5
Audio Generation with NSynth and GANSynth

In this chapter, we'll be looking into audio generation. We'll first provide an overview of WaveNet, an existing model for audio generation, especially efficient in text-to-speech applications. In Magenta, we'll use NSynth, a WaveNet autoencoder model, to generate small audio clips that can serve as instruments for a backing MIDI score. NSynth also enables audio transformations such as scaling, time stretching, and interpolation. We'll also use GANSynth, a faster approach based on **Generative Adversarial Network (GAN)**.

The following topics will be covered in this chapter:

- Learning about WaveNet and temporal structures for music
- Neural audio synthesis with NSynth
- Using GANSynth as a generative instrument

Technical requirements

In this chapter, we'll use the following tools:

- The **command line** or **Bash** to launch Magenta from the Terminal
- **Python** and its libraries to write music generation code using Magenta
- **Magenta** to generate audio clips
- **Audacity** to edit audio clips
- Any media player to listen to the generated WAV files

In Magenta, we'll make the use of the **NSynth** and **GANSynth** models. We'll be explaining these models in depth, but if you feel like you need more information, the models' README in Magenta's source code (`github.com/tensorflow/magenta/tree/master/magenta/models`) is a good place to start. You can also take a look at Magenta's code, which is well documented. We also provide additional content in the *Further reading* section.

The code for this chapter is in this book's GitHub repository in the `Chapter05` folder, located at `github.com/PacktPublishing/hands-on-music-generation-with-magenta/tree/master/Chapter05`. The examples and code snippets will suppose you are located in this chapter's folder. For this chapter, you should do `cd Chapter05` before you start.

Check out the following video to see the Code in Action:
`http://bit.ly/37QgQsI`

Learning about WaveNet and temporal structures for music

In the previous chapters, we've been generating symbolic content such as MIDI. In this chapter, we'll be looking at generating sub-symbolic content, such as **raw audio**. We'll be using the Waveform Audio File Format (WAVE or WAV, stored in a `.wav` file), a format containing uncompressed audio content, usable on pretty much every platform and device. See `Chapter 1`, *Introduction on Magenta and Generative Art*, for more information on waveforms in general.

Generating raw audio using neural nets is a rather recent feat, following the 2016 WaveNet paper, *A Generative Model For Raw Audio*. Other network architectures also perform well in audio generation, such as SampleRNN, also released in 2016 and used since to produce music tracks and albums (see databots for an example).

As stated in `Chapter 2`, *Generating Drum Sequences with DrumsRNN*, convolutional architectures are rather rare in music generation, given their shortcomings in handling sequential data. WaveNet uses a stack of causal convolution layers to address these problems, somewhat analogous to recurrent layers.

Modeling raw audio is hard—you have to handle 16,000 samples per second (at least) and keep track of the general structure at a bigger time scale. WaveNet's implementation is optimized to handle such data with the use of dilated convolution, where the convolution filter is applied over a large area by skipping input values with a certain step, enabling the network to preserve the input resolution throughout the network by using just a few layers. During training, the predictions can be made in parallel, while during generation, the predictions have to be made sequentially or **sample by sample**.

The WaveNet architecture has been used with excellent performance in text-to-speech application and recently in music generation but is computationally very expensive. Magenta's NSynth model is a **WaveNet autoregressive model**, an approach used to attain consistent long-term structure. Let's have a look into NSynth and its importance in generating music.

Looking at NSynth and WaveNet autoencoders

The NSynth model can be seen as a neural synthesizer—instead of having a synthesizer where you can define envelopes and specify the oscillator wave, pitch, and velocity, you have a model that generates new, realistic, instrument sounds. NSynth is **instrument-oriented**, or note-oriented, meaning it can be used to generate single notes of a generated instrument.

NSynth is a WaveNet-style autoencoder that learns the input data's temporal embedding. To understand the WaveNet Autoencoder (AE) network, you can refer to concepts explained in `Chapter 4`, *Latent Space Interpolation with MusicVAE*, since both networks are AEs. You'll see here many of the concepts we've previously shown, such as encoding, latent space, and interpolation.

Here is a simplified view of the WaveNet AE network:

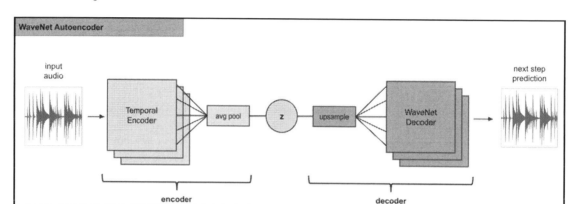

First, the encoder sees the whole input, which is the whole mono waveform (in the `.wav` format), and after 30 layers of computation, calculates an average pooling to create a temporal embedding (z in the diagram) of 16 dimensions for every 512 samples, which is a dimensionality reduction of 32 times. For example, a single audio input, with 16,000 samples (1 second of audio with a sample rate of 16,000), once encoded, will have a shape of 16 for the latent vector and 16,000/512 for the time (see the next section, *Encoding the WAV files*, for an example of this). Then, the WaveNet decoder will upsample the embedding to its original time resolution using a 1x1 convolution, trying to reproduce as closely as possible the input sound.

You can see WaveNet's implementation in the `Config` class of the `magenta.models.nsynth.wavenet.h512_bo16` module. The fastgen implementation used for the `synthesize` method is in the `FastGenerationConfig` class.

The z representation, or latent vector, has similar properties to what we saw in `Chapter 4`, *Latent Space Interpolation with MusicVAE*—similar sounds have similar z representations, and mixing or interpolation between two latent vectors is possible. This creates endless possibilities in terms of sound exploration. While traditional audio mixing revolves around the action of changing the volume of two audio clips to hear both at the same time, mixing two encodings together is about creating a sound that is a **hybrid of two original sounds.**

During this chapter, you'll get to listen to a lot of generated sounds, which we recommend you do instead of just looking at spectrograms. You'll probably notice that the sounds have a grainy or lo-fi texture. This is because the model works on mu-law encoded 8-bit 16 kHz sounds, which are of lower quality than what you typically listen to and is necessary for computational reasons.

Due to its training, the model might sometimes fall short while reconstructing the audio, which leads to additional harmonics, approximations, or crazy sounds. While surprising, these results give an interesting twist to the generated audio.

In this chapter, we'll be generating audio clips using NSynth, which we can then sequence using a previously generated MIDI sequence, for example. We'll listen to the sound of the interpolation between a cat sound and a bass sound by adding the encodings of both clips and synthesizing the result. We'll be generating a handful of sound combinations so we get a feel of what is possible in terms of audio interpolation.

Visualizing audio using a constant-Q transform spectrogram

Before we start, we'll introduce an audio visualization plot called the **Constant-Q Transform (CQT)** spectrogram. We provide more information about plotting audio signals and CQT in the last section, *Further reading*. In the previous chapters, we've been representing MIDI as a pianoroll plot, and the representations are simple and easy to understand. Audio, on the other hand, is hard to represent: two spectrograms looking almost the same might sound different.

In Chapter 1, *Introduction to Magenta and Generative Art*, in the *Representing music with a spectrogram* section, we've shown how a spectrogram is a plot of time and frequency. In this chapter, we'll be looking at a CQT spectrogram, which is a spectrogram displayed with the magnitude represented by the intensity and the instantaneous frequency by color. The colors represent the 16 different dimensions of the embeddings. The intensity of lines is proportional to the log magnitude of the power spectrum, and the colors are given by the derivative of the phase, making the phase visible as rainbow colors, hence the nickname "rainbowgrams" given by the Magenta team.

For this section, we are providing four audio samples that we'll use for our example and show as a rainbowgram. As always, the figures are not a replacement for listening to the audio content. Those samples are shown in the following screenshot:

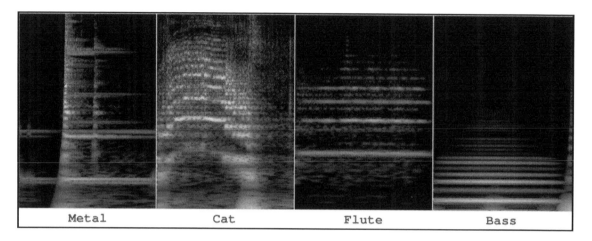

In the screenshot, you can notice a couple of things. First, the flute and the bass plots have a pretty well-defined harmonic series. Second, the metal plot, however, is more confused since it is a metal plate being struck. You can clearly see the attack of the sound and the following noise spanning the whole frequency range.

For our example, we'll be combining each pair of those sounds, for example, metal and cat, and cat and flute.

The NSynth dataset

Before we start, we'll have a brief look at the NSynth dataset, which was used to train the NSynth model. It is available at `magenta.tensorflow.org/datasets/nsynth` and is a high-quality and large-scale dataset, an order of magnitude larger than other similar datasets. Even if it is difficult to use for training with NSynth, it is interesting to look at for its content: over 300,000 musical notes that are classified by source, family, and quality. It can also serve as content for producing audio clips.

The audio clips are all 4 seconds long (the note was held for 3 seconds and given 1 second for the release) and represent a single note of different instruments. Each note has been recorded at every pitch of the standard MIDI piano range of 21 to 108 at five different velocities.

Since the instruments are classified by source, which is the method of sound production (such as acoustic, electronic, or synthetic), the dataset can be split for training on a specific instrument source. For example, the pre-trained GANSynth model we are going to use, `acoustic_only`, is useful for generating a more classical type of sound because the instruments in the training set are varied. The instruments are also classified by family, such as piano and bass, and qualities such as bright, dark, and percussive.

Interestingly, a dataset oriented on single notes like the NSynth dataset is really useful for producing neural audio synthesis of notes, which can in turn be sequenced with the other models in Magenta. In that sense, the NSynth model fits well in the Magenta ecosystem.

Neural audio synthesis with NSynth

In this section, we'll be combining different audio clips together. We'll learn to encode the audio, optionally saving the resulting encodings on disk, mix (add) them, and then decode the added encodings to retrieve a sound clip.

We'll be handling 1-second audio clips only. There are two reasons for this: first, **handling audio is costly**, and second, we want to **generate instrument notes** in the form of short audio clips. The latter is interesting for us because we can then sequence the audio clips using MIDI generated by the models we've been using in the previous chapters. In that sense, you can view NSynth as a generative instrument, and the previous models, such as MusicVAE or Melody RNN, as a generative score (partition) composer. With both elements, we can generate full tracks, with audio and structure.

To generate sound clips, we'll be using the `fastgen` module, an external contribution to Magenta, which now resides in NSynth's code, implementing optimizations for faster sound generation with an easy-to-use API.

Choosing the WaveNet model

Magenta provides two pre-trained NSynth models with included weights. We're going to be using the WaveNet pre-trained model. This model is very expensive to train, taking around 10 days on 32 K40 GPUs, so we won't be talking about training here.

You can follow this example in the `chapter_05_example_01.py` file in the source code of this chapter. There are more comments and content in the source code, so you should go check it out.

This chapter also contains audio clips in the `sounds` folders that you can use for this section.

To download the pre-trained model, use the following method, which will download the model and extract it:

```python
import os
import tarfile
import tensorflow as tf
from six.moves import urllib

def download_checkpoint(checkpoint_name: str,
                        target_dir: str = "checkpoints"):
  tf.gfile.MakeDirs(target_dir)
  checkpoint_target = os.path.join(target_dir, f"{checkpoint_name}.tar")
  if not os.path.exists(checkpoint_target):
    response = urllib.request.urlopen(
      f"http://download.magenta.tensorflow.org/"
      f"models/nsynth/{checkpoint_name}.tar")
    data = response.read()
    local_file = open(checkpoint_target, 'wb')
    local_file.write(data)
    local_file.close()
    tar = tarfile.open(checkpoint_target)
    tar.extractall(target_dir)
    tar.close()
```

This code downloads the proper checkpoint and then extracts it to the destination directory. This is similar to `download_checkpoint`, which we've written in the previous chapter. Using the `wavenet-ckpt` checkpoint name, the resulting checkpoint will be usable via the `checkpoints/wavenet-ckpt/model.ckpt-200000` path.

Note that this method might download rather big files (the pre-trained models in this chapter are big), so it will look as if the program is stuck for a while. It only means that the file is being downloaded (once only) locally.

Encoding the WAV files

First, we'll encode the WAV files using the `fastgen` library. Let's define the `encode` method and load the audio:

```
from typing import List
import numpy as np
from magenta.models.nsynth import utils
from magenta.models.nsynth.wavenet import fastgen

def encode(wav_filenames: List[str],
           checkpoint: str = "checkpoints/wavenet-ckpt/model.ckpt-200000",
           sample_length: int = 16000,
           sample_rate: int = 16000) -> List[np.ndarray]:
  # Loads the audio for each filenames
  audios = []
  for wav_filename in wav_filenames:
    audio = utils.load_audio(os.path.join("sounds", wav_filename),
                             sample_length=sample_length,
                             sr=sample_rate)
    audios.append(audio)

  # Encodes the audio for each new wav
  audios = np.array(audios)
  encodings = fastgen.encode(audios, checkpoint, sample_length)

  return encodings
```

In the preceding code, we first load the audio for each file in the `wav_filenames` parameter, using the `load_audio` method from the `magenta.models.nsynth.utils` module. To load the audio, two parameters are important, `sample_length` and `sample_rate`:

- The sample rate is set at `16000`, which is the sample rate used by the underlying model. Remember, the sample rate is the number of discrete samples for 1 second of audio.
- The sample length can be calculated by multiplying the desired number of seconds by the sample rate. For our example, we'll be using audio clips of 1 second for a sample length of 16,000.

We first convert the `audios` list into `ndarray` for the `encode` method, which has a shape of (4, 16000), because we have 4 samples of 16,000 samples each. The `encode` method from `magenta.models.nsynth.wavenet` returns the encodings for the provided audio clips. The returned encodings has a shape of (4, 31,16), with a length of 4 representing the number of elements, 31 representing the time, and 16 representing the size of the latent vector, z.

> You might be wondering why we have a length of 31 for the time in `encodings`. Remember our model reduces every 512 samples to 16 (see the *Looking at NSynth and WaveNet autoencoders* section), but our number of samples, 16,000, is not divisible by 512, so we end up with 31.25. This also impacts the decoding, which will result in WAV files of 0.992 seconds long.

Another important point here is that all the encodings are calculated at once in the same batch (the batch size is defined in the encode method by taking `audios.shape[0]`), which will be faster than doing them one by one.

Visualizing the encodings

The encodings can be visualized by plotting them, with the abscissa being the time and the ordinate being the encoded value. Each curve in the figure represents a z dimension, with 16 different colors. Here is a diagram for each of the encoded sounds of our example:

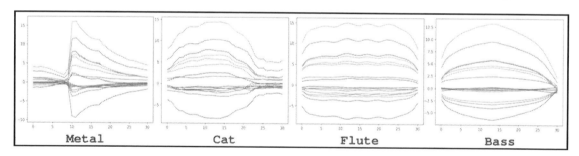

You can use the `save_encoding_plot` plot method in the `audio_utils.py` file from this chapter's code to produce the encodings plot.

Saving the encodings for later use

Saving and loading the encodings once they have been calculated is a good practice since it will speed up your program, even if the longer part of it is still the synthesizing.

 You can find this code in the `audio_utils.py` file in the source code of this chapter. There are more comments and content in the source code, so you should go check it out.

To save the encodings, we're using NumPy `.npy` files as follows:

```
import os
import numpy as np

def save_encoding(encodings: List[np.ndarray],
                  filenames: List[str],
                  output_dir: str = "encodings") -> None:
    os.makedirs(output_dir, exist_ok=True)
    for encoding, filename in zip(encodings, filenames):
        filename = filename if filename.endswith(".npy") else filename + ".npy"
        np.save(os.path.join(output_dir, filename), encoding)
```

You can see here we are using the `save` method from the `numpy` module. And we're retrieving the encodings from the files using the `load` method as follows:

```
def load_encodings(filenames: List[str],
                   input_dir: str = "encodings") -> List[np.ndarray]:
    encodings = []
    for filename in filenames:
        encoding = np.load(os.path.join(input_dir, filename))
        encodings.append(encoding)
    return encodings
```

We can then use the returned encodings instead of calling `fastgen.encode(...)`. Now that we have our encodings ready, we'll see how to mix them together.

Mixing encodings together by moving in the latent space

Now that we have the encodings of our sound files, we can mix them. The term mixing is common in audio production and usually refers to superposing two sounds and adjusting their volume so that both can be heard properly. This is not what we are doing here; we are effectively **adding** the sounds together, resulting in a new sound that is more than their mere superposition.

Let's define a `mix_encoding_pairs` method for that purpose:

```
def mix_encoding_pairs(encodings: List[np.ndarray],
                       encodings_name: List[str]) \
    -> Tuple[np.ndarray, List[str]]:
  encodings_mix = []
  encodings_mix_name = []
  # Takes the pair of encodings two by two
  for encoding1, encoding1_name in zip(encodings, encodings_name):
    for encoding2, encoding2_name in zip(encodings, encodings_name):
      if encoding1_name == encoding2_name:
        continue
      # Adds the encodings together
      encoding_mix = encoding1 + encoding2 / 2.0
      encodings_mix.append(encoding_mix)
      # Merges the beginning of the track names
      if "_" in encoding1_name and "_" in encoding2_name:
        encoding_name = (f"{encoding1_name.split('_', 1)[0]}_"
                         f"{encoding2_name.split('_', 1)[0]}")
      else:
        encoding_name = f"{encoding1_name}_{encoding2_name}"
      encodings_mix_name.append(encoding_name)
  return np.array(encodings_mix), encodings_mix_name
```

The important bit is `encoding1 + encoding2 / 2.0`, where we add the encodings together, producing a new encoding that we'll later synthesize. In the rest of the method, we iterate on the encodings two by two, producing a new encoded mix for each pair without computing the mix of a sample with itself, resulting in 12 elements in the method's return.

We also keep the name prefix in the `<encoding-prefix-1>_<encoding-prefix-2>` format to better identify them when we save the WAV on disk (we're splitting using the _ character because the samples from Freesound have them to split with the unique ID).

Finally, we return `ndarray` containing the mixed encodings as well a corresponding list of names for the encodings.

Synthesizing the mixed encodings to WAV

Finally, we'll now define the `synth` method that takes the encodings and turns them into sound:

```
def synthesize(encodings_mix: np.ndarray,
               encodings_mix_name: List[str],
               checkpoint: str = "checkpoints/wavenet-
ckpt/model.ckpt-200000") \
    -> None:
  os.makedirs(os.path.join("output", "nsynth"), exist_ok=True)
  encodings_mix_name = [os.path.join("output", "nsynth",
                                     encoding_mix_name + ".wav")
                        for encoding_mix_name in encodings_mix_name]
  fastgen.synthesize(encodings_mix,
                     checkpoint_path=checkpoint,
                     save_paths=encodings_mix_name)
```

Basically, all that method is doing is calling the `synthesize` method on the `magenta.models.nsynth.wavenet.fastgen` module. The `encodings_mix` shape is (12, 31, 16), where 12 is our `batch_size` (the number of final output audio clips), 31 is the time, and 16 is the dimensionality of the latent space.

To understand what the `synthesize` method is doing, take a look at this excerpt:

```
for sample_i in range(total_length):
  encoding_i = sample_i // hop_length
  audio = generate_audio_sample(sess, net,
                                audio, encodings[:, encoding_i, :])
  audio_batch[:, sample_i] = audio[:, 0]
  if sample_i % 100 == 0:
    tf.logging.info("Sample: %d" % sample_i)
  if sample_i % samples_per_save == 0 and save_paths:
    save_batch(audio_batch, save_paths)
```

Here, `total_length` is 15,872, just short of our 16,000 sample length for a time of 1 second, because the length is calculated by multiplying the time (31) by the hop length (512). See the information box in the previous section, *Encoding the WAV files*, for more information. This will result in audio files that won't be exactly 1 second long.

The other thing to notice here is that the process **generates one sample at a time**. This might seem inefficient, and that's because it is: the model is really good at reconstructing audio, but also painfully slow. You can see here that the bulk of the operation is executed in a serial loop in Python, not in parallel on the GPU.

In the following section, *Using GANSynth as a generative instrument*, we look at a similar, but faster, model.

Putting it all together

Now that we have our three methods, `encode`, `mix`, and `synth`, we can call them to create new sounds and textures.

Preparing the audio clips

For this example, we provided some audio clips in the `sounds` folder that you can use. While we recommend you experiment with your own sound, you can test your method first with those and experiment with yours later.

There are many places you can find audio clips from:

- Make your own! It is as easy as opening your mic and hitting a plate with a stick (see the following list for how to record with Audacity).
- The Freesound website, `freesound.org`, is an amazing community that's passionate about sharing audio clips. Freesound is a website for sharing copyright-free audio clips (most are under CC0 1.0 Universal (CC0 1.0) Public Domain Dedication).
- There's also the NSynth dataset, `magenta.tensorflow.org/datasets/nsynth`.

You can use any sample you want, but we recommend keeping it short (1 or 2 seconds) since this is a time-consuming process.

Whatever source you choose, having a simple digital audio editor and recording application software will help you a lot with cutting, normalizing, and handling your sounds. As stated in the introduction, Audacity is amazing open source cross-platform (Windows, Linux, and macOS) software for that purpose.

For example, if you downloaded your audio clips from Freesound, they might not all be the same length and volume, or they might be badly aligned. Audacity is easy to use for such tasks:

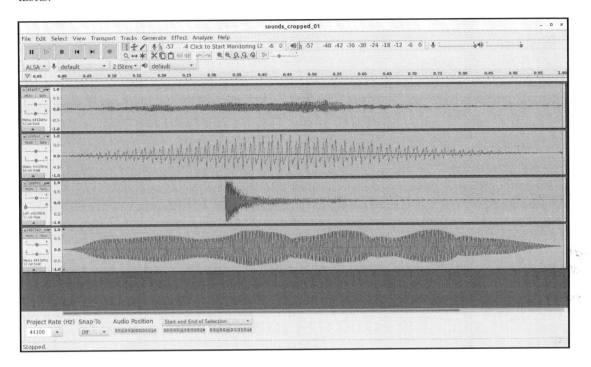

In this screenshot, we see each line corresponds to an audio clip. All of them are cropped to 1 second, ready for our example. Here are some pointers for using Audacity proficiently:

- To **record** your own sounds, click first on the **Click to Start Monitoring** option. If you see red bars, you're good. Then, click on the red record button on the left.
- To **cut** your recording, use the **Selection Tool** (*F1*) at the top, select a part, and press the *Delete* key to remove that part. You can use the audio position at the bottom for a precise selection of 1 second, for example.
- To **shift** the content of the audio (move a sharp noise to the beginning of the clip, for example), use the **Time Shift Tool** (*F5*) at the top, select a part, and drag and drop the part you want to move.
- You will want your tracks to be in **mono** for this chapter (a single channel instead of two channels). If you see two wave lines for a single file, your audio is in stereo. On the left, click on the filename. In the dropdown menu, use **Split stereo track**, then remove the left or right track. You'll also need to put the track panning in the center between **L** and **R**.

- **Normalizing** is the act of making something louder or quieter without modifying the content of the audio, which might be useful if you have a sample that doesn't have the proper volume. To do that, select the whole track and use **Effect > Normalize**, then change the maximum amplitude to what you want.
- To **export** in WAV, using the **File > Export > Export as WAV** menu. You can use the **Solo** button on the left if you have multiple tracks because if you don't, they'll be mixed together.

Now that we know how to produce our audio clips, let's write the code to use them.

Generating new instruments

We are now ready to render audio clips by mixing the pairs of audio clips. This part is an expensive process, depending on the speed of your PC and whether you have a GPU or not; this might vary greatly. At the time of writing, a moderately powerful i7 laptop will take 20 minutes to compute all of the 12 samples, and a PC with an entry-level GPU such as an NVIDIA RTX 2060 will do it in 4 minutes.

You can start by taking only two samples from WAV_FILENAMES if you find the generation takes too long. We'll see in a later section, *Using GANSynth as a generative instrument*, that there are faster alternatives.

Finally, let's call our encode, mix, and synth methods:

```
WAV_FILENAMES = ["83249__zgump__bass-0205__crop.wav",
                 "160045__jorickhoofd__metal-hit-with-metal-bar-resonance"
                 "__crop.wav",
                 "412017__skymary__cat-meow-short__crop.wav",
                 "427567__maria-mannone__flute__crop.wav"]

# Downloads and extracts the checkpoint to "checkpoints/wavenet-ckpt"
download_checkpoint("wavenet-ckpt")

# Encodes the wav files into 4 encodings (and saves them for later use)
encodings = encode(WAV_FILENAMES)

# Mix the 4 encodings pairs into 12 encodings
encodings_mix, encodings_mix_name = mix_encoding_pairs(encodings,
                                                       WAV_FILENAMES)

# Synthesize the 12 encodings into wavs
synthesize(encodings_mix, encodings_mix_name)
```

If you decide to use your own sound, make sure they are in the sounds folder. Also, you can prefix the sound filenames with an identifier before an underscore character; the resulting clips will keep those identifier pairs.

The resulting output will sit in the output/nsynth folder as WAV files; you should have one per unique input pair, so 12 WAV clips if you used 4 input clips. Go ahead and listen to them.

Visualizing and listening to our results

Now that we have our clips generated, we can also look at the rainbowgrams.

> You can find the code for the spectrograms and rainbowgrams in the audio_utils.py file in the source code of this chapter. There are more comments and content in the source code, so you should go check it out.

To generate the rainbowgrams for all of the generated audio files for our example, let's call the save_rainbowgram_plot method:

```
import os
import librosa
import glob
from audio_utils import save_rainbowgram_plot

for path in glob.glob("output/nsynth/*.wav"):
    audio, _ = librosa.load(path, 16000)
    filename = os.path.basename(path)
    output_dir = os.path.join("output", "nsynth", "plots")
    print(f"Writing rainbowgram for {path} in {output_dir}")
    save_rainbowgram_plot(audio,
                          filename=filename.replace(".wav",
"_rainbowgram.png"),
                          output_dir=output_dir)
```

The preceding code outputs the following plots in `output/nsynth/plots`:

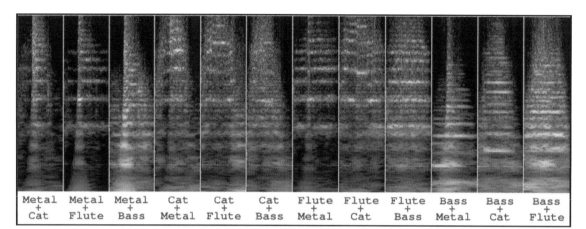

There are some things to note about the generated audio files and their corresponding spectrograms:

- First, the three metal-generated sounds on the left are interesting because they show that the generated sound kept the note's envelope since the original metal sound had a strong attack. The generated audio sounds like something is struck, like the original, but now with better harmonics.
- Then, the three cat generated sounds are also interesting. In them, the cute cat meow becomes an otherworldly growl. Since the NSynth model was trained on instrument notes and the cat sound is so different, the model has to guess, which results in an interesting sound. Experiment with sounds outside the training dataset, such as percussion; it's interesting to see what the model comes up with.
- In some of the clips, such as the flute + bass clip, we can hear some clicks in the generated audio. This happens when the model samples an extreme value and then corrects itself.

You should try and experiment with different sound combinations and durations. We've been using rather short samples to speed up the process, but you can use samples as long as you want. Just remember that the NSynth dataset contains only single notes that are 4 seconds long, meaning the generation of multiple consequent notes for longer samples will result in the model guessing the transition between them.

Using NSynth generated samples as instrument notes

Now that we have a bunch of generated samples from NSynth, we can sequence them using MIDI. The easiest way to do this is to use a **Digital Audio Workstation (DAW)**. Since this requires writing specific code to make Magenta send MIDI to the DAW, we'll be dedicating a section on this topic in `Chapter 9`, *Making Magenta Interact with Music Applications*. If you want to try that now, you can skip ahead and return here later.

Using the command line

The command line is limited for NSynth, but you can still generate audio clips. If you haven't done already, you'll need to download and extract the checkpoint in the `checkpoints/wavenet-ckpt` folder. While in this chapter's code, use the following command to generate audio from the audio clips in the `sounds` folder (warning: this process takes a long time):

```
nsynth_generate --checkpoint_path="checkpoints/wavenet-
ckpt/model.ckpt-200000" --source_path="sounds" --save_path="output/nsynth"
--batch_size=4 --sample_length=16000
```

By using `batch_size=4` and `sample_length=16000`, you make sure that code runs as fast as possible. The resulting files will be in the `output/nsynth` folder, with names in the `gen_FILENAME.wav` format, where `FILENAME` is the source filename. You'll see a generated audio clip for each source sound, resulting in four audio clips.

The generated clips were produced by encoding the audio and then synthesizing it. Compare them with the original audio: it will give you a feel of the NSynth sound.

More of NSynth

There is more to NSynth than we've shown here, such as more advanced use of interpolation and mixing, time stretching, and more. NSynth has produced interesting projects, such as a mobile application (mSynth) and physical hardware (NSynth Super). Refer to the *Further reading* section for more information on NSynth.

Using GANSynth as a generative instrument

In the previous section, we used NSynth to generate new sound samples by combining existing sounds. You may have noticed that the audio synthesis process is very time-consuming. This is because autoregressive models, such as WaveNet, focus on a single audio sample, which makes the resulting reconstruction of the waveform really slow because it has to process them iteratively.

GANSynth, on the other hand, uses upsampling convolutions, making the training and generation processing in parallel possible for the entire audio sample. This is a major advantage over autoregressive models such as NSynth since those algorithms tend to be I/O bound on GPU hardware.

The results of GANSynth are impressive:

- **Training** on the NSynth dataset converges in ~3-4 days on a single V100 GPU. For comparison, the NSynth WaveNet model converges in 10 days on 32 K40 GPUs.
- **Synthesizing** a 4-second audio sample takes 20 milliseconds in GANSynth on a TitanX GPU. For comparison, the WaveNet baseline takes 1,077 seconds, which is 50,000 times slower.

Another important implication of GANs is that the model has a spherical Gaussian prior, which is decoded to produce the entire sound, making the interpolations between two samples smoother and without additional artifacts, unlike WaveNet interpolation. This is because WaveNet autoencoders such as NSynth have limited scope when learning local latent codes that control generation on the scale of milliseconds.

In this section, we'll be making use of GANSynth to generate a 30-second audio clip by taking a MIDI file and playing it using random instruments sampled from the model's latent space. Each instrument will be played for a limited amount of time over the course of the audio track, for example, for 5 seconds each, blending between one another when the instrument changes happen.

Choosing the acoustic model

Magenta provides two pre-trained GANSynth models: `acoustic_only`, where the model was trained only on acoustic instruments, and `all_instruments`, where the model was trained on the whole NSynth dataset (see the previous section, *The NSynth dataset*, for more information on the dataset).

We're going to use the `acoustic_only` dataset for our example since the resulting audio track of a Bach score will sound more natural in terms of instrument choices. If you want to produce a wider generation, use the `all_instruments` model.

> You can follow this example in the `chapter_05_example_02.py` file in the source code of this chapter. There are more comments and content in the source code, so you should go check it out.
>
> This chapter also contains a MIDI clip in the `midi` folder that we'll use for this section.

To download the model, use the following method, which will download the model and extract it:

```
def download_checkpoint(checkpoint_name: str,
                        target_dir: str = "checkpoints"):
  tf.gfile.MakeDirs(target_dir)
  checkpoint_target = os.path.join(target_dir, f"{checkpoint_name}.zip")
  if not os.path.exists(checkpoint_target):
    response = urllib.request.urlopen(
      f"https://storage.googleapis.com/magentadata/"
      f"models/gansynth/{checkpoint_name}.zip")
    data = response.read()
    local_file = open(checkpoint_target, 'wb')
    local_file.write(data)
    local_file.close()
    with zipfile.ZipFile(checkpoint_target, 'r') as zip:
      zip.extractall(target_dir)
```

Using the `acoustic_only` checkpoint name, the resulting checkpoint will be usable using the `checkpoints/acoustic_only` path.

Getting the notes information

To start this example, we'll be loading a MIDI file that will serve as the backing score for the audio generation.

First, we load the MIDI file using the `load_midi` method in the `magenta.models.gansynth.lib.generate_util` module:

```
import os
from magenta.models.gansynth.lib.generate_util import load_midi
from note_sequence_utils import save_plot
```

```
def get_midi(midi_filename: str = "cs1-1pre-short.mid") -> dict:
    midi_path = os.path.join("midi", midi_filename)
    _, notes = load_midi(midi_path)
    return notes
```

We've provided a MIDI file in the `midi` folder, but you can also provide a MIDI file you like, for example, a generation from a previous chapter. The `load_midi` method then returns a dictionary of information about the notes in the MIDI file, such as a list of pitches, velocities, and start and end times.

The provided `cs1-1pre-short.mid` file looks like this:

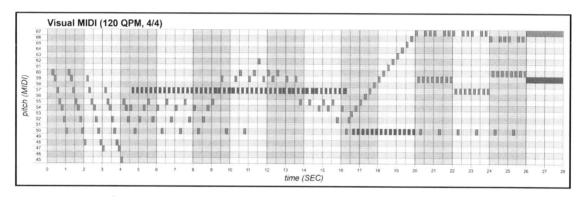

You can see the MIDI file is 28 seconds long (14 bars at 120 QPM) and contains two instruments.

Gradually sampling from the latent space

Now that we have the information about the MIDI file (in the `notes` variable), we can generate the audio from it.

Let's define the `generate_audio` method:

```
from magenta.models.gansynth.lib import flags as lib_flags
from magenta.models.gansynth.lib import model as lib_model
from magenta.models.gansynth.lib.generate_util import combine_notes
from magenta.models.gansynth.lib.generate_util import
get_random_instruments
from magenta.models.gansynth.lib.generate_util import get_z_notes

def generate_audio(notes: dict,
                   seconds_per_instrument: int = 5,
                   batch_size: int = 16,
```

```
                    checkpoint_dir: str = "checkpoints/acoustic_only") \
    -> np.ndarray:
flags = lib_flags.Flags({"batch_size_schedule": [batch_size]})
model = lib_model.Model.load_from_path(checkpoint_dir, flags)

# Distribute latent vectors linearly in time
z_instruments, t_instruments = get_random_instruments(
    model,
    notes["end_times"][-1],
    secs_per_instrument=seconds_per_instrument)

# Get latent vectors for each note
z_notes = get_z_notes(notes["start_times"], z_instruments, t_instruments)

# Generate audio for each note
audio_notes = model.generate_samples_from_z(z_notes, notes["pitches"])

# Make a single audio clip
audio_clip = combine_notes(audio_notes,
                           notes["start_times"],
                           notes["end_times"],
                           notes["velocities"])

return audio_clip
```

This method has four important parts, which we'll explain in the following three subsections—getting the random instrument, getting the latent vectors, generating the samples from the latent vectors, then combining the notes into a full audio clip.

Generating random instruments

The `get_random_instruments` method from `magenta.models.gansynth.lib.generate_util` looks like this:

```
def get_random_instruments(model, total_time, secs_per_instrument=2.0):
    """Get random latent vectors evenly spaced in time."""
    n_instruments = int(total_time / secs_per_instrument)
    z_instruments = model.generate_z(n_instruments)
    t_instruments = np.linspace(-.0001, total_time, n_instruments)
    return z_instruments, t_instruments
```

Using a sample of 28 seconds with 5 seconds per instrument gives us `n_instruments` of 5, then the latent vectors get initialized by the model's `generate_z` method, which is a sampling of the normal distribution:

```
np.random.normal(size=[n, self.config['latent_vector_size']])
```

This results in a `z_instruments` shape of (5, 256), 5 being the number of instruments and 256 the size of the latent vector. Finally, we take five steps of equal distance between the start and end time of the sequence in `t_instruments`.

Getting the latent vectors

The `get_z_notes` method from `magenta.models.gansynth.lib.generate_util` looks like this:

```
def get_z_notes(start_times, z_instruments, t_instruments):
  """Get interpolated latent vectors for each note."""
  z_notes = []
  for t in start_times:
    idx = np.searchsorted(t_instruments, t, side='left') - 1
    t_left = t_instruments[idx]
    t_right = t_instruments[idx + 1]
    interp = (t - t_left) / (t_right - t_left)
    z_notes.append(slerp(z_instruments[idx], z_instruments[idx + 1],
interp))
  z_notes = np.vstack(z_notes)
  return z_notes
```

This method takes each start note times and finds which instrument (previous instrument, `t_left`, and the next instrument, `t_right`) should be used for it. It then finds at what position the note is between the two instruments, in `interp`, to call the `slerp` method, which will find the proper latent vector that corresponds to the instrument between the two nearest vectors. This enables smooth transition from one instrument to the other.

Generating the samples from the encoding

We won't be looking into the details of the `generate_samples_from_z` method from `magenta.models.gansynth.lib.model`. We'll just use this code snippet to illustrate what we introduced in the *Using GANSynth as a generative instrument* section about the model generating the audio clip as a whole:

```
# Generate waves
start_time = time.time()
```

```
waves_list = []
for i in range(num_batches):
  start = i * self.batch_size
  end = (i + 1) * self.batch_size

  waves = self.sess.run(self.fake_waves_ph,
                        feed_dict={self.labels_ph: labels[start:end],
                                   self.noises_ph: z[start:end]})
  # Trim waves
 for wave in waves:
    waves_list.append(wave[:max_audio_length, 0])
```

For our example, this method will iterate 27 times to process all of the labels by chunks of 8 `labels` and `z` at the same time (our `batch_size` is 8). The bigger the batch size, the more waves it can generate in parallel. You can see that, contrary to NSynth, the audio samples are not generated one by one.

Finally, once all of the audio chunks are generated, `combine_notes` from the `magenta.models.gansynth.lib.generate_util` module will generate the audio using the audio clip and the MIDI notes. Basically, what the method does is calculate an envelope for each MIDI note that will let the proper portion of the audio clip be heard when a note is triggered.

Putting it all together

Now that we've defined and explained the different parts of the code, let's call the corresponding method to generate the audio clip from the MIDI file using gradually interpolated instruments:

```
# Downloads and extracts the checkpoint to "checkpoint/acoustic_only"
download_checkpoint("acoustic_only")

# Loads the midi file and get the notes dictionary
notes = get_midi_notes()

# Generates the audio clip from the notes dictionary
audio_clip = generate_audio(notes)

# Saves the audio plot and the audio file
save_audio(audio_clip)
```

The generated rainbowgram looks like this:

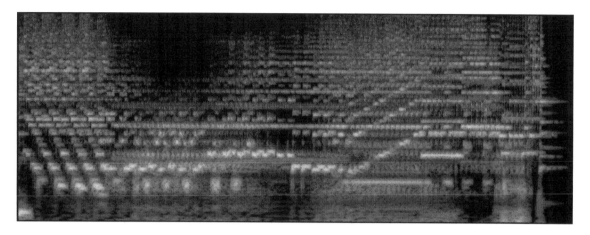

The diagram doesn't tell us much about the sound, apart from seeing the progression of the notes in the whole audio clip. Go and listen to the generated clip. Multiple generations will introduce different instruments; make sure you test it multiple times and with multiple MIDI files to get a feel of the possibilities in terms of instrument generation.

Using the command line

The GANSynth command-line utility makes it possible to generate an audio clip from a MIDI file, like we've done with the Python code. If you haven't done already, you'll need to download and extract the checkpoint into the `checkpoints/wavenet-ckpt` folder. While in this chapter's code, use the following command and an audio clip from the MIDI file from the `midi` folder (warning: this process takes a long time):

```
gansynth_generate --ckpt_dir="checkpoints/acoustic_only" --
output_dir="output/gansynth" --midi_file="midi/cs1-1pre-short.mid"
```

The resulting file will be in the `output/gansynth` folder and will be called `generated_clip.wav`. As in our example, the generated clip contains multiple instruments that are gradually blending together. You can use the `secs_per_instrument` parameter to change the time each instrument will play.

Summary

In this chapter, we looked at audio generation using two models, NSynth and GANSynth, and produced many audio clips by interpolating samples and generating new instruments. We started by explaining what WaveNet models are and why they are used in audio generation, particularly in text-to-speech applications. We also introduced WaveNet autoencoders, an encoder and decoder network capable of learning its own temporal embedding. We talked about audio visualization using the reduced dimension of the latent space in rainbowgrams.

Then, we showed the NSynth dataset and the NSynth neural instrument. By showing an example of combining pairs of sounds, we learned how to mix two different encodings together in order to then synthesize the result into new sounds. Finally, we looked at the GANSynth model, a more performant model for audio generation. We showed the example of generating random instruments and smoothly interpolating between them.

This chapter marks the end of the music generation content of this book—you can now generate a full song using MIDI as the backing score and neural instruments as the audio. During the course of the previous chapters, we've been using pre-trained models to show that the models in Magenta are ready to use and quite powerful.

Nonetheless, there are many reasons to train your own models, as we'll see in the following chapters. In Chapter 6, *Data Preparation for Training*, we'll be looking into preparing datasets for specific genres of music and for specific instruments. In Chapter 7, *Training Magenta Models*, we'll be using those datasets to train our own models that we can then use to generate new genres and instruments.

Questions

1. Why is generating audio hard?
2. What makes the WaveNet autoencoder interesting?
3. What are the different colors in a rainbowgram? How many are there?
4. How would you timestretch an audio clip, slowing it down by 2 seconds, using NSynth?
5. Why is GANSynth faster that NSynth?
6. What code is required to sample 10 instruments from GANSynth latent space?

Further reading

- **Audio Signals in Python:** An article on plotting audio signals in Python, explaining how to create a CQT plot (myinspirationinformation.com/uncategorized/audio-signals-in-python/)
- **Constant-Q transform toolbox for music processing:** A paper (2010) on implementing CQTs for music (www.researchgate.net/publication/228523955_Constant-Q_transform_toolbox_for_music_processing)
- **WaveNet: A generative model for raw audio:** A DeepMind article on WaveNet models for raw audio (deepmind.com/blog/article/wavenet-generative-model-raw-audio)
- **WaveNet: A Generative Model for Raw Audio:** A WaveNet paper (2016) (arxiv.org/abs/1609.03499)
- **SampleRNN**: An article explaining the differences between WaveNet and SampleRNN (deepsound.io/samplernn_first.html)
- **NSynth: Neural Audio Synthesis:** A Magenta article on the NSynth model (magenta.tensorflow.org/nsynth)
- **Making a Neural Synthesizer Instrument:** More ideas on sound combinations and modifications (magenta.tensorflow.org/nsynth-instrument)
- **Generate your own sounds with NSynth:** An article on fastgen and examples of timestretching and mixing (magenta.tensorflow.org/nsynth-fastgen)
- **Neural Audio Synthesis of Musical Notes with WaveNet Autoencoders:** An NSynth paper (2017) (arxiv.org/abs/1704.01279)
- **GANSynth: Making music with GANs:** Magenta article on GANSynth (magenta.tensorflow.org/gansynth)
- **GANSynth: Adversarial Neural Audio Synthesis:** A GANSynth paper (2019) (openreview.net/forum?id=H1xQVn09FX)
- **Using NSynth to win the Outside Hacks Music Hackathon 2017:** A Magenta article on mSynth (magenta.tensorflow.org/blog/2017/09/12/outside-hacks/)
- **What is NSynth Super?:** An article on NSynth Super, the NSynth hardware synthesizer (nsynthsuper.withgoogle.com/)

Section 3: Training, Learning, and Generating a Specific Style

3

This section includes information on how to prepare data from different input formats and then train an existing model on that data. By the end of this section, you will understand how to generate music that fits a specific style.

This section contains the following chapters:

- Chapter 6, *Data Preparation for Training*
- Chapter 7, *Training Magenta Models*

Data Preparation for Training

6

So far, we've used existing Magenta pre-trained models since they are quite powerful and easy to use. But training our own models is crucial since it allows us to generate music in a specific style or generate specific structures or instruments. Building and preparing a dataset is the first step before training our own model. To do that, we need to look at existing datasets and APIs that will help us to find meaningful data. Then, we need to build two datasets in MIDI for specific styles—dance and jazz. Finally, we will need to prepare the MIDI files for training using data transformations and pipelines.

The following topics will be covered in this chapter:

- Looking at existing datasets
- Building a dance music dataset
- Building a jazz dataset
- Preparing the data using pipelines

Technical requirements

In this chapter, we'll use the following tools:

- **A command line** or **Bash** to launch Magenta from the Terminal
- **Python** and its libraries
- The Python **multiprocessing** module for multi-threaded data preparation
- **Matplotlib** to plot our data preparation results
- **Magenta** to launch data pipeline conversion
- **MIDI**, **ABCNotation**, and **MusicXML** as data formats
- External APIs such as **Last.fm**

In Magenta, we'll make use of **data pipelines**. We will explain these in depth later in this chapter, but if you feel like you need more information, the pipeline README file in Magenta's source code

(`github.com/tensorflow/magenta/tree/master/magenta/pipelines`) is a good place to start. You can also take a look at Magenta's code, which is well documented. There's also additional content in the *Further reading* section.

The code for this chapter can be found in this book's GitHub repository, in the `Chapter06` folder, which is located at `github.com/PacktPublishing/hands-on-music-generation-with-magenta/tree/master/Chapter06`. For this chapter, you should use the `cd Chapter06` command before you start.

Check out the following video to see the Code in Action: `http://bit.ly/3aXWLmC`

Looking at existing datasets

In this chapter, we'll be preparing some data for training. Note that this will be covered in more detail in `Chapter 7`, *Training Magenta Models*. Preparing data and training models are two different activities that are done in tandem—first, we prepare the data, then train the models, and finally go back to preparing the data to improve our model's performance.

First, we'll start by looking at symbolic representations other than MIDI, such as MusicXML and ABCNotation, since Magenta also handles them, even if the datasets we'll be working with in this chapter will be in MIDI only. Then, we'll provide an overview of existing datasets, including datasets from the Magenta team that were used to train some models we've already covered. This overview is by no means exhaustive but can serve as a starting point when it comes to finding training data.

The main dataset we'll be focusing on is the **Lakh MIDI dataset** (**LMD**), a recent and well crafted MIDI dataset that will serve as a basis for most of our examples. You can also use other datasets; the code we are providing here can be easily adapted to other content.

Looking at symbolic representations

There are three main symbolic representations: MIDI, MusicXML, and ABCNotation. We've already covered MIDI in detail, but we haven't talked about MusicXML and ABCNotation yet. While we won't be using these two in this chapter, it is nice to know they exist and that Magenta can handle them as well as MIDI files.

MusicXML, as its name suggests, is an XML-based musical representation format. It has the advantage of being text-based, meaning it doesn't require an external library such as PrettyMIDI to be processed and is supported in many sheet music editors, such as MuseScore. You can find the MusicXML specification on its official website: www.musicxml.com.

Here's an example of a MusicXML file:

```
<?xml version="1.0" encoding="UTF-8" standalone="no"?>
<!DOCTYPE score-partwise PUBLIC
    "-//Recordare//DTD MusicXML 3.1 Partwise//EN"
    "http://www.musicxml.org/dtds/partwise.dtd">
<score-partwise version="3.1">
 <part-list>
    <score-part id="P1">
      <part-name>Music</part-name>
    </score-part>
  </part-list>
  <part id="P1">
    <measure number="1">
      <attributes>
...
      </attributes>
      <note>
        <pitch>
          <step>C</step>
          <octave>4</octave>
        </pitch>
        <duration>4</duration>
        <type>whole</type>
      </note>
    </measure>
  </part>
</score-partwise>
```

ABCNotation, as its name suggests, is a text-based musical representation format based on the letter notation (A-G). The format is rather compact, with some header information concerning the whole file, followed by the content of the song using the letter notation. The notation is also well supported in sheet music software. Here's an example of an ABCNotation file:

```
<score lang="ABC">
X:1
T:The Legacy Jig
M:6/8
L:1/8
R:jig
```

```
K:G
GFG BAB | gfg gab | GFG BAB | d2A AFD |
GFG BAB | gfg gab | age edB |1 dBA AFD :|2 dBA ABd |:
efe edB | dBA ABd | efe edB | gdB ABd |
efe edB | d2d def | gfe edB |1 dBA ABd :|2 dBA AFD |]
</score>
```

We will provide some ABCNotation content in the *Looking at other datasets* section of this chapter.

The tools Magenta provides for preparing datasets for training handle MIDI, MusicXML, and ABCNotation in a single command, which is really handy. The convert_dir_to_note_sequences command will parse the content depending on its type and return NoteSequence regardless.

We'll look at these tools in more detail in Chapter 7, *Training Magenta Models*.

Building a dataset from the ground up

Using an existing dataset and trimming it down is the easiest way to start building and preparing a dataset for training since it is a rather fast method of getting enough data for training.

Another option is to build the dataset from scratch, either by creating new data for it or by incorporating data from various sources. While requiring more work, this method might give better results during training since the resulting data is carefully selected. This is a process you should follow if you are a musician and have your own MIDI files ready.

Using the LMD for MIDI and audio files

The LMD (colinraffel.com/projects/lmd) is one of the most complete and easy-to-use MIDI datasets. If you don't have anything handy right now, we recommend using it. This chapter's code will use this dataset, but you can also follow the examples using another dataset since even if the information is different, most of the techniques we will use here can still be used.

The dataset has various distributions, but we'll be looking at the following ones in particular:

- **LMD-full**: This is the full dataset, which contains 176,581 MIDI files.
- **LMD-matched**: The dataset is partially matched to another dataset, the **million song dataset** (**MSD**), which contains 45,129 MIDI files. This subset is useful because the matched files contain metadata such as artist and title.
- **LMD-aligned**: The LMD-matched dataset is aligned with an audio MP3 preview.

Using the MSD for metadata information

The MSD (`millionsongdataset.com`) is a large scale dataset that has over a million entries containing audio features and metadata information. We won't be using the MSD dataset directly; instead, we'll be using the matched content included in the LMD-matched dataset.

Using the MAESTRO dataset for performance music

The **MIDI and Audio Edited for Synchronous TRacks and Organization** (**MAESTRO**) dataset (`magenta.tensorflow.org/datasets/maestro`) is curated by the Magenta team and is based on live performances that have been recorded to both audio and MIDI, for over 200 hours of content. Since the recorded performances have been played by humans, the notes have expressive timing and dynamics (effects pedals are also represented).

The dataset's content comes from the International Piano-e-Competition (`piano-e-competition.com/`), which mainly contains classical music. This dataset has multiple usages, such as automatic audio to symbolic representation transcription, which has been used to train the Magenta Onsets and Frames model. It has also been used to train the Performance RNN model we covered in `Chapter 3`, *Generating Polyphonic Melodies*.

Similar to MAESTRO but with less content, you also have the MusicNet and MAPS datasets available. We won't be using the MAESTRO dataset for our examples, but it is an important dataset you might want to look at. For more information, take a look at the *Further reading* section at the end of this chapter.

Using the Groove MIDI Dataset for groovy drums

The **Groove MIDI Dataset** (`www.tensorflow.org/datasets/catalog/groove`) is composed of 13.6 hours of aligned MIDI and (synthesized) audio of human-performed, tempo-aligned expressive drumming captured on an electronic drum. The dataset is also split into 2-bars and 4-bars MIDI segments and has been used to train the GrooVAE model, which we presented in `Chapter 4`, *Latent Space Interpolation with MusicVAE*.

The GMD is an impressive dataset of recorded performances from professional drummers, who also improvised for the occasion, resulting in a diverse dataset. The performances are annotated with a genre, which can be used to filter and extract certain MIDI files.

While not quantized, the GMD can also be used to train quantized models, such as the drums RNN. The pipelines, which will be shown in the *Preparing the data using pipelines* section, can transform input data such as unquantized MIDI into quantized MIDI.

Using the Bach Doodle Dataset

Bach Doodle is a web application made by Google to celebrate the anniversary of the German composer and musician, Johann Sebastian Bach. Doodle allows the user to compose a 2-bars melody and ask the application to harmonize the input melody in Bach's style using Coconet and TensorFlow.js running in the browser.

The resulting Bach Doodle Dataset (`magenta.tensorflow.org/datasets/bach-doodle`) of harmonized composition is impressive: 21.6 million harmonizations for about 6 years of user-entered music. It contains the user input sequence and the output sequence from the network in note sequence format, as well as some metadata, such as the country of the user and the number of times it was played.

See the *Further reading* section for more information about data visualization regarding the dataset.

Using the NSynth dataset for audio content

We covered the NSynth dataset (`www.tensorflow.org/datasets/catalog/nsynth`) in the previous chapter, *Audio Generation with NSynth and GANSynth*. We won't be covering audio training in this book, but this is a good dataset to use for training the GANSynth model.

Using APIs to enrich existing data

Using APIs is a good way of finding more information about MIDI tracks. We'll be showing an example of this in this chapter, where we'll query an API using the song artist and title to find genres and tags associated with the song.

There are multiple services you can use to find such information. We won't list all of them, but two good starting points are **Last.fm** (`www.last.fm/`) and Spotify's **Echo Nest** (`static.echonest.com/enspex/`). The **tagtraum** dataset (`www.tagtraum.com/msd_genre_datasets.html`) is another good dataset for genre, which is based on MSD.

In this chapter, we'll be using the **Last.fm** API to fetch song information, and we'll learn how to use its API in an upcoming section, *Building a jazz dataset*.

Looking at other data sources

Outside of curated datasets, there are tons of other sources for music files on the internet—mainly websites offering searchable databases. The downside of using such sources is that you'll have to download and verify each file by hand, which might be time-consuming but necessary if you want to build your own dataset from the ground up.

Websites such as **MidiWorld** (`www.midiworld.com`) and **MuseScore** (`musescore.com`) contain a lot of MIDI files, often classified by style, composer, and instrument. There are also posts on Reddit that list pretty big MIDI datasets of varying quality.

For formats other than MIDI, you have the ABCNotation website (`abcnotation.com`), which features over 600,000 files of mainly folk and traditional music, but with links to other sources.

Building a dance music dataset

Now that we have datasets available so that we can build our own dataset, we'll look at different ways of using the information contained in a MIDI file. This section will serve as an introduction to the different tools that can be used for dataset creation using only MIDI files. In this section, we'll use the **LMD-full** distribution.

In the next section, *Building a jazz dataset*, we will delve deeper into using external information.

Threading the execution to handle large datasets faster

When building datasets, we want our code to execute fast because of the amount of data we'll be handling. In Python, using threading and multiprocessing is one way to go. There are many ways of executing code in parallel in Python, but we'll be using the `multiprocessing` module because of its simple design, which is also similar to other popular techniques such as using the `joblib` module.

 You can find this code in the `multiprocessing_utils.py` file, in the source code of this chapter. There are more comments and content in the source code, so check it out.

For our examples, we'll be using the following code to start four threads that will execute in parallel:

```python
from itertools import cycle
from multiprocessing import Manager
from multiprocessing.pool import Pool

with Pool(4) as pool:
  # Add elements to process here
  elements = []
  manager = Manager()
  counter = AtomicCounter(manager, len(elements))
  results = pool.starmap(process, zip(elements, cycle([counter])))
  results = [result for result in results if result]
```

Let's explain this code block in more detail:

- You can modify the number of threads in `Pool(4)` to fit your hardware. One thread per physical CPU is often a proper value for good performance.
- We instantiate `Manager`, which is needed to share resources inside threads, and `AtomicCounter`, which is available in the `multiprocessing_utils` module from this book's code, to share a counter between the threads.
- Finally, we use the `pool.starmap` method to launch the `process` method on the `elements` list (we'll be defining this method soon). The `starmap` method calls the `process` method with two parameters, the first one being **one element** of the `elements` list, with the second being `counter`.
- The `process` method will handle one element at the time and will increment the counter at each call.

- The `process` method should be able to return `None`, making it possible to filter out elements.
- The thread's life cycle and the split of the elements list is handled by the `multiprocessing` module.

Extracting drum instruments from a MIDI file

MIDI files can contain many instruments—multiple percussion instruments, pianos, guitars, and more. Extracting specific instruments and saving the result in a new MIDI file is a necessary step when building a dataset.

In this example, we'll be using `PrettyMIDI` to fetch the instruments information into a MIDI file, extract the drum instruments, merge them into a single drum instrument, and save the resulting instrument in a new MIDI file. Some MIDI files have multiple drum instruments to split the drum into multiple parts, such as bass drum, snare, and so on. For our example, we've chosen to merge them, but depending on what you are trying to do, you might want to keep them separate or keep only some parts.

 You can find this code in the `chapter_06_example_00.py` file, in the source code of this chapter. There are more comments and content in the source code, so check it out.

The `extract_drums` method takes `midi_path` and returns a single `PrettyMIDI` instance containing one merged drum instrument:

```python
import copy
from typing import Optional

from pretty_midi import Instrument
from pretty_midi import PrettyMIDI

def extract_drums(midi_path: str) -> Optional[PrettyMIDI]:
  pm = PrettyMIDI(midi_path)
  pm_drums = copy.deepcopy(pm)
  pm_drums.instruments = [instrument for instrument in pm_drums.instruments
                          if instrument.is_drum]
  if len(pm_drums.instruments) > 1:
    # Some drum tracks are split, we can merge them
    drums = Instrument(program=0, is_drum=True)
    for instrument in pm_drums.instruments:
      for note in instrument.notes:
        drums.notes.append(note)
```

```
      pm_drums.instruments = [drums]
  if len(pm_drums.instruments) != 1:
    raise Exception(f"Invalid number of drums {midi_path}: "
                    f"{len(pm_drums.instruments)}")
  return pm_drums
```

First, we use `copy.deepcopy` to copy the whole MIDI file content because we still want to keep the time signatures and tempo changes from the original file. That information is kept in the `PrettyMIDI` instance that's returned in the `copy.deepcopy` method from the `pm_drums` variable. Then, we filter the instruments using the `is_drum` property. If there are multiple drum instruments, we merge them together into a new `Instrument` by copying the notes.

Detecting specific musical structures

Now that we can extract specific instruments from the MIDI files, we can also find specific structures in the MIDI files to further refine our dataset. Dance and techno music, in most cases, have a bass drum on each beat, giving you that inescapable urge to dance. Let's see whether we can find that in our MIDI files.

The `get_bass_drums_on_beat` method returns the proportion of bass drums that fall directly on the beat:

```
import math
from pretty_midi import PrettyMIDI

def get_bass_drums_on_beat(pm_drums: PrettyMIDI) -> float:
  beats = pm_drums.get_beats()
  bass_drums = [note.start for note in pm_drums.instruments[0].notes
                if note.pitch == 35 or note.pitch == 36]
  bass_drums_on_beat = []
  for beat in beats:
    beat_has_bass_drum = False
    for bass_drum in bass_drums:
      if math.isclose(beat, bass_drum):
        beat_has_bass_drum = True
        break
    bass_drums_on_beat.append(True if beat_has_bass_drum else False)
  num_bass_drums_on_beat = len([bd for bd in bass_drums_on_beat if bd])
  return num_bass_drums_on_beat / len(bass_drums_on_beat)
```

The `get_beats` method from `PrettyMIDI` returns an array stating the start time of each beat. For example, on a 150 QPM file, we have the following array:

```
[  0.     0.4    0.8    1.2    1.6    2.     2.4    2.8    3.2    3.6    4.     4.4
   4.8    5.2    5.6    6.     6.4    6.8    7.2    7.6    8.     8.4    8.8    9.2
 ...
 201.6 202.   202.4 202.8 203.2 203.6 204.   204.4 204.8 205.2 205.6 206.
 206.4 206.8 207.2 207.6]
```

Then, we take only the bass drum pitches (35 or 36) in the given MIDI and make the assumption that we have exactly one instrument because our previous method, `extract_drums`, should have been called before. Then, we check whether, for each beat, a bass drum was played at that time and return the proportion as `float`.

Analyzing the beats of our MIDI files

Let's put everything together to check our results.

First, we'll add some arguments to our program using the `argparse` module:

```python
import argparse

parser = argparse.ArgumentParser()
parser.add_argument("--path_output_dir", type=str, required=True)
parser.add_argument("--bass_drums_on_beat_threshold",
                    type=float, required=True, default=0)
args = parser.parse_args()
```

Here, we've declared two command-line arguments, `--path_output_dir` and `--bass_drums_on_beat_threshold`, using the `argparse` module. The output directory is useful if we wish to save the extracted MIDI files in a separate folder, while the threshold is useful for filtering more or less of the extracted MIDI sequences.

Writing the process method

Now that we have our arguments ready, we can write the processing method.

Here is the `process` method that will be called by our multi-threaded code:

```
import os
from typing import Optional
from multiprocessing_utils import AtomicCounter

def process(midi_path: str, counter: AtomicCounter) -> Optional[dict]:
  try:
    os.makedirs(args.path_output_dir, exist_ok=True)
    pm_drums = extract_drums(midi_path)
    bass_drums_on_beat = get_bass_drums_on_beat(pm_drums)
    if bass_drums_on_beat >= args.bass_drums_on_beat_threshold:
      midi_filename = os.path.basename(midi_path)
      pm_drums.write(os.path.join(args.path_output_dir,
f"{midi_filename}.mid"))
    else:
      raise Exception(f"Not on beat {midi_path}: {bass_drums_on_beat}")
    return {"midi_path": midi_path,
            "pm_drums": pm_drums,
            "bass_drums_on_beat": bass_drums_on_beat}
  except Exception as e:
    print(f"Exception during processing of {midi_path}: {e}")
  finally:
    counter.increment()
```

The `process` method will create the output directory if it doesn't already exist. Then, it will call the `extract_drums` method with the given MIDI path, and then call the `get_bass_drums_on_beat` method using the returned `PrettyMIDI` drum, which returns the `bass_drums_on_beat` as a proportion. Then, if the value is over the threshold, we save that MIDI file on disk; otherize, we exit the method.

The return values of the `process` method are important – by returning the `PrettyMIDI` file and the proportion of bass drums on beat, we'll be able to make statistics about our dataset to make informed decisions about its size and content. The `process` method can also return an empty (`None`) value or raise an exception, which will make the caller drop that MIDI file.

Calling the process method using threads

Now that we have a processing method, we can use it to launch the execution.

Let's create an `app` method that calls the `process` method using threads:

```python
import shutil
from itertools import cycle
from multiprocessing import Manager
from multiprocessing.pool import Pool
from typing import List
from multiprocessing_utils import AtomicCounter

def app(midi_paths: List[str]):
    shutil.rmtree(args.path_output_dir, ignore_errors=True)

    with Pool(4) as pool:
        manager = Manager()
        counter = AtomicCounter(manager, len(midi_paths))
        results = pool.starmap(process, zip(midi_paths, cycle([counter])))
        results = [result for result in results if result]
        results_percentage = len(results) / len(midi_paths) * 100
        print(f"Number of tracks: {len(MIDI_PATHS)}, "
              f"number of tracks in sample: {len(midi_paths)}, "
              f"number of results: {len(results)} "
              f"({results_percentage:.2f}%)")
```

The `app` method will be called with a list of MIDI paths when the program launches. First, we clean up the output directory for the process method so that we can write in it. Then, we start four threads using `Pool(4)` (refer to the previous section, *Threading the execution to handle large datasets*, for more information). Finally, we calculate how many results were returned for information purposes.

Plotting the results using Matplotlib

Using the returned results, we can find statistics about our dataset. As an example, let's plot the drum length:

```python
import matplotlib.pyplot as plt

pm_drums = [result["pm_drums"] for result in results]
pm_drums_lengths = [pm.get_end_time() for pm in pm_drums]
plt.hist(pm_drums_lengths, bins=100)
plt.title('Drums lengths')
plt.ylabel('length (sec)')
plt.show()
```

We are using Matplotlib (`matplotlib.org/`), a popular and easy to use plotting library for Python. This will result in the following output:

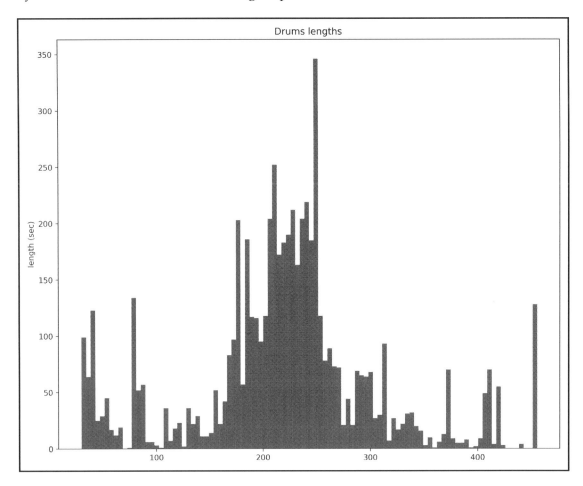

Making plots of different statistics helps you visualize the content and size of your dataset.

Processing a sample of the dataset

Now that we have everything in place, we can call the `app` method using a subset of our dataset.

First, we'll use a smaller sample size to make sure our code works properly:

```
parser.add_argument("--sample_size", type=int, default=1000)
parser.add_argument("--path_dataset_dir", type=str, required=True)

MIDI_PATHS = glob.glob(os.path.join(args.path_dataset_dir, "**", "*.mid"),
                       recursive=True)

if __name__ == "__main__":
  if args.sample_size:
    # Process a sample of it
    MIDI_PATHS_SAMPLE = random.sample(list(MIDI_PATHS), args.sample_size)
  else:
    # Process all the dataset
    MIDI_PATHS_SAMPLE = list(MIDI_PATHS)
  app(MIDI_PATHS_SAMPLE)
```

Let's explain the preceding code in more detail:

- We declare two new arguments, `--sample_size` and `--path_dataset_dir`. The first declares the size of the sample, while the second declares the location of the dataset.
- Then, we use `glob.glob` on the root folder of the dataset, which will return a list of paths, with one element per MIDI file.
- Because this operation takes a while on big datasets, you can also cache the result on disk (using the `pickle` module, for example) if you execute it often.
- We use `random.sample` to take a subset of the MIDI paths and use the resulting MIDI paths to call the `app` method.

You can use one of the distributions of LMD to launch the following code. You need to download it (for example, the **LMD-full** distribution) and extract the ZIP file. See the *Using the Lakh MIDI Dataset* section for the download links.

To launch this code with a small sample size, in a Terminal, use the following command (by replacing PATH_DATASET with the root folder of the extracted dataset and PATH_OUTPUT):

```
python chapter_06_example_00.py --sample_size=1000 --
path_dataset_dir="PATH_DATASET" --path_output_dir="PATH_OUTPUT"
```

The extracted MIDI file will be in PATH_OUTPUT, resulting in the following statistics:

```
Number of tracks: 116189, number of tracks in sample: 116189, number of
results: 12634 (10.87%)
Time:  7197.6346254
```

Here, we can see that approximately 10% of the MIDI file has a `--bass_drums_on_beat_threshold` over 0.75. This returns 12,634 results on the whole LMD dataset, which is more than enough to train our model later. We'll look at training in the next chapter.

Building a jazz dataset

In the previous section, we introduced the tools that are necessary for building a dataset based on information contained in the MIDI files from the full LMD dataset. In this section, we'll delve deeper into building a custom dataset by using external APIs such as the Last.fm API.

In this section, we'll use the **LMD-matched** distribution since it is (partially) matched with the MSD containing metadata information that will be useful for us, such as artist and title. That metadata can then be used in conjunction with Last.fm to get the song's genre. We'll also be extracting drum and piano instruments, just like we did in the previous section.

The LMD extraction tools

Before we start, we'll look at how to handle the LMD dataset. First, we need to download the following three elements from `colinraffel.com/projects/lmd/`:

- **LMD-matched**: A subset of LMD that is matched with MDS
- **LMD-matched metadata**: The H5 database containing the metadata information
- **Match scores**: The dictionary of match scores

Once extracted in the same folder, you should have the following elements: the `lmd_matched` directory, the `lmd_matched_h5` directory, and the `match_scores.json` file.

 You can find this code in the `lakh_utils.py` file, in the source code of this chapter. There are more comments and content in the source code, so check it out.

In the `lakh_utils.py` file, you have the utilities to find metadata and MIDI file paths from a unique identifier, `MSD_ID`. Our starting point will be the `match_scores.json` file, a dictionary of matched files in the following format:

```
{
...
  "TRRNARX128F4264AEB": {"cd3b9c8bb118575bcd712cffdba85fce":
0.7040202098544246},
  "TRWMHMP128EF34293F": {
    "c3da6699f64da3db8e523cbbaa80f384": 0.7321245522741104,
    "d8392424ea57a0fe6f65447680924d37": 0.7476196649194942
  },
...
}
```

As the key, we have the `MSD_ID`, and as the value, we have a dictionary of matches, each with a score. From an `MSD_ID`, we can get the highest score match using the `get_matched_midi_md5` method. From that MD5, we'll be able to load the corresponding MIDI file using the `get_midi_path` method.

Fetching a song's genre using the Last.fm API

The first part of our example uses the Last.fm API to fetch each song's genre. There are other APIs, such as Spotify's Echo Nest, that can be used to fetch such information. You can choose another service provider for this section if you feel like it.

The first step is to create an account on `www.last.fm/api/`. Since we won't be making any changes using the API, once you have an account, you only need to keep the **API key**.

 You can find this section's code in the `chapter_06_example_01.py` file, in the source code of this chapter. There are more comments and content in the source code, so check it out.

Reading information from the MSD

Before we call Last.fm to get the song's genre, we need to find the artist and title of each song. Because LMD is matched with MSD, finding that information is easy. Follow these steps to do so:

1. First, let's define a `process` method, as we did in the previous chapter, that can be called using threads, and that fetches the artist's information from the H5 database:

```python
import argparse
import tables
from typing import List, Optional
from lakh_utils import msd_id_to_h5
from threading_utils import AtomicCounter

parser = argparse.ArgumentParser()
parser.add_argument("--sample_size", type=int, default=1000)
parser.add_argument("--path_dataset_dir", type=str, required=True)
parser.add_argument("--path_match_scores_file", type=str,
required=True)
args = parser.parse_args()

def process(msd_id: str, counter: AtomicCounter) -> Optional[dict]:
  try:
    with tables.open_file(msd_id_to_h5(msd_id,
args.path_dataset_dir)) as h5:
      artist =
h5.root.metadata.songs.cols.artist_name[0].decode("utf-8")
      title = h5.root.metadata.songs.cols.title[0].decode("utf-8")
      return {"msd_id": msd_id, "artist": artist, "title": title}
  except Exception as e:
    print(f"Exception during processing of {msd_id}: {e}")
  finally:
    counter.increment()
```

This code looks just like the code we wrote in the previous section. Here, we use the `tables` module to open the H5 database. Then, we use the `msd_id_to_h5` method from our `lakh_utils` module to get the path to the H5 file. Finally, we fetch the artist and title in the H5 database before returning the result in a dictionary.

2. Now, we can call the `process` method, just like we did in the previous chapter. Before doing that, we need to load the score matches dictionary, which contains all the matches between LMD and MSD:

```
from lakh_utils import get_msd_score_matches

MSD_SCORE_MATCHES =
get_msd_score_matches(args.path_match_scores_file)

if __name__ == "__main__":
  if args.sample_size:
    # Process a sample of it
    MSD_IDS = random.sample(list(MSD_SCORE_MATCHES),
args.sample_size)
  else:
    # Process all the dataset
    MSD_IDS = list(MSD_SCORE_MATCHES)
  app(MSD_IDS)
```

To do that, we need to use the `get_msd_score_matches` method, which loads the dictionary in memory. Then, we take a sample of the full dataset using our `app` method.

3. Finally, to launch this code with a small sample size, in a Terminal, use the following command (by replacing PATH_DATASET and PATH_MATCH_SCORES):

```
python chapter_06_example_01.py --sample_size=1000 --
path_dataset_dir="PATH_DATASET" --
path_match_score="PATH_MATCH_SCORES"
```

You should receive the following output:

```
Number of tracks: 31034, number of tracks in sample: 31034, number of
results: 31034 (100.00%)
Time:  21.0088559
```

Now, we can plot the 25 most common artists, which should result in the following diagram:

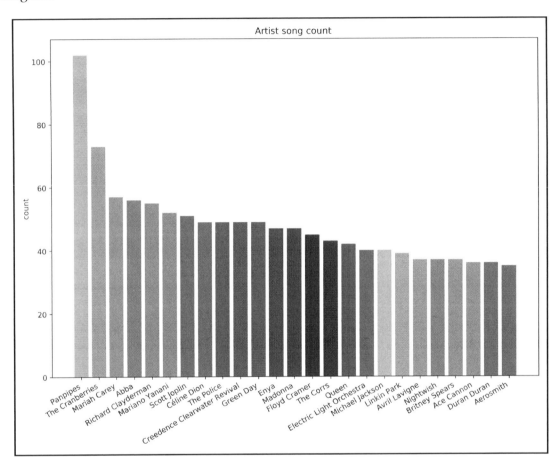

You could create a dataset based on one or multiple artists you like if you wanted to. You might end up with too few MIDI files for the training process, but it might be worth a shot.

Using top tags to find genres

Now that we know how to fetch information in the matched MSD database, we can call Last.fm to fetch the genre information for a track.

You can find this section's code in the `chapter_06_example_02.py` file, in the source code of this chapter. There are more comments and content in the source code, so check it out.

Let's get started:

1. The easiest way to call the Last.fm API is to perform a simple GET request. We'll do this in a `get_tags` method that takes the H5 database as a parameter:

```python
import argparse
from typing import List, Optional
import requests
from threading_utils import AtomicCounter

parser = argparse.ArgumentParser()
parser.add_argument("--sample_size", type=int, default=1000)
parser.add_argument("--path_dataset_dir", type=str, required=True)
parser.add_argument("--path_match_scores_file", type=str,
required=True)
parser.add_argument("--last_fm_api_key", type=str, required=True)
args = parser.parse_args()

def get_tags(h5) -> Optional[list]:
    title = h5.root.metadata.songs.cols.title[0].decode("utf-8")
    artist =
h5.root.metadata.songs.cols.artist_name[0].decode("utf-8")
    request = (f"https://ws.audioscrobbler.com/2.0/"
               f"?method=track.gettoptags"
               f"&artist={artist}"
               f"&track={title}"
               f"&api_key={args.last_fm_api_key}"
               f"&format=json")
    response = requests.get(request, timeout=10)
    json = response.json()
    if "error" in json:
        raise Exception(f"Error in request for '{artist}' - '{title}':
"
                        f"'{json['message']}'")
    if "toptags" not in json:
        raise Exception(f"Error in request for '{artist}' - '{title}':
"
                        f"no top tags")
    tags = [tag["name"] for tag in json["toptags"]["tag"]]
    tags = [tag.lower().strip() for tag in tags if tag]
    return tags
```

This code makes a request to the `track.gettoptags` API endpoint, which returns an ordered list of genres for the track, ordered from most tag count to less tag count, where the tag count is calculated from the user's submissions. The correct classification of those tags varies greatly from one artist to the other.

 You can find a lot of information on a track, artist, or release using APIs such s Last.fm or Echo Nest. Make sure you check out what information they provide when building your own dataset.

While a bit naive (we don't clean up the track name an artist name, or retry using another matching), most of the tracks (over 80%) are found on Last.fm, which is good enough for the purpose of our example.

2. Here's a simple process method that we can use to call our `get_tags` method:

```python
from typing import Optional
import tables
from threading_utils import AtomicCounter
from lakh_utils import msd_id_to_h5

def process(msd_id: str, counter: AtomicCounter) -> Optional[dict]:
  try:
    with tables.open_file(msd_id_to_h5(msd_id,
args.path_dataset_dir)) as h5:
        tags = get_tags(h5)
        return {"msd_id": msd_id, "tags": tags}
  except Exception as e:
    print(f"Exception during processing of {msd_id}: {e}")
  finally:
    counter.increment()
```

3. This example is based on jazz music, but you can use other genres for this example if you wish. You can plot the most popular common genres in LMD using the following code:

```
from collections import Counter

tags = [result["tags"][0] for result in results if result["tags"]]
most_common_tags_20 = Counter(tags).most_common(20)
plt.bar([tag for tag, _ in most_common_tags_20],
        [count for _, count in most_common_tags_20])
plt.title("Most common tags (20)")
plt.xticks(rotation=30, horizontalalignment="right")
plt.ylabel("count")
plt.show()
```

This should produce a plot that looks similar to the one shown in the following diagram:

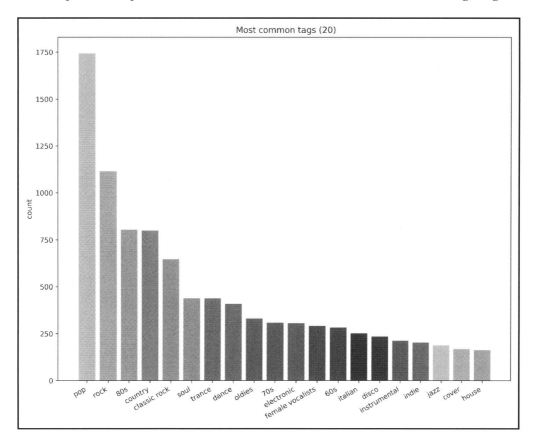

We'll be using the **jazz** genre, but you might want to combine multiple genres, such as **jazz** and **blues**, so that you have more content to work with or to create hybrid styles. We'll look at how much data you actually need for your models so that you can train them properly in the next chapter.

Finding instrument classes using MIDI

We'll be training on two instruments for our example, but you can do something else if you feel like it:

- **Percussion**: We'll be extracting drum tracks from the MIDI file to train a Drums RNN model
- **Piano**: We'll be extracting piano tracks to train a Melody RNN model

Here, the first step is finding the instruments that we have in our dataset. In the `PrettyMIDI` module, the `Instrument` class contains a `program` property that can be used to find such information. As a reminder, you can find more information about the various programs in the General MIDI 1 Sound Set specification (`www.midi.org/specifications/item/gm-level-1-sound-set`).

Each program corresponds to an instrument, and each instrument is classified in an instrument class. We'll be using this classification to find statistics about our dataset. Let's get started:

> You can find this section's code in the `chapter_06_example_04.py` file, in the source code of this chapter. There are more comments and content in the source code, so check it out.

1. First, let's write the `get_instrument_classes` method for this purpose:

```
from typing import List, Optional
from pretty_midi import PrettyMIDI, program_to_instrument_class
from lakh_utils import get_midi_path
from lakh_utils import get_matched_midi_md5

def get_instrument_classes(msd_id) -> Optional[list]:
  midi_md5 = get_matched_midi_md5(msd_id, MSD_SCORE_MATCHES)
  midi_path = get_midi_path(msd_id, midi_md5,
args.path_dataset_dir)
  pm = PrettyMIDI(midi_path)
  classes = [program_to_instrument_class(instrument.program)
            for instrument in pm.instruments
```

```
          if not instrument.is_drum]
  drums = ["Drums" for instrument in pm.instruments if
instrument.is_drum]
  classes = classes + drums
  if not classes:
    raise Exception(f"No program classes for {msd_id}: "
                    f"{len(classes)}")
  return classes
```

First, we load a `PrettyMIDI` instance and then convert the `program` into its instrument class. Here, you can see that we are handling the drums separately since there is no `program` property for drums.

2. Now, we can write our `process` method as follows:

```
from typing import Optional
import tables
from threading_utils import AtomicCounter
from lakh_utils import msd_id_to_h5

def process(msd_id: str, counter: AtomicCounter) -> Optional[dict]:
  try:
    with tables.open_file(msd_id_to_h5(msd_id,
args.path_dataset_dir)) as h5:
      classes = get_instrument_classes(msd_id)
      return {"msd_id": msd_id, "classes": classes}
  except Exception as e:
    print(f"Exception during processing of {msd_id}: {e}")
  finally:
    counter.increment()
```

3. The most common instrument classes can be found using the following code:

```
from collections import Counter

classes_list = [result["classes"] for result in results]
classes = [c for classes in classes_list for c in classes]
most_common_classes = Counter(classes).most_common()
plt.bar([c for c, _ in most_common_classes],
        [count for _, count in most_common_classes])
plt.title('Instrument classes')
plt.xticks(rotation=30, horizontalalignment="right")
plt.ylabel('count')
plt.show()
```

You should have similar results to what can be seen in the following diagram on the LMD:

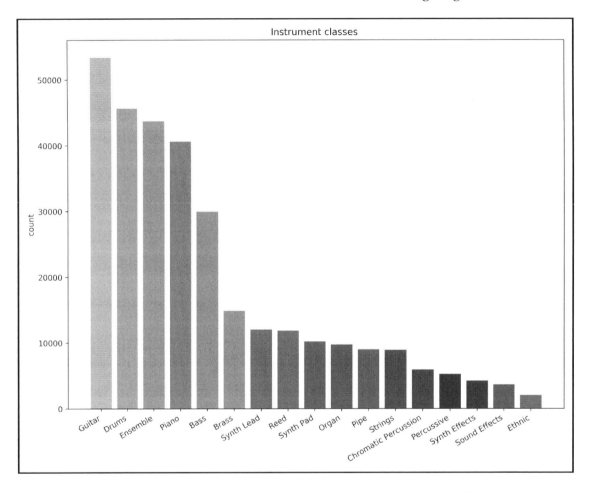

Here, we can see that the most used instrument classes in the LMD are **Guitar**, **Drums**, **Ensemble**, and **Piano**. We'll be using the **Drums** and **Piano** classes in the upcoming sections, but you can use another class if you feel like it.

Extracting jazz, drums, and piano tracks

Now that we are able to find the instrument tracks we want, filter the song by genre, and export the resulting MIDI files, we can put everything together to create two jazz datasets, one containing percussion and the other containing piano.

Extracting and merging jazz drums

We've already implemented most of the code for extracting jazz drums, namely the get_tags method and the extract_drums method.

You can find this section's code in the chapter_06_example_07.py file, in the source code of this chapter. There are more comments and content in the source code, so check it out.

The process method should call the get_tags and extract_drums methods like this:

```
import argparse
import ast
from typing import Optional
import tables
from multiprocessing_utils import AtomicCounter

parser = argparse.ArgumentParser()
parser.add_argument("--tags", type=str, required=True)
args = parser.parse_args()

TAGS = ast.literal_eval(args.tags)

def process(msd_id: str, counter: AtomicCounter) -> Optional[dict]:
  try:
    with tables.open_file(msd_id_to_h5(msd_id, args.path_dataset_dir)) as h5:
      tags = get_tags(h5)
      matching_tags = [tag for tag in tags if tag in TAGS]
      if not matching_tags:
        return
      pm_drums = extract_drums(msd_id)
      pm_drums.write(os.path.join(args.path_output_dir, f"{msd_id}.mid"))
      return {"msd_id": msd_id,
              "pm_drums": pm_drums,
              "tags": matching_tags}
  except Exception as e:
    print(f"Exception during processing of {msd_id}: {e}")
  finally:
    counter.increment()
```

Here, we are using the ast module to parse the tags argument. This is useful because it allows us to use the Python list syntax for the value of a flag, that is, --tags="['jazz', 'blues']". Then, we can check if the tags coming from Last.fm match with one of the required tags and write the resulting MIDI drums file to disk if so.

The drum's lengths and genre repartition can be seen in the following plots:

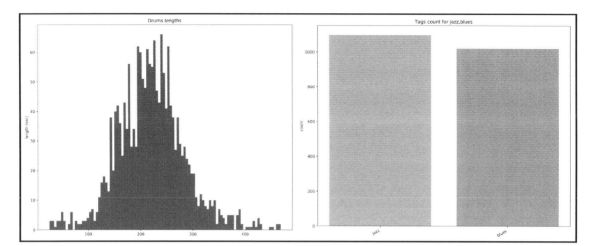

Here, we can see that we have around 2,000 MIDI files when combining both "**jazz**" and "**blues**".

Extracting and splitting jazz pianos

The last method we need to write is the piano extraction method. The `extract_pianos` method is similar to the previous `extract_drums` method, but instead of merging the tracks together, it splits them into separate piano tracks, potentially returning multiple tracks for each song. Let's get started:

 You can find this section's code in the `chapter_06_example_08.py` file, in the source code of this chapter. There are more comments and content in the source code, so check it out.

1. First, we'll write the `extract_pianos` method, as follows:

```
from typing import List
from pretty_midi import Instrument
from pretty_midi import PrettyMIDI
from lakh_utils import get_matched_midi_md5
from lakh_utils import get_midi_path

PIANO_PROGRAMS = list(range(0, 8))

def extract_pianos(msd_id: str) -> List[PrettyMIDI]:
```

```
      os.makedirs(args.path_output_dir, exist_ok=True)
      midi_md5 = get_matched_midi_md5(msd_id, MSD_SCORE_MATCHES)
      midi_path = get_midi_path(msd_id, midi_md5,
  args.path_dataset_dir)
      pm = PrettyMIDI(midi_path)
      pm.instruments = [instrument for instrument in pm.instruments
                        if instrument.program in PIANO_PROGRAMS
                        and not instrument.is_drum]
      pm_pianos = []
      if len(pm.instruments) > 1:
        for piano_instrument in pm.instruments:
          pm_piano = copy.deepcopy(pm)
          pm_piano_instrument =
  Instrument(program=piano_instrument.program)
          pm_piano.instruments = [pm_piano_instrument]
          for note in piano_instrument.notes:
            pm_piano_instrument.notes.append(note)
          pm_pianos.append(pm_piano)
      else:
        pm_pianos.append(pm)
      for index, pm_piano in enumerate(pm_pianos):
        if len(pm_piano.instruments) != 1:
          raise Exception(f"Invalid number of piano {msd_id}: "
                          f"{len(pm_piano.instruments)}")
        if pm_piano.get_end_time() > 1000:
          raise Exception(f"Piano track too long {msd_id}: "
                          f"{pm_piano.get_end_time()}")
      return pm_pianos
```

We've already covered most of the code in this snippet. The difference here is that we are filtering the instrument on any of the piano programs, ranging from 0 to 8. We're also returning multiple piano MIDI files.

2. Now, we can call our method using the following `process` method:

```
import argparse
import ast
from typing import Optional
import tables
from lakh_utils import msd_id_to_h5
from multiprocessing_utils import AtomicCounter

parser = argparse.ArgumentParser()
parser.add_argument("--tags", type=str, required=True)
args = parser.parse_args()

TAGS = ast.literal_eval(args.tags)
```

```
def process(msd_id: str, counter: AtomicCounter) -> Optional[dict]:
  try:
    with tables.open_file(msd_id_to_h5(msd_id,
args.path_dataset_dir)) as h5:
        tags = get_tags(h5)
        matching_tags = [tag for tag in tags if tag in TAGS]
        if not matching_tags:
          return
        pm_pianos = extract_pianos(msd_id)
        for index, pm_piano in enumerate(pm_pianos):
          pm_piano.write(os.path.join(args.path_output_dir,
                                      f"{msd_id}_{index}.mid"))
        return {"msd_id": msd_id,
                "pm_pianos": pm_pianos,
                "tags": matching_tags}
  except Exception as e:
    print(f"Exception during processing of {msd_id}: {e}")
  finally:
    counter.increment()
```

This code was covered in the previous section on drums, except here, each piano file is written separately using an index. The piano's lengths and genres can be plotted like so:

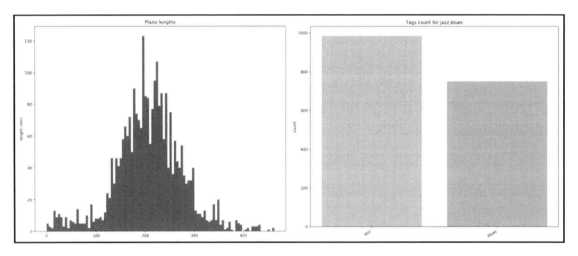

Here, we've found just under 2,000 piano tracks for **jazz** and **blues**.

Preparing the data using pipelines

In the previous sections, we looked at existing datasets and developed tools so that we can find and extract specific content. By doing so, we've effectively built a dataset we want to train our model on. But building the dataset isn't all – we also need to **prepare** it. By preparing, we mean the action of removing everything that isn't useful for training, cutting, and splitting tracks, and also automatically adding more content.

In this section, we'll be looking at some built-in utilities that we can use to transform the different data formats (MIDI, MusicXML, and ABCNotation) into a training-ready format. These utilities are called `pipelines` in Magenta, and are a sequence of operations that are executed on the input data.

An example of an operation that is already implemented in pipelines includes discarding melodies with too many pitches that are too long or too short. Another operation is transposing melodies, which consists of taking a melody and creating a new one by shifting the note's pitches up or down. This is a common practice in machine learning called **dataset augmentation**, which is useful if we wish to make the model train better by providing it with variations of the original data.

Let's take a look at what pipelines are and how they can be used. In this section, we'll be using the Melody RNN pipeline as an example, but each model has its own pipeline with its own specifics. For example, the Drums RNN pipeline does not transpose the drums sequences because it wouldn't make sense to do so.

Before we start talking about pipelines, we'll have a brief look at manually refining the dataset we built previously.

Refining the dataset manually

This might sound obvious, but we'll stress it because it is also really important: verify the MIDI files you've extracted. The dataset's content should correspond to what you were looking for in terms of music.

The easiest way of verifying a track's content is by opening the content in MuseScore and listening to it:

Let's have a look a the things we can verify for each of these files:

- The first thing to verify is whether the **instruments** we've extracted are present in the resulting MIDI files, meaning that, for our jazz piano example, we should have only one instrument track and that it should be any of the eight piano programs.
- Another thing to verify is whether the **genre** of the tracks fits our requirements. Does the piano sound like jazz music? Does the music actually sound good to you?
- Other problems to look out for include tracks that are **incomplete**, too short, too long, or full of silence. Some of those tracks will be filtered by the data preparation pipeline, but a manual pass on the data is also important.
- If some of the tracks you like are filtered by the data preparation pipeline, for example, for being too short, you can manually fix this issue by copying and pasting parts of it to make it longer. You can also write a pipeline to automatically do that.

If some of the tracks don't fit your requirements, remove them from the dataset.

Once you've validated the dataset's content and removed all the unwanted tracks, you can also cut and clean the content of each file. The easiest way of doing that is by going into MuseScore, listening to the track, removing the parts you don't like, and exporting the file back to MIDI.

Looking at the Melody RNN pipeline

Once we've manually refined the dataset, we are ready to prepare it using a pipeline, resulting in data that has been prepared for training. As an example, we'll be looking at the Melody RNN pipeline.

Launching the data preparation stage on our dataset

The first step when it comes to preparing the data is to call the `convert_dir_to_note_sequences` command, which is the same regardless of the model you will be using. This command will take a directory containing MIDI files, MusicXML files, or ABCNotation files as input and convert them into TensorFlow records of `NoteSequence`.

We recommend that you create another folder for your training data (separate from the dataset folder you created previously). Now, let's get started:

1. First, change directory to the folder you've created and call the `convert_dir_to_note_sequences` command using the following command (replace `PATH_OUTPUT_DIR` with the directory you used in the previous section):

   ```
   convert_dir_to_note_sequences --input_dir="PATH_OUTPUT_DIR" --
   output_file="notesequences.tfrecord"
   ```

   This will output a bunch of "Converted MIDI" files and produce a `notesequences.tfrecord`. From now on, the data is in the same format, regardless of the symbolic representation we used when building the dataset.

2. Now, we can launch the pipeline on our data using the following code:

   ```
   melody_rnn_create_dataset --config="attention_rnn" --
   input="notesequences.tfrecord" --output_dir="sequence_examples" --
   eval_ratio=0.10
   ```

   First, we need to give `--config` as an argument. This is necessary because the encoder and decoder are defined in the configuration (see Chapter 3, *Generating Polyphonic Melodies*, for a refresher on how encoding and decoding works).

   We also pass the `--eval_ratio` argument, which will give the pipeline the number of elements in the training and evaluation sets. When executed, the pipeline will output statistics and warnings about the files it encounters.

The statistics are printed on the console for each increment of 500 files that are processed, but only the last part (after the **Completed.** output) is of interest to us. The following is the output of the 500 samples of the jazz piano dataset:

```
Processed 500 inputs total. Produced 122 outputs.
DAGPipeline_MelodyExtractor_eval_melodies_discarded_too_few_pitches
: 7
DAGPipeline_MelodyExtractor_eval_melodies_discarded_too_long: 0
DAGPipeline_MelodyExtractor_eval_melodies_discarded_too_short: 42
DAGPipeline_MelodyExtractor_eval_melodies_truncated: 2
DAGPipeline_MelodyExtractor_eval_melody_lengths_in_bars:
   [7,8): 4
   [8,10): 2
   [10,20): 2
   [30,40): 2
DAGPipeline_MelodyExtractor_eval_polyphonic_tracks_discarded: 113
DAGPipeline_MelodyExtractor_training_melodies_discarded_too_few_pit
ches: 45
DAGPipeline_MelodyExtractor_training_melodies_discarded_too_long: 0
DAGPipeline_MelodyExtractor_training_melodies_discarded_too_short:
439
DAGPipeline_MelodyExtractor_training_melodies_truncated: 20
DAGPipeline_MelodyExtractor_training_melody_lengths_in_bars:
   [7,8): 22
   [8,10): 21
   [10,20): 42
   [20,30): 11
   [30,40): 16
DAGPipeline_MelodyExtractor_training_polyphonic_tracks_discarded:
982
DAGPipeline_RandomPartition_eval_melodies_count: 49
DAGPipeline_RandomPartition_training_melodies_count: 451
DAGPipeline_TranspositionPipeline_eval_skipped_due_to_range_exceede
d: 0
DAGPipeline_TranspositionPipeline_eval_transpositions_generated:
317
DAGPipeline_TranspositionPipeline_training_skipped_due_to_range_exc
eeded: 0
DAGPipeline_TranspositionPipeline_training_transpositions_generated
: 2387
```

The statistics of interest here are as follows::

- `Processed 500 inputs total`. **`Produced 122 outputs`**.: This gives us the input size or the number of provided MIDI files, as well as the number of resulting `SequenceExample` that will be used for training (122, counting both evaluation and training sets). This is the most important statistic.
- `DAGPipeline_MelodyExtractor_MODE_melody_lengths_in_bars`: This gives you the length of the resulting `SequenceExample` elements for each "MODE".

The `SequenceExample` encapsulates the data that will be fed to the network during training. Those statistics are useful because the quantity (as well as the quality) of the data is important for the model's training. If a model doesn't train properly on 122 outputs, we'll need to make sure we have more data for the next time we train.

In that sense, it is really important to look at the produced outputs, which tells us about the exact amount of data the network will receive. It doesn't matter whether we feed 100,000 MIDI files to the data preparation pipeline if a small amount of `SequenceExample` is produced because the input data isn't good. If a pipeline produces a small number of outputs for a big input, look at the statistics and find out which part of the processing step is removing the elements.

Now, let's have a look at how the pipeline is defined and executed for our example.

Understanding a pipeline execution

The statistics we provided in the previous section are a bit confusing because they are not shown in the order they are executed. Let's have a proper look at how this is really executed to understand what's going on:

- `DagInput` initiates the pipeline's execution, taking each `NoteSequence` of the TensorFlow records as input (500 elements).
- `RandomPartition` randomly splits the elements into training and evaluation sets given the ratio provided in the command (450 elements in the training set and 50 elements in the evaluation set).
- `TimeChangeSplitter` splits the elements at each time change (doesn't output statistics).

- `Quantizer` quantizes the note sequence on the closest step defined by the `steps_per_quarter` attribute in the configuration and discards elements with multiple tempos and time signatures (doesn't output statistics).
- `TranspositionPipeline` transposes the note sequence into multiple pitches, adding new elements in the process (2,387 elements generated by transposition for the training set).
- `MelodyExtractor` extracts the melodies from the `NoteSequence`, returning a `Melody` and removing elements if needed, such as polyphonic tracks and tracks that are too short or too long (1,466 elements are removed for the training set). This part also outputs the lengths of the melodies in bars:
  - The minimum and maximum length of the melody are defined by `min_bars` and `max_steps`, respectively. See the next section to learn how to change them.
  - `ignore_polyphonic_notes`, which is set `True`, discards polyphonic tracks.
- `EncoderPipeline` encodes`Melody` into `SequenceExample` using `KeyMelodyEncoderDecoder` defined for the attention configuration (doesn't output statistics). The encoder pipeline receives the configuration passed as an argument; for example, `LookbackEventSequenceEncoderDecoder` for the `lookback_rnn` configuration.
- `DagOutput` finishes the execution.

If you want to look at the implementation of the `Pipeline`, have a look at the `get_pipeline` method in the `melody_rnn_pipeline` module.

Writing your own pipeline

As you might have noticed from the code in the `get_pipeline` method, most of the configurations cannot be changed. However, we can write our own pipeline and call it directly.

You can find this section's code in the `melody_rnn_pipeline_example.py` file, in the source code of this chapter. There are more comments and content in the source code, so check it out.

For this example, we'll take the existing Melody RNN pipeline, copy it, and change the transposition and sequence length. Let's get started:

1. First, copy the `get_pipeline` method and call it using the following Python code (replacing INPUT_DIR and OUTPUT_DIR with the proper values):

```
from magenta.pipelines import pipeline

pipeline_instance = get_pipeline("attention_rnn", eval_ratio=0.10)
pipeline.run_pipeline_serial(
    pipeline_instance,
    pipeline.tf_record_iterator(INPUT_DIR,
pipeline_instance.input_type),
    OUTPUT_DIR)
```

You should see the same output that we received previously when we used the pipeline method. By taking a small sample (500 pieces of data) of the piano jazz dataset, we received the following output:

```
INFO:tensorflow:Processed 500 inputs total. Produced 115 outputs.
...
INFO:tensorflow:DAGPipeline_MelodyExtractor_training_melody_lengths
_in_bars:
  [7,8): 31
  [8,10): 9
  [10,20): 34
  [20,30): 11
  [30,40): 17
  [50,100): 2
...
INFO:tensorflow:DAGPipeline_TranspositionPipeline_training_transpos
itions_generated: 2058
...
```

2. Now, let's change some parameters to see how it works. In the following code, we've added some transpositions (the default transposition value is (0,), which means no transposition shifts):

```
...
transposition_pipeline =
note_sequence_pipelines.TranspositionPipeline(
    (0,12), name='TranspositionPipeline_' + mode)
...
```

By using the transpositions (0,12), we're telling the transposition pipeline to create, for each existing sequence, a sequence 12 pitches higher, corresponding to a full octave shift up. Keep the rest of the code as is.

 Transposition values should follow musical intervals expressed in semitones (a pitch value in MIDI). The simplest interval is the perfect interval that we are using, which corresponds to an octave, or 12 semitones or MIDI pitches. Other intervals can be used, such as the Major third, which is used in the Polyphony RNN pipeline, with a transposition range of (-4, 5).

Now, the output should look as follows:

```
. . .
INFO:tensorflow:Processed 500 inputs total. Produced 230 outputs.
. . .
INFO:tensorflow:DAGPipeline_MelodyExtractor_training_melody_lengths
_in_bars:
  [7,8): 66
  [8,10): 14
  [10,20): 64
  [20,30): 22
  [30,40): 34
  [50,100): 4
. . .
INFO:tensorflow:DAGPipeline_TranspositionPipeline_training_transpos
itions_generated: 4297
. . .
```

Notice how we now have approximately twice as much data to work with. Data augmentation is important for handling small datasets.

3. We can also change the minimum and maximum lengths of the sequences in the melody extractor, like so:

```
. . .
melody_extractor = melody_pipelines.MelodyExtractor(
  min_bars=15, max_steps=1024, min_unique_pitches=5,
  gap_bars=1.0, ignore_polyphonic_notes=False,
  name='MelodyExtractor_' + mode)
. . .
```

The preceding code will output a total of 92 outputs (instead of our previous 230).

We can also write our own pipeline class. For example, we could automatically cut sequences that are too long or duplicate sequences that are too short, instead of discarding them. For a note sequence pipeline, we need to extend the NoteSequencePipeline class and implement the transform method, as shown in the following code:

```
from magenta.pipelines.note_sequence_pipelines import
NoteSequencePipeline

class MyTransformationClass(NoteSequencePipeline):
    def transform(self, note_sequence):
        # My transformation code here
        pass
```

Take a look at the sequences_lib module in Magenta, which contains tons of utilities for handling note sequences. Each dataset needs to be prepared and the easiest way to prepare the data is by creating new pipelines.

Looking at MusicVAE data conversion

The MusicVAE model doesn't use pipelines – actually, it doesn't even have a dataset creation script. Compared to our previous example with Melody RNN, it still uses similar transformations (such as data augmentation) and is more configurable since some of the transformations can be configured, instead of us needing to write a new pipeline.

Let's have a look at a simple MusicVAE configuration contained in the configs module of the music_vae module. Here, you can find the following cat-mel_2bar_small configuration:

```
# Melody
CONFIG_MAP['cat-mel_2bar_small'] = Config(
    model=MusicVAE(lstm_models.BidirectionalLstmEncoder(),
                   lstm_models.CategoricalLstmDecoder()),
    hparams=merge_hparams(
        lstm_models.get_default_hparams(),
        HParams(
            batch_size=512,
            max_seq_len=32,  # 2 bars w/ 16 steps per bar
            z_size=256,
            enc_rnn_size=[512],
            dec_rnn_size=[256, 256],
            free_bits=0,
            max_beta=0.2,
            beta_rate=0.99999,
```

```
            sampling_schedule='inverse_sigmoid',
            sampling_rate=1000,
        )),
    note_sequence_augmenter=data.NoteSequenceAugmenter(transpose_range=(-5,
5)),
    data_converter=data.OneHotMelodyConverter(
        valid_programs=data.MEL_PROGRAMS,
        skip_polyphony=False,
        max_bars=100,   # Truncate long melodies before slicing.
        slice_bars=2,
        steps_per_quarter=4),
    train_examples_path=None,
    eval_examples_path=None,
)
```

The following list further explains the code:

- By looking at the NoteSequenceAugmenter class, you can see that it takes note of sequence augmentation by using shifting (like in our custom pipeline) and stretching, another data augmentation technique.
- It also limits the maximum length of the melody to max_bars=100, but remember that MusicVAE handles limited size samples because of its network type. In this example, each sample is sliced to a length of slice_bars=2.
- The note sequence augmenter lets you decide a transposition range that it will randomly choose a value from.
- Stretching isn't used for Melody RNN because most stretching ratios don't work for quantized sequences. Stretching can be used for Performance RNN, for example.

We won't be looking at creating a new configuration just now. See Chapter 7, *Training Magenta Models*, for more information on how to do that.

Summary

In this chapter, we looked at how to build and prepare a dataset that will be used for training. First, we looked at existing datasets and explained how some are more suitable than others for a specific use case. We then looked at the LMD and the MSD, which are useful for their size and completeness, and datasets from the Magenta team, such as the MAESTRO dataset and the GMD. We also looked at external APIs such as Last.fm, which can be used to enrich existing datasets.

Then, we built a dance music dataset and used information contained in MIDI files to detect specific structures and instruments. We learned how to compute our results using multiprocessing and how to plot statistics about the resulting MIDI files.

After, we built a jazz dataset by extracting information from the LMD and using the Last.fm API to find the genre of each song. We also looked at how to find and extract different instrument tracks in the MIDI files.

Finally, we prepared the data for training. By using pipelines, we were able to process the files we extracted, remove the files that weren't of the proper length, quantize them, and use data augmentation techniques to create a proper dataset, ready for training. By doing this, we saw how different models have different pipelines, depending on their network type.

In the next chapter, we'll use what we produced in this chapter to train some models on the datasets we've produced. You'll see that training is an empirical process that requires a lot of back and forth between preparing the data and training the model. During this process, you will likely come back to this chapter for more information.

Questions

1. What are the advantages and disadvantages of the different symbolic representations?
2. Write a piece of code that will extract cello instruments from MIDI files.
3. How many rock songs are present in LMD? How many match one of the "jazz", "blues", "country" tags?
4. Write a piece of code that will extend MIDI files that are too short for the Melody RNN pipeline.
5. Extract the jazz drums from GMD. Can we train a quantized model with this?
6. Why is data augmentation important?

Further reading

- **The MAESTRO Dataset and Wave2Midi2Wave:** A Magenta team blog post on the MAESTRO dataset and its usage in the Wave2Midi2Wave method (`magenta.tensorflow.org/maestro-wave2midi2wave`)

- **Enabling Factorized Piano Music Modeling and Generation with the MAESTRO Dataset:** A paper (2019) about MAESTRO and Wave2Midi2Wave (`arxiv.org/abs/1810.12247`)

- **Celebrating Johann Sebastian Bach:** The Bach Doodle, which gave us the Bach Doodle Dataset (`www.google.com/doodles/celebrating-johann-sebastian-bach`)

- **Visualizing the Bach Doodle Dataset:** An amazing visualization of the Bach Doodle Dataset (`magenta.tensorflow.org/bach-doodle-viz`)

- **The Bach Doodle: Approachable music composition with machine learning at scale:** A paper (2019) about the Bach Doodle dataset (`arxiv.org/abs/1907.06637`)

Training Magenta Models 7

In this chapter, we'll use the prepared data from the previous chapter to train some of the RNN and VAE networks. Machine learning training is a finicky process involving a lot of tuning, experimentation, and back and forth between your data and your model. We'll learn to tune hyperparameters, such as batch size, learning rate, and network size, to optimize network performance and training time. We'll also show common training problems such as overfitting and models not converging. Once a model's training is complete, we'll show how to use the trained model to generate new sequences. Finally, we'll show how to use Google Cloud Platform to train models faster on the cloud.

The following topics will be covered in this chapter:

- Choosing the model and configuration
- Training and tuning a model
- Using Google Cloud Platform

Technical requirements

In this chapter, we'll use the following tools:

- A **command line** or **Bash** to launch Magenta from the Terminal
- **Python** and its libraries to write specific training configuration for a model
- **Magenta** and **Magenta GPU** to train our models
- **TensorBoard** to verify the training metrics
- **Google Cloud Platform** to offload the training in the cloud

In Magenta, we'll make the use of the **Drums RNN**, **Melody RNN**, and **MusicVAE** models for training. We'll be explaining the training for those models, but if you feel like you need more information, the model's README in Magenta's source code (`github.com/tensorflow/magenta/tree/master/magenta/models`) is a good place to start. You can also take a look at Magenta's code, which is well documented. We have also provided additional content in the last section, *Further reading*.

The code for this chapter is in this book's GitHub repository in the `Chapter07` folder, located at `github.com/PacktPublishing/hands-on-music-generation-with-magenta/tree/master/Chapter07`. The examples and code snippets will assume you are located in the chapter folder. For this chapter, you should go to `cd Chapter07` before you start.

Check out the following video to see the Code in Action:
`http://bit.ly/2OcaY5p`

Choosing the model and configuration

In `Chapter 6`, *Data Preparation for Training*, we looked at how to build a dataset. The datasets we produced were symbolic ones composed of MIDI files containing specific instruments, such as percussion or piano, and from specific genres, such as dance music and jazz music.

We also looked at how to prepare a dataset, which corresponds to the action of preparing the input formats (MIDI, MusicXML, or ABCNotation) into a format that can be fed to the network. That format is specific to a Magenta model, meaning the preparation will be different for the Drums RNN and MusicVAE models, even if both models can train on percussion data.

The first step before starting the training is to choose the proper model and configuration for our use case. Remember, a model in Magenta defines a deep neural network architecture, and each network type has its advantages and disadvantages. Let's have a look at how to choose a model, configure it, and train it from scratch.

Comparing music generation use cases

Let's take the example of training a percussion model. If we want to train a model that generates rhythmic percussion, we can either choose the Drums RNN model or the MusicVAE model:

- The first model, Drums RNN, will be more efficient at **generating longer sequences** that keep the global musical structure because the model can learn long-term dependencies using the attention mechanism (refer to `Chapter 2`, *Generating Drum Sequences with Drums RNN*, for a refresher on that).
- The second model, MusicVAE, won't be able to do that but will be able to sample from the latent space and **interpolate between sequences** (refer to `Chapter 4`, *Latent Space Interpolation with MusicVAE*, for a refresher on that).

Depending on your use case, you might want to train one or the other or both, but keep in mind their strengths and weaknesses.

If we take the example of training a melody model, we can use a monophonic model, such as Melody RNN or MusicVAE (with the same restrictions as previously mentioned) if we want the resulting generation to be monophonic. We can also use a polyphonic model, such as Polyphony RNN if we want the generation to be polyphonic.

Sometimes, we know what model to use, but the configuration doesn't fit our use case. Let's look at how to create a new configuration.

Creating a new configuration

We'll take the example of a bass dataset we would like to train using the Music VAE model. Looking at the `configs` module in the `magenta.models.music_vae` module, we find the `cat-mel_2bar_small` configuration, which is close to what we want to achieve, but when the dataset is converted, the notes that don't correspond to a melody program (defined as 0 to 32 in Magenta) are thrown out.

You can find this code in the `chapter_07_example_01.py` file in the source code of this chapter. There are more comments and content in the source code, so you should go check it out.

To achieve that, we'll create a new configuration called `cat-bass_2bar_small` and we'll change the valid programs to `bass` programs:

1. First, let's create a new `Config` instance with the following content:

```
from magenta.common import merge_hparams
from magenta.models.music_vae import Config
from magenta.models.music_vae import MusicVAE
from magenta.models.music_vae import lstm_models
from magenta.models.music_vae.data import BASS_PROGRAMS
from magenta.models.music_vae.data import NoteSequenceAugmenter
from magenta.models.music_vae.data import OneHotMelodyConverter
from tensorflow.contrib.training import HParams

cat_bass_2bar_small = Config(
  model=MusicVAE(lstm_models.BidirectionalLstmEncoder(),
                 lstm_models.CategoricalLstmDecoder()),
  hparams=merge_hparams(
    lstm_models.get_default_hparams(),
    HParams(
      batch_size=512,
      max_seq_len=32,
      z_size=256,
      enc_rnn_size=[512],
      dec_rnn_size=[256, 256],
      free_bits=0,
      max_beta=0.2,
      beta_rate=0.99999,
      sampling_schedule="inverse_sigmoid",
      sampling_rate=1000,
    )),
note_sequence_augmenter=NoteSequenceAugmenter(transpose_range=(-5,
5)),
  data_converter=OneHotMelodyConverter(
    valid_programs=BASS_PROGRAMS,
    skip_polyphony=False,
    max_bars=100,
    slice_bars=2,
    steps_per_quarter=4),
  train_examples_path=None,
  eval_examples_path=None,
)
```

The only part we've changed here is the `valid_programs=BASS_PROGRAMS` argument in `OneHotMelodyConverter`, but we could have changed other elements, such as `NoteSequenceAugmenter` that we talked about in the previous chapter. Hyperparameters can be changed using the `hparams` flag, but we can also define them in a configuration if we want to define default values for a model.

2. To use the new configuration, we can call the `run` method of the `music_vae_train` module:

    ```
    import tensorflow as tf
    from magenta.models.music_vae.configs import CONFIG_MAP
    from magenta.models.music_vae.music_vae_train import run

    def main(unused_argv):
      CONFIG_MAP["cat-bass_2bar_small"] = cat_bass_2bar_small
      run(CONFIG_MAP)

    if __name__ == "__main__":
      tf.app.run(main)
    ```

    Here, we import the whole configuration map and add our new configuration before calling the `run` method, so that we can still pass other configurations in the `--config` flag.

3. We can then call this code the same way as we would call the `music_vae_train` command:

    ```
    python chapter_07_example_01.py --config="cat-bass_2bar_small"
    [FLAGS]
    ```

Here, `FLAGS` are the training flags we need to pass, such as `--run_dir` and `--sequence_example_file`.

Other models, such as the Drums RNN or Melody RNN models, will be configured in the same manner. Refer to the next section for examples on how to do that.

Now that we know how to choose a model and a configuration (or create a new one), let's look at how to start and configure the training.

Training and tuning a model

Training a machine model is an empirical and iterative approach, where we first prepare the data and the configuration, then train the model, fail, and restart again. Getting models to train on the first try is rare, but we'll persevere through hardship together.

When launching a **training phase**, we'll be looking at specific metrics to verify that our model is training properly and converging. We'll also be launching an **evaluation phase**, which executes on a separate, smaller dataset, to verify that the model can properly generalize on data that it hasn't seen yet.

The **evaluation** dataset is often called the **validation** dataset in machine learning in general, but we'll keep the term evaluation since it is used in Magenta.

The validation dataset is different than the **test** dataset, which is an external dataset, often curated by hand, and contains hard examples, giving a final test to measure the network performance. The test dataset is often used to compare different models' performance. We won't be looking at test datasets here.

We'll break down and explain each step of the process. Let's start by looking at some best practices and conventions we'll be using for this chapter.

Organizing datasets and training data

Because of the iterative nature of training, we'll get to produce many datasets and many **training runs**. The best way to proceed is to keep both separate, for example, in two folders named `datasets` and `training`.

In the `datasets` folder, we can copy what we produced from the previous chapter in separate folders, for example, `dance_drums`, `jazz_drums`, `piano_drums`, and so on, with the folders containing the MIDI files:

- We keep the `notesequences.tfrecords` file in the proper dataset folder since it is produced only once per dataset.
- We keep the `sequence_examples` folder outside of this folder because it is model dependent, meaning we'll be regenerating this folder for each model, for example, once for Drums RNN and once for MusicVAE (even if we use the same data).

In the `training` folder, we'll be creating a new folder for each model and dataset, for example, `drums_rnn_dance_drums`:

- We'll be executing the `MODEL_create_dataset` command (if available), creating the `sequence_examples` directory (if any) for the model.
- Then, we'll be launching multiple training runs, with proper naming, for example, `run1_with_dropout`, or other configuration we might want to use:

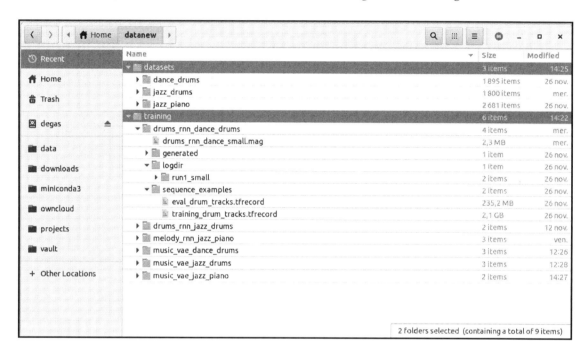

Having a single training folder with multiple runs is useful because we can load multiple training runs in TensorBoard and compare how each model has performed.

Training on a CPU or a GPU

Training is a computationally extensive activity. Training a simple model, such as the Drums RNN model, on an entry-level GPU (for example, an RTX 2060) will take around 5 hours. Training on the CPU takes a lot more time since the operations needed in network training (namely, vector arithmetic) are optimized to be executed in parallel on a GPU. To use a GPU, we also need to have properly installed the `magenta-gpu` package, as well as the CUDA libraries (see `Chapter 1`, *Introduction on Magenta and Generative Art*, for more information on that).

If you don't have a GPU, don't despair, you can follow this chapter anyway. You can do the data preparation steps and launch the training on a small network (see the first training example later on how to do that). Then, let the network train for a while, and if you see encouraging results, follow the steps in the last section, *Using Google Cloud Platform*, to restart the training on a faster machine. This will enable you to test the commands and datasets locally and then offload the bulk of the work to GCP. Even if you have a GPU, this might be a good way to proceed, especially if you want to train multiple models at the same time, or test different hyperparameters at the same time.

The following sections and commands still apply to both CPU and GPU training, as well as GCP.

Training RNN models

We now have all of the elements to start training a model. Let's take a simple example, we'll use the dance_drums dataset from the previous chapter and train the Drums RNN model.

You can find this code in the README.md file in the source code of this chapter. Since most of the code snippets in this chapter are command line, we are not providing example files for each example.

From the previous chapter, we should now have a datasets/dance_drums folder ready with the MIDI files. We've already executed the convert_dir_to_note_sequences command, which produces a notesequences.tfrecord file.

Creating the dataset and launching the training

We'll now create the dataset (an operation we've already done in the previous chapter, but we show it again here as a refresher) and launch the training.

1. First, let's create the sequence examples. In the training folder, create and change directory to a new folder called drums_rnn_dance_drums, and execute (replacing PATH_TO_NOTE_SEQUENCES with the proper file):

   ```
   drums_rnn_create_dataset --config="drum_kit" --
   input="PATH_TO_NOTE_SEQUENCES" --output_dir="sequence_examples" --
   eval_ratio=0.10
   ```

   This should create a sequence_examples folder containing two files, a training set and an evaluation set for the drum sequences.

Ideally, the `drums_rnn_create_dataset` command should be called only once for all of the training runs. Since we are going to tune the hyperparameters between each run, and that the hyperparameters are sensible to the training data, changing the training and evaluation dataset while tuning the model is not a good idea.

2. We'll now start the training using a small network:

```
drums_rnn_train --config="drum_kit" --run_dir="logdir/run1_small" --
sequence_example_file="sequence_examples/training_drum_tracks.tfrec
ord" --hparams="batch_size=64,rnn_layer_sizes=[64,64]" --
num_training_steps=20000
```

On Windows, the `--run_dir` flag should use a backslash. For this example and all of the following examples, instead of writing `--run_dir="logdir/run1_small"`, use `--run_dir="logdir\run1_small"`.

We use an output directory named `run1_small`, so we can remember later what run it is, and an input file named `training_drum_tracks.tfrecord`. The hyperparameters are a batch size of 64 and a two-layer RNN network of 64 units for each layer, the number of elements in the list defining the number of layers. For a 3 layers RNN network, use [64, 64, 64].

You should see in the Terminal the complete list of hyperparameters and their values, which are taken from the configuration when not overridden by a flag:

```
INFO:tensorflow:hparams = {'batch_size': 64, 'rnn_layer_sizes':
[64, 64], 'dropout_keep_prob': 0.5, 'attn_length': 32, 'clip_norm':
3, 'learning_rate': 0.001, 'residual_connections': False,
'use_cudnn': False}
```

We'll soon see how hyperparameters affect training in the following sections. If you are using a GPU, make sure TensorFlow can use your GPU by checking this output:

```
2019-11-20 01:56:12.058398: I
tensorflow/core/common_runtime/gpu/gpu_device.cc:1304] Created
TensorFlow device (/job:localhost/replica:0/task:0/device:GPU:0
with 5089 MB memory) -> physical GPU (device: 0, name: GeForce GTX
1060 6GB, pci bus id: 0000:01:00.0, compute capability: 6.1)
```

3. Now, the network will start training, and you should see outputs like this:

```
INFO:tensorflow:Accuracy = 0.27782458, Global Step = 10, Loss =
5.4186254, Perplexity = 225.56882 (16.487 sec)
INFO:tensorflow:global_step/sec: 0.586516
```

We'll be talking about the different metrics soon. When we launched the training, we've used the `--num_training_steps=20000` flag, meaning the network will stop its training after reaching 20,000 global steps. We won't be talking about epoch here, which consists of a full cycle through the training data since we only handle steps in Magenta. The model should converge before that, but giving an upper bound is good so that it doesn't execute for too long for no reason.

If you want to have an approximation on the time the training will take to reach 20,000 steps, you can use the `global_step/sec` output. For the previous output, our job should finish in approximately 9 hours, but this is an upper bound, so chances are we can stop it before.

Now that the training is launched, we can launch the evaluation.

Launching the evaluation

The evaluation job executes on the evaluation dataset, which is a smaller (we previously used a `--eval_ratio=0.10` flag, meaning 10%) and separate dataset from the training set. The evaluation job evaluates the model and computes the loss function, without updating any of the weights in the network. Therefore, the evaluation process is fast and can be executed at the same time as the training job on the CPU.

To launch the evaluation, we use the same command, using the `--eval` flag. If you are using a GPU, you'll need to deactivate the GPU for that execution, using the `CUDA_VISIBLE_DEVICES=""` environment variable, because the previous TensorFlow process takes all of the available memory.

On Windows, don't forget to use a backslash in the `--run_dir` flag. Also on Windows, use the `set` command to set an environment variable for the current command-line session. On Linux and macOS, you can set the environment variable for a single command by prefixing the variable value before the command.

On Windows, use the following:

```
set CUDA_VISIBLE_DEVICES=""
drums_rnn_train --config="drum_kit" --run_dir="logdir\run1_small" --
sequence_example_file="sequence_examples/eval_drum_tracks.tfrecord" --
hparams="batch_size=64,rnn_layer_sizes=[64,64]" --num_training_steps=20000
--eval
```

On Linux and macOS, use the following:

```
CUDA_VISIBLE_DEVICES="" drums_rnn_train --config="drum_kit" --
run_dir="logdir/run1_small" --
sequence_example_file="sequence_examples/eval_drum_tracks.tfrecord" --
hparams="batch_size=64,rnn_layer_sizes=[64,64]" --num_training_steps=20000
--eval
```

For this command, the provided network size needs to correspond to the training network size. If you used `rnn_layer_sizes=[64,64]` in the training command, then you need to use the same here. The two flags we've changed from the previous command are the `--eval` and `--sequence_example_file` flags.

The evaluation will execute when a new checkpoint (which happens approximately every 40 steps) is added in the running directory. When that happens, you'll see outputs similar to this:

```
Starting evaluation at 2019-11-25-23:38:24
INFO:tensorflow:Accuracy = 0.0, Global Step = 35, Loss = 0.0, Perplexity =
1.0
INFO:tensorflow:Evaluation [1/3]
INFO:tensorflow:Evaluation [2/3]
INFO:tensorflow:Evaluation [3/3]
Finished evaluation at 2019-11-25-23:38:30
```

The evaluation job will stop automatically when the training job hasn't produced a checkpoint for a while.

Looking at TensorBoard

During and after training, we can launch TensorBoard, which helps to visualize the network metrics. We'll be using TensorBoard to tune the hyperparameters and iterate with the data preparation phase.

To launch TensorBoard, use the following command:

```
tensorboard --logdir=logdir
```

Notice that we pass the parent output directory, meaning we'll have access to all of the contained runs (currently, there's only one). We can find the URL of TensorBoard in the console. Once opened, the page will look like this:

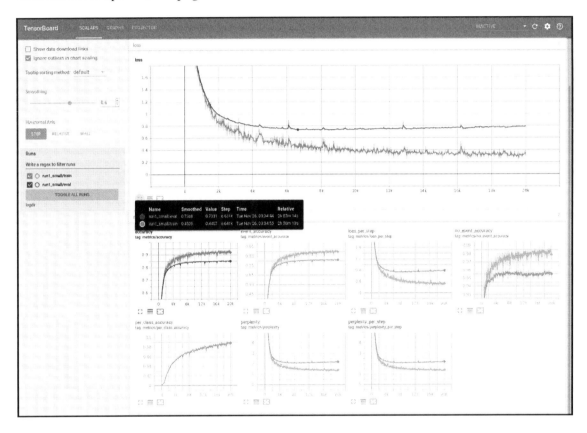

This is the result of our trained model after 20,000 steps. On the left, we have the training and evaluation jobs, which can be toggled. On the right, different metrics are shown in the screenshot, with the abscissa being the global step count, which goes to 20,000 steps. The two most interesting metrics for us are **loss** and **accuracy**. We want the **loss to go down**, both for the training and evaluation sets, and the **accuracy to go up**.

We notice that this model has converged, meaning we have a successful training at hand, but we need to verify that the resulting model is good, by looking at the loss metric. Let's have a look at the loss function, comparing the training loss and the evaluation loss:

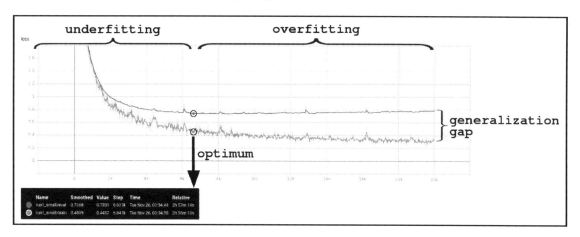

We can see here that the model is slightly overfitting the training data. You can find the model optimum by taking the **evaluation loss curve at its lowest point** before it starts going up. On the left of that point, the model is underfitting the training data; on the right, the model is overfitting the data. The difference between both curves is called the generalization gap.

Let's explain underfitting and overfitting before continuing on to other examples.

Explaining underfitting and overfitting

Understanding underfitting and overfitting and how to prevent them is important for proper network training. When a model is too simple and cannot learn from the training dataset, we say the model is **underfitting**. On the other hand, when a model is learning properly from the training dataset but cannot generalize to data outside of it, we say the model is **overfitting**.

We show underfitting, optimal solution, and overfitting in the following diagram:

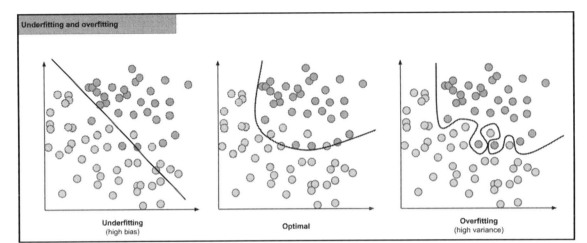

On the left, we show underfitting, meaning the model didn't learn on the dataset. In the middle, we show an optimal solution, and on the right, we show overfitting, where the resulting model is overly complex for the given data, meaning the model won't generalize to other datasets.

Remember that the objective of a neural network is to perform well on the training dataset as well as **new data that it has never seen**, which will be used to make predictions. Achieving that is hard since it requires a proper combination of quality and quantity of data, as well as proper network size and learning parameters.

Let's have a look at how to fix those issues.

Fixing underfitting

Underfitting is easy to address and can be solved by **increasing the capacity of the model**—basically, by adding more layers and units. By increasing the model's capacity, the network can learn more types of functions for mapping inputs to outputs.

For our previous example, we can increase the capacity of the model by adding more units (neurons) in each of the two layers:

```
drums_rnn_train --config="drum_kit" --run_dir="logdir/run1_small" --
sequence_example_file="sequence_examples/training_drum_tracks.tfrecord" --
hparams="batch_size=64,rnn_layer_sizes=[128,128]" --
num_training_steps=20000
```

We also need to train long enough, which might be hardware dependent, since if we are training on slow hardware, it might take a lot of time to reach the optimal point.

See the section, *Defining proper network size and hyperparameters*, for more information on network size.

Fixing overfitting

Overfitting, on the other hand, is harder to address since it comes from a variety of factors. The two most common causes are as follows:

- When a model overfits, it is because it has the capacity of overfitting the training dataset. By keeping the same training dataset, you can **reduce the network capacity**, so that the network won't have the necessary resources to overfit the training data anymore. To reduce the network capacity, use the `rnn_layer_sizes` hyperparameter as in the previous example.
- By keeping the same network capacity, you can **augment the training dataset size** so that, with more data, the network might not have the capacity to overfit it anymore. The added data needs to be varied enough to fix overfitting and might not always work. To augment the training dataset size, go back to Chapter 6, *Data Preparation for Training*, and add content to the dataset. Be aware that augmenting the dataset with data that isn't diverse enough won't help to resolve overfitting.

There is a relationship between the training dataset and the network size: **the bigger and more diverse the dataset, the bigger the network has to be**. A bigger network won't necessarily produce better results if the training dataset isn't big enough or qualitative enough.

There are other ways of fixing overfitting that can be used in Magenta models:

- **Early stopping** of the training phase at the optimal point is one way since all of the training after that point makes the resulting network worse. To use early stopping, see the next section, *Using a specific checkpoint to implement early stop*.
- Using regularization techniques such as **dropout**, which randomly and temporarily drops a unit/neuron out of the network, is another way. To use dropout, use the `dropout_keep_prob` hyperparameter.

Regularization techniques are a class of approach that aims at constraining the size of the weights in a neural network and is widely used as a way to prevent overfitting.

As you might have noticed by now, there's a relationship between our dataset and our model that needs to be taken into account when tuning the training phase. Let's have a more detailed look into network size and hyperparameters.

Defining network size and hyperparameters

Defining a proper network size is a trial and error process, but a good starting point, if your hardware is good enough, are the values in the configuration of the model you want to use.

Let's take an example using the `attention_rnn` configuration of the Melody RNN model, using `batch_size=128`, `rnn_layer_sizes=[128, 128]`, `dropout_keep_prob=0.5`, `learning_rate=0.001`, and `clip_norm=3`:

1. If the model is overfitting, we can try the following:
    1. Using more dropout, for example, `dropout_keep_prob=0.4` and lower values
    2. Adding more data
    3. Reducing the network size using `rnn_layer_sizes=[64, 64]`
2. If the model is converging and not overfitting, we can try using a bigger model, `rnn_layer_sizes=[256, 256]`. If we have good data, using a bigger model will yield better results, so we want to optimize that.

When changing something, we need to make sure we are making a single modification and then testing the result before making any other change. Changing multiple parameters at the same time will prevent us from knowing the direct impact of each one.

Sometimes, when increasing the network size, we might stumble into a model that doesn't converge, meaning the loss function starts increasing again, which will result in a training error. That can be fixed by changing `learning_rate` or `clip_norm`. See the next section, *Fixing a model not converging*, for more information.

Determining the batch size

We haven't talked about `batch_size` yet. The batch size is the amount of data the network will handle at once. A bigger batch size may improve the training time by making the model parameters converge faster. It also should remove some computational overhead from transferring a larger chunk of data to the GPU memory at once.

A rule of thumb is that when you increase the batch size, you'll also need to **increase the learning rate**. Since more data is taken into account at the same time, the model's weight can get updated using a bigger ratio.

Increasing the batch size might improve training time, but it might as well **decrease the performance of the model**, so using a too big batch size might not be a good idea. Overall, the batch size is often a trade-off between execution time and the resulting quality of the model.

We provide more information on this in the last section, *Further reading*.

Fixing out of memory errors

Sometimes, when using a batch size or network size too big, you might end up with the following error:

```
[tensorflow/stream_executor/cuda/cuda_driver.cc:890] failed to alloc
8589934592 bytes on host: CUDA_ERROR_OUT_OF_MEMORY: out of memory
```

Reduce the batch size and network size until the out of memory error disappears. Sometimes, the error is not fatal, in which case it will negatively impact the training performance.

Fixing a wrong network size

When using an existing run directory, either from continuing a previous training, starting an evaluation job, or starting a generation job, we need to provide the same network size as when it was first launched.

If the training run was first started using `rnn_layer_sizes=[256,256,256]` and then restarted using `rnn_layer_sizes=[128,128,128]`, we'll end up with the following error:

```
Invalid argument: Assign requires shapes of both tensors to match. lhs
shape= [128] rhs shape= [256]
```

In this case, we'll need to use the network size that was first used when we started the training.

Fixing a model not converging

A model that converges is defined by a **decreasing loss function** on both the training and evaluation sets. If our loss function goes up at some point, the model is unstable and isn't properly converging. There are many reasons as to why a model might not converge.

Let's take a simple example (this example uses the `jazz_drums` dataset we created in the previous chapter):

```
drums_rnn_train --config="drum_kit" --run_dir="logdir/run1_diverge" --
sequence_example_file="sequence_examples/training_drum_tracks.tfrecord" --
hparams="batch_size=128,rnn_layer_sizes=[128,128,128]" --
num_training_steps=20000
```

When a model is diverging, we might get an error at some point:

```
E1112 20:03:08.279203 10460 basic_session_run_hooks.py:760] Model diverged
with loss = NaN.
...
  File "c:\users\magenta\appdata\local\programs\python\python35\lib\site-
packages\tensorflow\python\training\basic_session_run_hooks.py", line 761,
in after_run
    raise NanLossDuringTrainingError
tensorflow.python.training.basic_session_run_hooks.NanLossDuringTrainingErr
or: NaN loss during training.
```

The resulting TensorBoard graph will show the loss function going up. Let's fix the problem by using a smaller learning rate. The default learning rate value that was used in the previous command is `learning_rate=0.001`, so we'll make that 10 times smaller:

```
drums_rnn_train --config="drum_kit" --run_dir="logdir/run2_learning_rate" -
-sequence_example_file="sequence_examples/training_drum_tracks.tfrecord" --
hparams="learning_rate=0.0001,batch_size=128,rnn_layer_sizes=[128,128,128]"
--num_training_steps=20000
```

Here is the resulting TensorBoard graph with both runs:

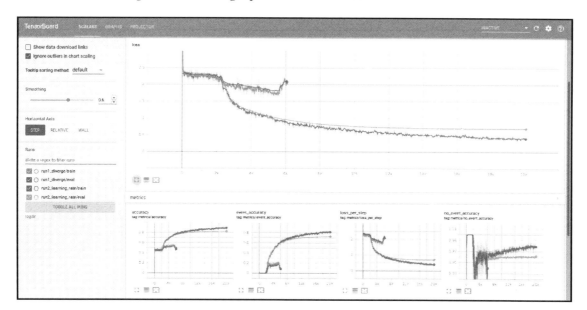

You can see that `run1_diverge` has a loss function that goes up, and `run2_learning_rate` is training properly.

There are many ways of fixing a diverging model, but since the problem is dependent on the data and the network size, you'll have to test various methods:

- Try **reducing the learning rate**, like in our previous example. Learning rate decay (available in the Music VAE model), where the learning rate is gradually reduced, can also help.
- Try **changing the network size**. In this example, using a network size of `rnn_layer_sizes=[256,256,256]` will also fix the problem.
- Try **decreasing the gradient clipping**. In our previous example, the gradient clipping default value is `clip_norm=3`, so you will want to decrease the `clip_norm` hyperparameter, for example, to `clip_norm=2`. Remember, default hyperparameter values are in the configurations for each model (see the previous section, *Creating a new configuration*, for more information on this).

> Sometimes, fixing a diverging model will make another problem arise. For example, fixing the problem using a bigger network size might result in the network overfitting. Make sure you test multiple solutions so that the chosen one is best.

Most often than not, the NaN loss during training error is caused by the exploding gradients problem we've already talked about in Chapter 4, *Generating Polyphonic Melodies*. This problem is common in RNNs, and even if LSTM cells helps a lot to make the model converge, the exploding gradient problem can still occur, given the accumulation of gradients unrolled over hundreds of input time steps.

During training, the loss is calculated on the training examples, and then its derivative is backpropagated through the network, updating the weights by a fraction of the propagated error, this fraction being the learning rate. When the weights get updated over and over by large values, they tend to explode, or overflow, which is why using a smaller learning rate might fix the problem.

Gradient clipping has a similar effect but is useful if we prefer not changing the learning rate. By using gradient clipping, we can rescale, or clip to a maximum value, the gradient vector (the error derivative) that will be backpropagated through the network. The parameter we have available in Magenta is clip_norm, which is used by TensorFlow as tf.clip_by_norm(t, clip_norm). By decreasing the parameter's value, we effectively normalize the error gradient so that the norm is equal or less than the provided value.

Fixing not enough training data

Let's now train the Melody RNN model using our previous chapter's jazz piano dataset:

1. We first create the dataset using the attention_rnn configuration. In the training folder, create and change the directory to a new folder called melody_rnn_jazz_piano, and execute (replacing PATH_TO_NOTE_SEQUENCES with the proper file, which should be in your datasets folder):

```
melody_rnn_create_dataset --config="attention_rnn" --
input="PATH_TO_NOTE_SEQUENCES" --output_dir="sequence_examples" --
eval_ratio=0.10
```

2. We then train the model using the following:

```
melody_rnn_train --config="attention_rnn" --
run_dir="logdir/run1_few_data" --
sequence_example_file="sequence_examples/training_melodies.tfrecord
" --hparams="batch_size=128,rnn_layer_sizes=[128,128]" --
num_training_steps=20000
```

When checked in TensorFlow, we can look at the `run1_few_data` run:

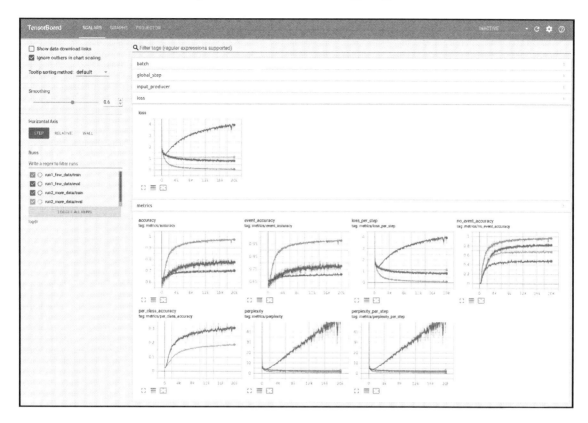

In the **loss** diagram, the first two lines at the top are the train and evaluation metrics for the run, `run1_few_data`. The evaluation loss goes up, meaning the model is overfitting really fast. This is because we don't have a lot of data (659 outputs to be exact).

Fixing this problem requires us to go back to preparing the data. For the `run2_more_data` run, in the loss diagram, the two lowest curves show us that the problem is fixed. To get more data, we came back to the pipeline from the previous chapter, `melody_rnn_pipeline_example.py`, and changed `ignore_polyphonic_notes=False` to `True` in the `MelodyExtractor` pipeline. This means that, instead of throwing out polyphonic melodies, the pipeline converts them into a monophonic one, keeping the highest note. The conversion method is in the `melodies_lib` module, so if we want to change that behavior, we'll have to write our own pipeline.

Because this change modifies the musical content of our dataset, we'll need to carefully listen to the generated results, to verify that the trained model outputs interesting samples. Here is a generated sample from the `run2_more_data` trained model:

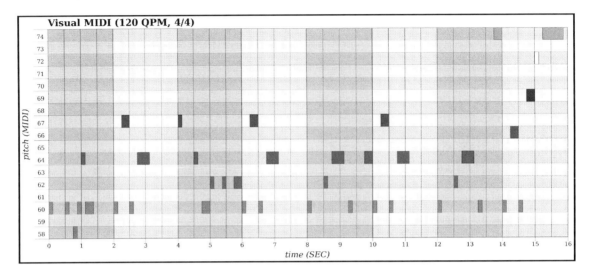

This example is a good example of the necessity of going back and forth between the data preparation step and the training step. See the next section, *Generating sequences from a trained model*, for more information on how to generate sequences from a trained model.

Configuring attention and other hyperparameters

The Melody RNN model uses attention during training to look at previous steps (see `Chapter 3`, *Generating Polyphonic Melodies*, for a refresher on that). You can use the `attn_length` hyperparameter to configure the length of the attention spawn.

Each model has its own configuration. Make sure you check them out in their respective configuration files to see what parameter you can tune during training.

Generating sequences from a trained model

Now that we have a trained model, `run1_small`, and we understand that it slightly overfits, let's try and generate a sequence out of it to see how it goes. To generate a sequence when the network has finished training or during training, we can use the model's `generate` command.

Let's call the `drums_rnn_generate` method using the following parameters (if you are launching this command during training and you are using a GPU, don't forget to use `CUDA_VISIBLE_DEVICES=""`):

```
drums_rnn_generate --config="drum_kit" --run_dir="logdir/run1_small" --
hparams="rnn_layer_sizes=[64,64]" --output_dir="generated/generated1_small"
```

The `generate` command will take the latest checkpoint in the run directory and use it to generate a sequence. We need to use the same network size as for the training phase.

Here is a generated sequence from our training phase:

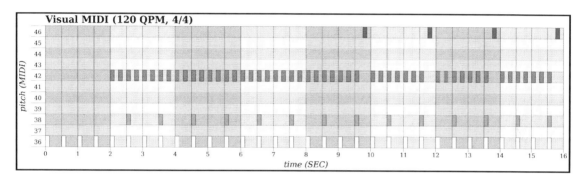

The model should have generated 10 sequences; we should listen to hear what it sounds like. Congratulations! You've heard the first notes of your own generated model.

The advantage of using the `dance` dataset is that it is easy to verify that the training model is generating what we expected: in the resulting 10 sequences, each of them mostly has a bass drum on beat. Now, we need to ask ourselves whether the resulting generation is diverse and interesting. If not, we should go back to prepare a new dataset and iterate on it.

Using a specific checkpoint to implement early stops

We previously talked about early stopping, which is the action of stopping training at the optimum, instead of letting the model degrade further, as a way to prevent overfitting. There are multiple ways of doing that, such as coding a stop condition that checks whether the evaluation loss function starts going up, but the easiest approach is to keep only the checkpoint that is nearest to the optimum after the training phase is over.

Going back to our previous example, we find the evaluation loss curve minimum to be at around 7,000 steps. In the `logdir/run1_small` directory, we find that we have a checkpoint near our optimum that we can use: `model.`**`ckpt-6745`**`.data-00000.`

To use that checkpoint, we need to use the `--checkpoint_file` flag instead of the `--run_dir` flag:

```
drums_rnn_generate --config="drum_kit" --
checkpoint_file="logdir/run1_small/train/model.ckpt-6745" --
hparams="batch_size=64,rnn_layer_sizes=[64,64]" --
output_dir="generated/generated1_small"
```

Notice we don't pass the full filename (only `model.ckpt-6745` and not `model.ckpt-6745.data-00000-of-00001`) because TensorFlow expects only the first part. The command should generate 10 new elements using that checkpoint.

Packaging and distributing the result using bundles

When we are satisfied with our trained model, we can package it using Magenta's bundle for distribution. Remember that bundles are available for RNN models only, but we'll provide ways of bundling other models such as Music VAE when we get there. Follow these steps:

1. To package a bundle, we call the generate command using the `--bundle_file` and `--save_generator_bundle` flags:

   ```
   drums_rnn_generate --config="drum_kit" --
   run_dir="logdir/run1_small" --
   hparams="batch_size=64,rnn_layer_sizes=[64,64]" --
   bundle_file="drums_rnn_dance_small.mag" --save_generator_bundle
   ```

   This will save the bundle in the `drums_rnn_dance_small.mag` file using the latest checkpoint. We can also use the `--checkpoint_file` flag from the previous command if we need another checkpoint that is not the latest.

2. We can now use the bundle as follows:

   ```
   drums_rnn_generate --config="drum_kit" --
   bundle_file="drums_rnn_dance_small.mag" --
   output_dir="generated/generated1_small"
   ```

Notice how the hyperparameters are left out—this is because they are configured in the bundle file. This also means the bundle hyperparameters overrides the ones configured in the `drum_kit` configuration.

Now that we have our first model trained, tuned, and packaged, we'll have a look at training other models.

Training MusicVAE

Let's now train the MusicVAE model so that we can compare the sampling with an RNN generation. One thing that differs for the MusicVAE training is that the data preparation step (the `create dataset` command) doesn't exist because the data conversion is made right before the model starts training. We'll manually create the dataset using a pipeline and then start the training.

Splitting the dataset into evaluation and training sets

Since there is no dataset creation command but we still need to split the dataset into training and evaluation data, we're going to write a pipeline to do that.

You can find this code in the `chapter_07_example_02.py` file in the source code of this chapter. There are more comments and content in the source code, so you should go check it out.

We'll also convert the note sequences into tensors, which will help us to validate the data before we start the training:

1. First, let's write the `partition` method that will split the dataset into training and evaluation data:

```
from magenta.music.protobuf.music_pb2 import NoteSequence
from magenta.pipelines.dag_pipeline import DAGPipeline
from magenta.pipelines.dag_pipeline import DagInput
from magenta.pipelines.dag_pipeline import DagOutput
from magenta.pipelines.pipeline import run_pipeline_serial
from magenta.pipelines.pipeline import tf_record_iterator
from magenta.pipelines.pipelines_common import RandomPartition

def partition(config: str, input: str, output_dir: str, eval_ratio:
int):
  modes = ["eval", "train"]
  partitioner = RandomPartition(NoteSequence, modes, [eval_ratio])
  dag = {partitioner: DagInput(NoteSequence)}
  for mode in modes:
    validator = TensorValidator(NoteSequence,
f"{mode}_TensorValidator", config)
```

```
        dag[validator] = partitioner[f"{mode}"]
        dag[DagOutput(f"{mode}")] = validator

    pipeline = DAGPipeline(dag)
    run_pipeline_serial(
        pipeline, tf_record_iterator(input, pipeline.input_type),
    output_dir)
```

We've already seen similar code in the previous chapter; we are actually reusing the RandomPartition class we've already covered, which will split the input into two sets using a given ratio.

2. Then, let's write the TensorValidator class:

```
from magenta.models.music_vae.configs import CONFIG_MAP
from magenta.pipelines.pipeline import Pipeline

class TensorValidator(Pipeline):

    def __init__(self, type_, name, config):
        super(TensorValidator, self).__init__(type_, type_, name)
        self._model = CONFIG_MAP[config]
        self._data_converter = self._model.data_converter

    def transform(self, note_sequence):
        tensors = self._data_converter.to_tensors(note_sequence)
        if not tensors.lengths:
            path = str(note_sequence).split('\n')[0:2]
            print(f"Empty tensor for {path}")
            return []
        return [note_sequence]
```

What is interesting here is that we are using the configuration to find the data converter (drums conversion, melody conversion, and so on) and then converting into tensors, a step that will be done before the model starts training. This step validates our input data and can help us to make statistics about the number of "valid" tensors as well as how much data we have. Unfortunately, the fact that we don't have a "create dataset" command makes it harder for us to know exactly what kind of data will be fed to the network, which is why this class is useful.

3. Finally, we'll call the partition method and declare some flags for the command line:

```
import argparse

parser = argparse.ArgumentParser()
parser.add_argument("--config", type=str, required=True)
```

```
parser.add_argument("--input", type=str, required=True)
parser.add_argument("--output_dir", type=str, required=True)
parser.add_argument("--eval_ratio", type=float, default=0.1)

def main():
    args = parser.parse_args()
    partition(args.config, args.input, args.output_dir,
args.eval_ratio)

if __name__ == "__main__":
    main()
```

4. Now, let's create a new training directory and then call our new Python script (replacing PATH_TO_PYTHON_SCRIPT and PATH_TO_DATASET_TFRECORDS with proper values):

```
python PATH_TO_PYTHON_SCRIPT --config="cat-drums_2bar_small" --
input="PATH_TO_DATASET_TFRECORDS" --output_dir="sequence_examples"
```

This will create a `sequence_examples` directory containing the `eval.tfrecords` and `train.tfrecords` datasets.

Launching the training and evaluation

Now that we have validated our data and split it into two datasets, we can start the training.

Launching the training, evaluation, and TensorBoard is similar to the previous sections:

```
# Start the training job
music_vae_train --config="cat-drums_2bar_small" --run_dir="logdir/run1" --
mode="train" --examples_path="sequence_examples/train.tfrecord"

# Start the evaluation job
music_vae_train --config="cat-drums_2bar_small" --run_dir="logdir/run1" --
mode="eval" --examples_path="sequence_examples/eval.tfrecord"

# Start the TensorBoard
tensorboard --logdir=logdir
```

Like for the previous models, you can pass hyperparameters using the `--hparams=FLAGS` flag. Here, we are using the "small" configuration since MusicVAE models can get big in terms of size pretty fast. A small model is enough for good performance, for example, the Magenta pre-trained drum model uses the `cat-drums_2bar_small` configuration.

When training Music VAE, we'll also want to tune the following two hyperparameters: `free_bits` and `max_beta`. By increasing `free_bits` or decreasing `max_beta`, we are decreasing the effect of the KL loss, resulting in a model that is better at reconstruction, with potentially worse random samples. See the previous chapter, `Chapter 4`, *Latent Space Interpolation with MusicVAE*, if you don't remember how **Kulback-Leibler** (**KL**) divergence affects the model performance.

Distributing a trained model

Unfortunately, for MusicVAE, we cannot create a Magenta bundle. The simplest way to distribute a TensorFlow checkpoint is to copy the checkpoint files and zip them for the transfer:

1. First, let's copy the corresponding files (replace `STEP` with the checkpoint step you want to keep):

   ```
   mkdir "trained/cat-drums_2bar_small"
   cp logdir/run1/train/model.ckpt-STEP* "trained/cat-
   drums_2bar_small"
   ```

   You should now have three files in the `complete/cat-drums_2bar_small` directory. Remember, TensorFlow checkpoints should be loaded using their prefix, for example, `model.ckpt-157780`.

2. Enter the following to use the checkpoint in a generation (replace `STEP` with the checkpoint you want to use):

   ```
   music_vae_generate --config="cat-drums_2bar_small" --
   checkpoint_file="trained/cat-drums_2bar_small/model.ckpt-STEP"
   ```

Remember that checkpoints do not contain information about the changes you've made to the hyperparameters (unlike Magenta bundles), so you'll need to pass the same hyperparameters you've used during training each time you use it.

Some hyperparameters can be changed. For example, there is no sense in using a batch size of 512 when you are sampling (unless you are sampling 512 sequences at once, perhaps), but it could be the value you've used for training.

You will want to keep everything related to the TensorFlow graph, which means the network size and anything related to encoding and decoding.

Creating a configuration for this specific training is probably the easiest way of keeping track of the hyperparameters that were used.

Training other models

We won't be training every model here, but training other models should be fairly similar to the one we've shown. The same model tuning, regarding overfitting, for example, can be applied to other models. Refer to the README files of the model you want to train for more information.

Using Google Cloud Platform

Using a cloud computing provider is useful to offload computing to faster machines. It can also be used if we want to make multiple runs at the same time. For example, we could try fixing exploding gradients by launching two runs: one with a lower learning rate and one with a lower gradient clipping. We could spawn two different VMs, each training its own model, and see which performs better.

We are going to use Google Cloud Platform (GCP), but other cloud providers, such as Amazon AWS or Microsoft Azure, will also work. We'll go through the different steps needed to train a Melody RNN model on the piano jazz dataset from the previous chapter, including the GCP account configuration and VM instance creation.

Creating and configuring an account

First, head to `console.cloud.google.com` and create a new Google account (or use an existing one). Once in GCP, follow these steps:

1. If this is your first time logging in, you will need to create a new project, which you can call `Magenta`. If not, find your current project at the top of the screen, and create a new one if you want.

2. Then, we'll need to set up quotas, since when a new account is created, it cannot create VM instances with GPUs. On the left, go to **IAM & Admin** > **Quotas**, and find the **GPUs (all regions)** quotas by searching GPU in the **Metrics** field. Click on the checkbox, then **Edit**, and change the quota to another value, like 5. The quota modification will take a bit of time to get validated.

3. Finally, we'll need to set up billing. On the left, go to **Billing** and then follow the instructions to add a **Billing Account**.

Our account being properly setup, we can now create a new VM instance.

Preparing an SSH key (optional)

Using an SSH key is useful to connect to the VM instance from a local Terminal. This is an optional step since, in GCP, you can connect to the VM instance using a Terminal in a browser, which works pretty well, but with really slow upload and download speeds.

If you already have an SSH key ready, you can skip this step. If you are unsure, check the file at ~/.ssh/id_rsa.pub.

On Linux and macOS, you can generate a new SSH key by entering the following in a Terminal:

```
ssh-keygen
```

This will save a key in ~/.ssh/id_rsa.pub. On Windows, the easiest way to do this is to install Git Bash (git-scm.com/download/win), which contains two commands we'll use—ssh-keygen and scp, which we'll be using in the next sections.

Once generated, the public key looks like this:

```
ssh-rsa AAAA... user@host
```

The user part before the host is important since it will be the user to provide to GCP when you log in.

Creating a VM instance from a Tensforflow image

Now, we return to GCP then, on the menu on the left, we go to **Compute Engine**:

1. Once in **Compute Engine**, choose **Images** from the left menu.
2. In the **Filter Images** search, type `TensorFlow` and find the most recent image. At the time of writing, the image is called **c3-deeplearning-tf-1-15-cu100-20191112**.
3. Choose the image and then choose **Create instance**; you will see the create instance screen:

We'll now fill the information as in the preceding diagram:

1. In **Name**, use `Magenta`.
2. In **Region** and **Zone**, find a place that is near you.
3. In **Machine Type**, use at least **n1-standard-4**, a 4 core CPU with 15 GB of RAM.
4. In **CPU platform and GPU**, click on **Add GPU** and choose a **GPU type**, using at least an **NVIDIA Tesla K80**.

Depending on the chosen region and the current availability, you'll have different GPUs available. The NVIDIA Tesla K80 GPUs have an average computing power (0.45 global step/second on Melody RNN) and the P100 GPUs are almost twice as powerful (0.75 global step/second on Melody RNN). As a comparison, an entry-level gaming GPU such as the RTX 2060 makes 0.6 global step/second on Melody RNN.

Now, let's go on to the disk content:

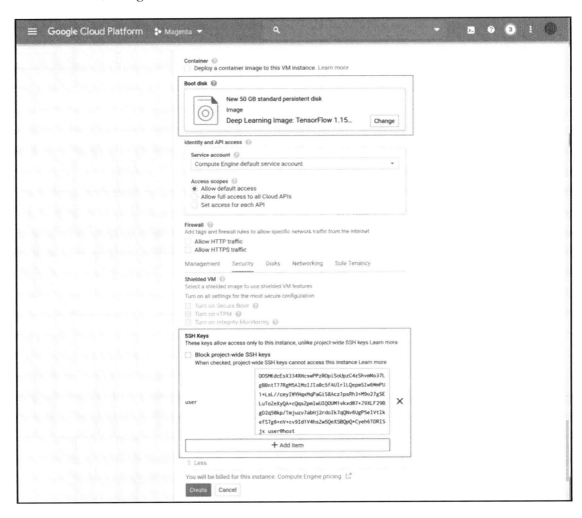

We will initialize the instance using the following steps:

1. The boot disk should be already filled with a **Deep Learning Image** of 50 GB.
2. After expanding the **Management, security, disks, networking, sole tenancy** section, in the **Security** tab, paste your public SSH key (if you have one). The resulting user (in this case, **user**) will be shown on the left.
3. Check the resulting price in the upper-right corner, which is **about $1.269 hourly** for this machine. Note that we are billed for the machine uptime. If we don't use the machine, we won't be billed for it, so we'll need to close it when we are finished.
4. Click on **Create**.

In the **VM instances** menu on the left, you should see the newly created VM.

Initializing the VM

Now that we have a new VM to work with, we need to install all of the required software. We can refer to Chapter 1, *Introduction on Magenta and Generative Art*, for the detailed installation instructions, but we'll also put the main commands here.

Installing the NVIDIA CUDA drivers

Fortunately, the VM image we are using does a lot of the installation for us. Let's first connect and install the required drivers:

1. First, we need to connect to the VM. If we don't have an SSH key, we use the **SSH** button on the right of the VM instance, which should start a new browser Terminal. If we have an SSH key, we can use the following command, on Linux, macOS, and Windows (using Git Bash):

   ```
   ssh USER@IP
   ```

   Here, we have to replace USER with the user in our SSH key and IP with the **external IP** shown in the VM instance page.

2. The VM will greet us with the following message, which we answer with y:

   ```
   This VM requires Nvidia drivers to function correctly. Installation
   takes ~1 minute.
   Would you like to install the Nvidia driver? [y/n] y
   ```

The NVIDIA drivers (CUDA drivers and cuDNN), in the proper versions for TensorFlow, should get installed. Unfortunately, there is a problem with the cuDNN versions, so we'll have to manually reinstall it.

3. Download the latest **cuDNN a.b.c for CUDA 10.0** at `developer.nvidia.com/rdp/cudnn-download` (download the full cuDNN Library) on your local machine.

4. Transfer the cuDNN archive to the VM instance. If we don't have an SSH key, we will use the interface to transfer the file (in the upper-right corner). If we have an SSH key, we use our Terminal:

```
scp PATH_TO_CUDNN_ARCHIVE USER@IP:
```

We'll have to replace `PATH_TO_CUDNN_ARCHIVE`, `USER`, and `IP` with proper values. The archive should now be in our home directory in the VM instance.

5. Now, log in to the machine using SSH (we don't have to do this if we are using the browser Terminal):

```
ssh USER@IP
```

We'll have to replace `USER` and `IP` with proper values.

6. Extract the archive:

```
# On the VM instance
tar -xzvf CUDNN_ARCHIVE_NAME
```

We'll have to replace `CUDNN_ARCHIVE_NAME` with the archive name.

7. Now let's override the current cuDNN installation with the new versions:

```
# On the VM instance
sudo cp cuda/include/cudnn.h /usr/local/cuda/include
sudo cp cuda/lib64/libcudnn* /usr/local/cuda/lib64
sudo chmod a+r /usr/local/cuda/include/cudnn.h
/usr/local/cuda/lib64/libcudnn*
```

Now that we have the CUDA drivers with the proper versions up and running, let's install the prerequisite software and Magenta GPU.

Installing Magenta GPU

Some packages are not installed by default on this image, so we'll have to install them manually:

1. First, we'll install some audio dependencies:

```
# On the VM instance
sudo apt install libasound2-dev libsndfile-dev
```

2. Then, we'll install Miniconda (`docs.conda.io/en/latest/miniconda.html`) and create a new environment:

```
# On the VM instance
conda create -n magenta python=3.6
conda activate magenta
```

3. Finally, let's install the Magenta GPU:

```
# On the VM instance
pip install magenta-gpu
```

We are now good to go, so let's start a training job on our new VM instance.

Launching the training

To start the training, we'll need to first transfer the dataset to the VM instance:

1. To transfer a dataset to the VM instance, first zip it, and then use the Terminal browser interface to upload it if you aren't using an SSH key. If you are using an SSH key, you can use `scp` to do that:

```
scp PATH_TO_DATASET USER@IP:
```

We'll have to replace `PATH_TO_DATASET`, `USER`, and `IP` with proper values. The archive should now be in our home directory in the VM instance.

2. Once uploaded, we unzip the archive, and then we start the training process as we would on a local machine, for example, for the Melody RNN model:

```
# On the VM instance
melody_rnn_create_dataset --config="attention_rnn" --
input="PATH_TO_NOTE_SEQUENCE_TFRECORDS" --
output_dir="sequence_examples" --eval_ratio=0.10
```

```
# On the VM instance
melody_rnn_train --config="attention_rnn" --run_dir="logdir/run1" -
-
sequence_example_file="sequence_examples/training_melodies.tfrecord
" --hparams="batch_size=128,rnn_layer_sizes=[128,128]" --
num_training_steps=20000
```

We'll have to replace PATH_TO_NOTE_SEQUENCE_TFRECORDS with a proper value.

3. To start the evaluation, we have to start a new Terminal; SSH again on the VM instance, and then we can launch the evaluation:

```
# On the VM instance
CUDA_VISIBLE_DEVICES="" melody_rnn_train --config="attention_rnn" -
-run_dir="logdir/run1" --
sequence_example_file="sequence_examples/eval_melodies.tfrecord" --
hparams="batch_size=62,rnn_layer_sizes=[128,128]" --
num_training_steps=20000 --eval
```

4. We can also see TensorBoard by using connection-forwarding in SSH. In a new Terminal, use the following command to connect to the VM instance:

```
ssh -L 16006:127.0.0.1:6006 USER@IP
```

We'll have to replace USER and IP with proper values. This command redirects the local port 16006 to port 6006 in the VM instance.

5. Then, in the previous Terminal, we can launch TensorBoard:

```
# On the VM instance
tensorboard --logdir=logdir
```

The TensorBoard can be opened locally by using the 127.0.0.1:16006 address in the browser. Once the training is finished, we can zip the training folder on the VM instance, and then get it back using scp or the browser Terminal.

6. Once this is finished, don't forget to **stop the running instance**. Remember, we are billed on usage on GCP; we don't want to keep our VM instance running without a reason.

At the time of writing, the cost of training a Melody RNN model for 20,000 steps on a P100 GPU is around $5.

Summary

In this chapter, we used the datasets that we prepared in the previous chapter to train the Magenta models on different instruments and genres. We first compared different models and configurations for specific use cases and then showed how to create a new one if necessary.

Then, we launched different training runs and looked at how to tune the model for better training. We showed how to launch the training and evaluation jobs and how to check the resulting metrics on the TensorBoard. Then, we saw a case of overfitting and explained how to fix overfitting and underfitting. We also showed how to define the proper network size and hyperparameters, by looking at problems such as incorrect batch size, memory errors, a model not converging, and not having enough training data. Using our newly trained model, we've generated sequences and showed how to package and handle checkpoints.

Finally, we've shown how to use GCP to train our model in the cloud on powerful machines. We've introduced how to create a Magenta VM instance and how to launch training, evaluation, and TensorBoard on it.

This chapter marks the end of the training content for this book. In the next chapters, we'll be looking at parts that are outside the core features of Magenta, such as Magenta.js, and making Magenta interact with a **Digital Audio Workstation (DAW)**.

Questions

1. Write a new configuration for the Drums RNN model that uses an attention length of 64 and that encodes only the snares and bass drums, but inverted.
2. We have a model that underfits: what does this mean and how do we fix the problem?
3. We have a model that overfits: what does this mean and how do we fix the problem?
4. What is a technique that makes sure that, for a given training run, we stop at the optimum?
5. Why might increasing batch size make the model worse in terms of performance? Will it make it worse in terms of efficiency or training time?

6. What is a good network size?
7. Does limiting the value of the error derivative before backpropagation help or worsen the problem of exploding gradients? What is another solution to that problem?
8. Why is using a cloud provider useful to train our models?

Further reading

- **How to Choose Loss Functions When Training Deep Learning Neural Networks**: A very thorough article on how to write a loss function (machinelearningmastery.com/how-to-choose-loss-functions-when-training-deep-learning-neural-networks/)

- **How to Avoid Overfitting in Deep Learning Neural Networks**: An article on underfitting and overfitting and its solutions (machinelearningmastery.com/introduction-to-regularization-to-reduce-overfitting-and-improve-generalization-error/)

- **How to Avoid Exploding Gradients With Gradient Clipping**: An article on exploding gradients and how to fix it using gradient clipping (machinelearningmastery.com/how-to-avoid-exploding-gradients-in-neural-networks-with-gradient-clipping/)

- **Use Weight Regularization to Reduce Overfitting of Deep Learning Models**: An article on weight regularization, which helps reduce overfitting (machinelearningmastery.com/weight-regularization-to-reduce-overfitting-of-deep-learning-models/)

- **A Gentle Introduction to Dropout for Regularizing Deep Neural Networks**: An article on dropout, which helps to reduce overfitting (machinelearningmastery.com/dropout-for-regularizing-deep-neural-networks/)

- **A Gentle Introduction to Early Stopping to Avoid Overtraining Neural Networks**: An article on early stopping, which helps to reduce overfitting (machinelearningmastery.com/early-stopping-to-avoid-overtraining-neural-network-models/)

- **On Large-Batch Training for Deep Learning: Generalization Gap and Sharp Minima**: A paper (2017) explaining why a larger batch size might lead to a less efficient network (arxiv.org/abs/1609.04836)

Section 4: Making Your Models Interact with Other Applications

4

This section explains the contextualization of Magenta in a music production environment by demonstrating how to make it communicate with other applications, such as the browser, a DAW, or a MIDI controller. By the end of this section, you will be able to use the MIDI interface and Magenta.js.

This section contains the following chapters:

- Chapter 8, *Magenta in the Browser with Magenta.js*
- Chapter 9, *Making Magenta Interact with Music Applications*

Magenta in the Browser with Magenta.js

8

In this chapter, we'll talk about Magenta.js, a JavaScript implementation of Magenta that has gained in popularity for its ease of use, since it runs in the browser and can be shared as a web page. We'll introduce TensorFlow.js, the technology upon which Magenta.js is built, and show which models are available in Magenta.js, including how to convert our previously trained models. Then, we'll create small web applications using GANSynth and MusicVAE, for sampling audio and sequences respectively. Finally, we'll see how Magenta.js can interact with other applications, using the Web MIDI API and Node.js.

The following topics will be covered in this chapter:

- Introducing Magenta.js and TensorFlow.js
- Creating a Magenta.js web application
- Making Magenta.js interact with other apps

Technical requirements

In this chapter, we'll use the following tools:

- **Command line** or **Bash** to launch Magenta from the terminal
- **Python** and **Magenta** to convert trained models for Magenta.js
- **TensorFlow.js** and **Magenta.js** to create music generation apps in the browser
- **JavaScript**, **HTML**, and **CSS** to write Magenta.js web applications
- A **recent browser** (Chrome, Firefox, Edge, Safari) for up-to-date web APIs
- **Node.js** and **npm** to install Magenta.js and its dependencies server side
- **FluidSynth** to listen to generated MIDI from the browser

In Magenta.js, we'll make the use of the **Music RNN** and **MusicVAE** models for MIDI sequence generation and **GANSynth** for audio generation. We'll cover their usage in depth, but if you feel like you need more information, the Magenta.js Music README in the Magenta.js source code (`github.com/tensorflow/magenta-js/tree/master/music`) is a good place to start. You can also take a look at the Magenta.js code, which is well documented. We also provide additional content in the last section, *Further reading*.

The code for this chapter is in the book's GitHub code repository in the `Chapter08` folder, located at `github.com/PacktPublishing/hands-on-music-generation-with-magenta/tree/master/Chapter08`. The examples and code snippets used assume you are located in the chapter folder. For this chapter, you should run `cd Chapter08`, before you start.

Check out the following video to see the Code in Action:
Placeholder link

Introducing Magenta.js and TensorFlow.js

In the previous chapters, we've covered Magenta in Python, its usage, and its inner workings. We'll now be looking at Google's Magenta.js, a smaller implementation of Magenta in JavaScript. Magenta and Magenta.js both have their advantages and disadvantages; let's compare them to see which one we should use, depending on the use case.

A Magenta.js application is easy to use and deploy since it executes in the browser. **Developing and deploying a web application is easy**: all you need is an HTML file and a web server, and your application is available for the whole world to see and use. This is a major advantage of making a browser-based application, since not only does it enable us to create our own music generation application easily, but it also makes it easy to use it collaboratively. See the *Further reading* section at the end of the chapter for great examples of popular Magenta.js web applications.

This is the power of a web browser: everyone has one, and a web page requires no installation to run. The downside of a Magenta.js web application is that it also runs in a browser: it isn't the best place to handle quality, real-time audio, and making your application interact with traditional music production tools, such as **digital audio workstations (DAWs)**, is harder.

We'll be looking at the specifics of working in the browser as we go along. First, we'll be looking at Tone.js in the *Introducing Tone.js for sound synthesis in the browser* section, which describes the usage of the Web Audio API. Then, we'll be looking at the Web Workers API in the *Using the Web Workers API to offload computations from the UI thread* section, to make real-time audio easier. Finally, we'll be looking at making Magenta.js interact with other music applications, in the *Making Magenta.js interact with other apps* section.

Introducing TensorFlow.js for machine learning in the browser

First, let's introduce TensorFlow.js (`www.tensorflow.org/js`), the project upon which Magenta.js is built. As its name suggests, TensorFlow.js is a JavaScript implementation of TensorFlow, making it possible to **use and train models in the browser**. Importing and running pre-trained models from TensorFlow SavedModel or Keras is possible.

Using TensorFlow.js is easy. You can use a `script` tag, as shown in the following code block:

```
<html>
<head>
  <script
src="https://cdn.jsdelivr.net/npm/@tensorflow/tfjs/dist/tf.min.js"></script
>
  <script>
    const model = tf.sequential();
    model.add(tf.layers.dense({units: 1, inputShape: [1]}));
    model.compile({loss: 'meanSquaredError', optimizer: 'sgd'});
  </script>
</head>
<body>
</body>
</html>
```

Alternatively, you can use the `npm` or `yarn` command to run the following code block:

```
import * as tf from '@tensorflow/tfjs';
const model = tf.sequential();
model.add(tf.layers.dense({units: 1, inputShape: [1]}));
model.compile({loss: 'meanSquaredError', optimizer: 'sgd'});
```

Notice in both code snippets the usage of the `tf` variable, which is imported with the script (we'll be seeing more `tf` usage in this chapter's examples). We won't be looking at TensorFlow.js specifically, but we are going to use it in our Magenta.js code.

Another nice thing about TensorFlow.js is that it uses WebGL (`www.khronos.org/registry/webgl/specs/latest/`) for its computation, meaning it is **graphics processing unit** (**GPU**) accelerated (if you have a GPU), without having to install CUDA libraries. The mathematical operations are implemented in WebGL shaders and the tensors are encoded in WebGL textures, which is a very clever use of WebGL. We don't have to do anything for GPU acceleration since the TensorFlow.js backend will handle it for us. When using the Node.js server side, the TensorFlow C API is used for hardware acceleration, meaning that the usage of CUDA libraries is possible.

Using WebGL has a few caveats, though, most notably that the computations might block the UI thread in some cases and that the memory used by a tensor allocation must be reclaimed (disposed) after usage. Regarding computation threading, we'll be looking at this in more depth when we look at web workers. Regarding memory management, we'll be showing proper usage in the code as we go along. See the *Further reading* section for more information on these issues.

Introducing Magenta.js for music generation in the browser

Now that we understand what Tensorflow.js is, let's talk about Magenta.js. First, we need to understand what Magenta.js can and cannot do. For now, models cannot be trained in Magenta.js (with the exception of the partial training in MidiMe), but the models we've trained in the previous chapter can be converted and imported easily. Another limitation of Magenta.js is that not all models are present, but the most important ones are. While writing Magenta.js code, we'll see that most of the concepts we've already covered are there, sometimes with a different syntax.

Here is an overview of some of the pre-trained models present in Magenta.js:

- **Onsets and Frames** for piano transcription, converting raw audio to MIDI
- **Music RNN (long short-term memory (LSTM)**-based networks) for monophonic and polyphonic MIDI generation, including the Melody RNN, Drums RNN, Improv RNN and Performance RNN models
- **MusicVAE** for single or trio sampling and interpolation, also including GrooVAE
- **Piano Genie** that maps an 8-key input to a full 88-key piano

We've already talked about these models in the previous chapters. We can find the pre-trained checkpoints list either in the Magenta.js source code, in the `music/checkpoints/checkpoints.json` file, or in the hosted version, at `goo.gl/magenta/js-checkpoints`. Most of the checkpoints (or bundles) we've used are present in Magenta.js, plus some new additions such as longer 4-bar MusicVAE and GrooVAE models.

Converting trained models for Magenta.js

Using pre-trained models is great, but we can also import our own trained models, such as the ones we trained in the previous chapter—Chapter 7, *Training Magenta Models*. We are doing that by using the `checkpoint_converted.py` script that dumps the weights from a Magenta checkpoint to a format Magenta.js can use.

 You can find this code in the `chapter_08_example_01.html` file in the source code of this chapter. There are more comments and content in the source code—you should go and check it out.

Let's convert a simple RNN model for Magenta.js, by following these steps:

1. First, we'll need the `checkpoint_converter.py` script from Magenta.js. The easiest way is to download the script directly from the source code on GitHub, as follows:

   ```
   curl -o "checkpoint_converter.py"
   "https://raw.githubusercontent.com/tensorflow/magenta-js/master/scr
   ipts/checkpoint_converter.py"
   ```

   This should create the `checkpoint_converter.py` file locally.

2. Now, we'll need the TensorFlow.js Python packaging on which the `checkpoint_converter.py` script depends. Run the following code:

   ```
   # While in your Magenta conda environment
   pip install tensorflowjs
   ```

3. We can now run the conversion script using, for example, one of our previously trained DrumsRNN models (replacing `PATH_TO_TRAINING_DIR` with a proper value), as follows:

   ```
   python checkpoint_converter.py
   "PATH_TO_TRAINING_DIR/drums_rnn_dance_drums/logdir/run1_small/train
   /model.ckpt-20000" "checkpoints/drums_rnn_dance_small"
   ```

This will create the `checkpoints/drums_rnn_dance_small` directory with a JSON metadata file and the checkpoint binary files that will get loaded by TensorFlow.js.

 Remember that when referencing checkpoints in TensorFlow, you need to provide the prefix—for example, `model.ckpt-20000`, but not followed by `.data`, `.index`, or `.meta`.

4. Then, we need to create a JSON configuration file that describes the model configuration. Open the `checkpoints/drums_rnn_dance_small/config.json` file and enter this content:

```
{
  "type": "MusicRNN",
  "dataConverter": {
    "type": "DrumsConverter",
    "args": {}
  }
}
```

This is a minimal example for the DrumsRNN model, without any further configuration. Note that the `args` key for the `dataConverter` key is necessary, even if no arguments are provided. The `type` of `dataConverter` is one of the subclasses of `DataConverter`, located in the `data.ts` file in `music/src/core` in the Magenta.js source code. Other possible data converters could be `MelodyConverter`, `TrioConverter`, or `GrooveConverter`.

Other models and converters will require more configuration. The easiest way to find the proper configuration for a specific model is to find a similar Magenta pre-trained model and use similar values. To do that, follow the *Downloading pretrained models locally* section, and find the information you want in the downloaded `config.json` file.

5. Our custom model is now converted to a format TensorFlow.js understands. Let's create a small web page that imports and initializes that model to test it, as follows:

```
<html lang="en">
<body>
<script
src="https://cdn.jsdelivr.net/npm/@magenta/music@1.12.0/dist/magent
amusic.js"></script>
```

```
<script>
  // Initialize a locally trained DrumsRNN model from the local
directory
  // at: checkpoints/drums_rnn_dance_small
  async function startLocalModel() {
    const musicRnn = new mm.MusicRNN("http://0.0.0.0:8000/" +
      "checkpoints/drums_rnn_dance_small");
    await musicRnn.initialize();
  }

  // Calls the initialization of the local model
  try {
    Promise.all([startLocalModel()]);
  } catch (error) {
    console.error(error);
  }
</script>
</body>
</html>
```

Don't worry too much about the content of the HTML page, since it will be thoroughly explained in the following sections. The important part here is that the MusicRNN constructor (mm.MusicRNN("URL")) is loading our converted DrumsRNN checkpoint in the MusicRNN model.

You might have noticed that the URL of the checkpoint is local, at http://0.0.0.0:8000. This is because most browsers implement **Cross-Origin Resource Sharing** (**CORS**) restrictions, one of them being that a local file can only fetch resources starting with a **Uniform Resource Identifier** (**URI**) scheme of http or https.

6. The easiest way of circumventing that is to start a web server locally, like this:

   ```
   python -m http.server
   ```

   This will start a web server serving the current folder at http://0.0.0.0:8000, meaning the HTML file from the previous snippet will be served at http://0.0.0.0:8000/example.html, and our checkpoint at http://0.0.0.0:8000/checkpoints/drums_rnn_dance_small.

7. Open the HTML file and check the console. You should see the following:

   ```
   * Tone.js v13.8.25 *
   MusicRNN  Initialized model in 0.695s
   ```

This means that our model was successfully initialized.

Downloading pre-trained models locally

Downloading pre-trained models locally is useful if we want to serve them ourselves or if we want to check the `config.json` content:

1. First, we'll need the `checkpoint_converter.py` script from Magenta.js. The easiest way is to download the script directly from the source code on GitHub, as follows:

   ```
   curl -o "checkpoint_downloader.py"
   "https://raw.githubusercontent.com/tensorflow/magenta-js/master/scr
   ipts/checkpoint_downloader.py"
   ```

   This should create the `checkpoint_converter.py` file locally.

2. We can then call the script by entering the following code:

   ```
   python checkpoint_downloader.py
   "https://storage.googleapis.com/magentadata/js/checkpoints/music_va
   e/mel_16bar_small_q2" "checkpoints/music_vae_mel_16bar_small_q2"
   ```

This will download the `mel_16bar_small_q2` MusicVAE pre-trained model in the `checkpoints` folder.

Introducing Tone.js for sound synthesis in the browser

In this chapter, you'll hear generated audio in the browser, which means that audio synthesis, analogous to when we used FluidSynth in the previous chapters to listen to MIDI files, is happening in the browser, using the Web Audio API.

The **Web Audio API** (`www.w3.org/TR/webaudio/`) provides fairly low-level concepts to handle sound sources, transformations, and routing, through the usage of audio nodes. First, we have a sound source that provides an array of sound intensities (see `Chapter 1`, *Introduction on Magenta and Generative Art*, for a refresher on that), which could be a sound file (a sample) or an oscillator. Then, the sound source node can be connected to a transformation node such as a gain (to change the volume). Finally, the result needs to be connected to a destination (an output) for the sound to be heard in the speakers.

The specification is quite mature, listed as *W3C Candidate Recommendation, September 18, 2018,* so some implementation details might change, but it can be considered stable. In terms of support, all the major browsers support the Web Audio API, which is great. See the *Further reading* section for more information.

We won't be using the Web Audio API directly. Rather, we'll be using **Tone.js** (`tonejs.github.io`), which is a JavaScript library built on top of the Web Audio API, providing higher-level functionalities. Another advantage of using Tone.js is that it can be resilient to change, in the event of the underlying Web Audio API changing.

Since the Web Audio API implementation changes from browser to browser, the quality of the audio might vary. For example, layering multiple audio samples from GANSynth resulted in audio clipping in Firefox but worked correctly in Chrome. Remember that for professional-grade audio quality, audio synthesis in the browser might not be the best choice.

Creating a Magenta.js web application

Now that we have introduced the concepts surrounding Magenta.js, we'll be creating a web application using Magenta.js. Let's create a web application where we generate a trio of instruments (the drum kit, the bass, and the lead) using MusicVAE, where we can change the lead instrument for a GANSynth-generated instrument.

We'll be building this application step by step. First, we'll make an app that generates instruments, using GANSynth. Then, we'll create an app in which we can sample a trio sequence. Finally, we'll merge the two apps together.

Generating instruments in the browser using GANSynth

For the first part of our example, we'll use GANSynth to sample single instrument notes, which are short audio clips of 4 seconds. We'll be able to layer multiple audio clips, for interesting effects.

First, we'll create the HTML page and import the required scripts. Then, we'll write the GANSynth sampling code and explain each step in detail. We'll finish the example by listening to the generated audio.

Writing the page structure

We'll be keeping the page structure and style at a minimum, to focus on the Magenta.js code.

 You can find this code in the `chapter_08_example_02.html` file in the source code of this chapter. There are more comments and content in the source code—you should go and check it out.

First, let's create the page structure and import the required scripts, as follows:

```
<html lang="en">
<body>
<div>
  <button disabled id="button-sample-gansynth-note">
    Sample GANSynth note
  </button>
  <div id="container-plots"></div>
</div>
<script
src="https://cdn.jsdelivr.net/npm/@magenta/music@1.12.0/dist/magentamusic.m
in.js"></script>
<script>
  // GANSynth code
</script>
</body>
</html>
```

The page structure contains only a button that will call the GANSynth generation and a container in which we'll draw the generated spectrogram.

There are two ways of using Magenta.js in the browser, as follows:

1. We can import the whole Magenta.js music distribution in `dist/magentamusic.min.js`. In the Magenta documentation, this is referred to as the **ES5 bundle** method. This will include Magenta.js (bound on `mm`) and all its dependencies, including TensorFlow.js (bound on `mm.tf`) and Tone.js (bound on `mm.Player.tone`).

2. We can import only the Magenta.js elements that we need, under the `es6` folder. In the Magenta documentation, this is referred to as the **ES6 bundle** method. For example, if we only need the GANSynth model, we will need to import Tone.js (bound on `Tone`), Tensorflow.js (bound on `tf`), Magenta.js core (bound on `core`), and Magenta.js GANSynth (bound on `gansynth`).

We won't talk about the differences between the ES5 and the ES6 bundles here. Just remember that the easiest way to go is to use the ES5 bundle method, importing one big file with everything. If you want more control over what is sent to the client (for performance reasons, for example), you'll want to use the ES6 bundle method. Remember that the module bindings are not the same between both methods, so you'll have to adapt your code if you change the imports.

Here are the ES6 bundle imports for the GANSynth model only:

```
<script
src="https://cdn.jsdelivr.net/npm/tone@13.8.25/build/Tone.min.js"></script>
<script
src="https://cdn.jsdelivr.net/npm/@tensorflow/tfjs@1.4.0/dist/tf.min.js"></
script>
<script
src="https://cdn.jsdelivr.net/npm/@magenta/music@^1.0.0/es6/core.js"></scri
pt>
<script
src="https://cdn.jsdelivr.net/npm/@magenta/music@^1.0.0/es6/gansynth.js"></
script>
```

This imports only the GANSynth model, which can be instantiated using `new gansynth.GANSynth(...)`. When using ES6 modules, we need to import each script individually. For our example, these are Tone.js, TensorFlow.js, Magenta.js core, and GANSynth.

We'll stick with ES5 bundles for our example, but feel free to use ES6 bundles if you feel like it. We'll be showing where the code differs between each approach in our examples.

 You can find the ES6 code for this example in the `chapter_08_example_02_es6.html` file, in the source code of this chapter.

Now, let's write the GANSynth code (in the `GANSynth code` comment), and explain each step.

Sampling audio using GANSynth

Now that we have properly imported Magenta.js, we can write the GANSynth audio generation code by following these steps:

1. First, we'll initialize the DOM elements and initialize GANSynth, like this:

```
// Get DOM elements
const buttonSampleGanSynthNote = document
    .getElementById("button-sample-gansynth-note");
const containerPlots = document
    .getElementById("container-plots");

// Starts the GANSynth model and initializes it. When finished,
enables
// the button to start the sampling
async function startGanSynth() {
  const ganSynth = new
mm.GANSynth("https://storage.googleapis.com/" +
      "magentadata/js/checkpoints/gansynth/acoustic_only");
  await ganSynth.initialize();
  window.ganSynth = gansynth;
  buttonSampleGanSynthNote.disabled = false;
}
```

Here, we instantiate GANSynth using `mm.GANSynth(...)`. Remember, the Magenta.js context is under the `mm` variable when imported using an ES5 module. The URL for the checkpoint is the same that we've used in the previous chapter—Chapter 5, *Audio Generation with NSynth and GANSynth*. Refer to that chapter if you want more information. We also make the reference to `ganSynth` globally so that we can call it later easily.

Using the Magenta.js ES6 bundle, we would have the following code:

```
const ganSynth = new
gansynth.GANSynth("https://storage.googleapis.com/" +
      "magentadata/js/checkpoints/gansynth/acoustic_only");
```

For the ES6 bundle, the module variable is `gansynth.GANSynth` instead of `mm.GANSynth`.

2. Now, let's write an asynchronous function that will insert the generated spectrogram in the web page using a `canvas`, like this:

```
// Plots the spectrogram of the given channel
// see music/demos/gansynth.ts:28 in magenta.js source code
async function plotSpectra(spectra, channel) {
  const spectraPlot = mm.tf.tidy(() => {
    // Slice a single example.
    let spectraPlot = mm.tf.slice(spectra, [0, 0, 0, channel], [1,
-1, -1, 1])
        .reshape([128, 1024]);
    // Scale to [0, 1].
    spectraPlot = mm.tf.sub(spectraPlot, mm.tf.min(spectraPlot));
    spectraPlot = mm.tf.div(spectraPlot, mm.tf.max(spectraPlot));
    return spectraPlot;
  });
  // Plot on canvas.
  const canvas = document.createElement("canvas");
  containerPlots.appendChild(canvas);
  await mm.tf.browser.toPixels(spectraPlot, canvas);
  spectraPlot.dispose();
}
```

This method creates a spectrogram plot and inserts it in a `canvas` element in the `containerPlots` elements we've previously declared. It will keep adding spectrograms for each generation.

You might have noticed the usage of `tf.tidy` and `dispose` in the example. Using those methods is necessary to avoid memory leaks in the TensorFlow.js code. This is because TensorFlow.js uses WebGL to make its computations, and **WebGL resources need to be explicitly reclaimed** after use. Any `tf.Tensor` needs to be disposed of after use by using `dispose`. The `tf.tidy` method can be used to dispose of all the tensors that are not returned by a function after executing it.

You might wonder what the `async` and `await` keywords are, in the previous JavaScript code. Those two keywords mark the usage of **asynchronous methods**. When calling a method that is marked with `async`, meaning it is asynchronous, the caller needs to mark the calls with `await`, meaning that it will wait (block) until a value is returned. The `await` keyword can be used only in `async` methods. In our example, the `mm.tf.browser.toPixels` method is marked with `async`, so we need to wait for its return using `await`. Calling an `async` method without using `await` can be done using the `Promise` syntax—`Promise.all([myAsyncMethod()])`.

Promises were introduced in JavaScript to fix a recurring problem when writing asynchronous code: the **callback hell**. The callback hell is a problem that arises when multiple linked calls are all asynchronous, resulting in nested callbacks (from hell).

Promises are great because they provide a clean mechanism to handle complex chains of asynchronous calls, as well as proper error handling. However, they are a bit verbose, which is why the `async` and `await` keywords were introduced as syntactic sugar, to alleviate some of the common use cases around using promises.

3. Then, we write an asynchronous function that samples a note from GANSynth, plays it, and plots it using our previous method, as follows:

```
// Samples a single note of 4 seconds from GANSynth and plays it
repeatedly
async function sampleGanNote() {
  const lengthInSeconds = 4.0;
  const sampleRate = 16000;
  const length = lengthInSeconds * sampleRate;

  // The sampling returns a spectrogram, convert that to audio in
  // a tone.js buffer
  const specgrams = await ganSynth.randomSample(60);
  const audio = await ganSynth.specgramsToAudio(specgrams);
  const audioBuffer = mm.Player.tone.context.createBuffer(
      1, length, sampleRate);
  audioBuffer.copyToChannel(audio, 0, 0);

  // Play the sample audio using tone.js and loop it
  const playerOptions = {"url": audioBuffer, "loop": true,
"volume": -25};
  const player = new
mm.Player.tone.Player(playerOptions).toMaster();
  player.start();

  // Plots the resulting spectrograms
  await plotSpectra(specgrams, 0);
  await plotSpectra(specgrams, 1);
}
```

We first sample from GANSynth using the `randomSample` method, using a base pitch of `60`, which is C4, as an argument. This tells the model to sample a value corresponding to that pitch. Then, the returned spectrogram is converted to audio using `specgramsToAudio`. Finally, we use a Tone.js audio buffer to play the sample, by instantiating a new player using the audio buffer. Since we instantiate a new player for each sample, each new audio sample will get layered on top of the others.

The code to instantiate the player, `mm.Player.tone.Player`, is a bit convoluted since we first need to find the reference to Tone.js that was already instantiated by the Magenta.js object using `mm.Player.tone` (here, the `Player` reference is a Magenta.js class).

Using ES6 bundles is more straightforward, as can be seen here:

```
const player = new Tone.Player(playerOptions).toMaster();
```

Since the Magenta.js ES6 bundle doesn't include Tone.js, it is initialized on its own and can be referenced directly, using the `Tone` variable.

4. Finally, let's wrap up our example by binding the button to an action and initializing GANSynth, like this:

```
// Add on click handler to call the GANSynth sampling
buttonSampleGanSynthNote.addEventListener("click", () => {
  sampleGanNote();
});

// Calls the initialization of GANSynth
try {
  Promise.all([startGanSynth()]);
} catch (error) {
  console.error(error);
}
```

First, we bind our button the `sampleGanNote` method, then we initialize GANSynth, using the `startGanSynth` method.

Launching the web application

Now that we have our web application ready, we can test our code. Let's open the HTML page we've created using a browser. We should see a page similar to the one shown in the following screenshot:

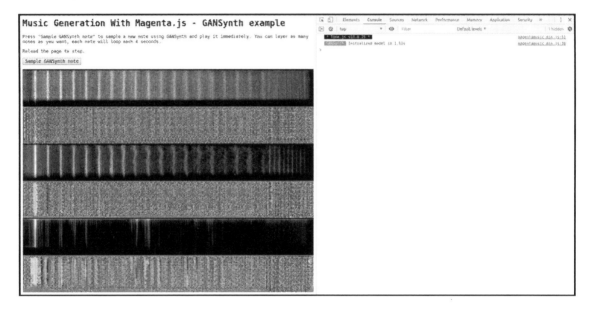

In the previous figure, we've already generated some GANSynth samples. Each generation plots two spectrograms and keeps the previous ones on the page. On the right side of the preceding screenshot, in the console debugger, you can see Tone.js and GANSynth initializing. When that is completed, the **Sample GANSynth note** button will get enabled.

Go ahead and generate sounds: you'll get pretty interesting effects when layering many of them. Congratulations—you've completed your first Magenta.js web application!

Generating a trio using MusicVAE

We'll now be using the MusicVAE model in Magenta.js to generate some sequences and play them directly in the browser, using Tone.js. The checkpoint we'll be using is a `trio` model, meaning we'll be generating three sequences at the same time: the drum kit, the bass, and the lead.

You can find this code in the chapter_08_example_03.html file in the source code of this chapter. There are more comments and content in the source code—you should go and check it out.

Since the code is similar to the last section, we won't be going through all the content, but we'll explain the major differences:

1. First, let's define the page structure and script imports, as follows:

```html
<html lang="en">
<body>
<div>
  <button disabled id="button-sample-musicae-trio">
    Sample MusicVAE trio
 </button>
  <canvas id="canvas-musicvae-plot"></canvas>
</div>
<script
src="https://cdn.jsdelivr.net/npm/@magenta/music@1.12.0/dist/magent
amusic.min.js"></script>
<script>
  // MusicVAE code
</script>
</body>
</html>
```

The page has the same structure as the previous section. We'll be filling in the code in the MusicVAE code comment.

2. Then, let's initialize the MusicVAE model, as follows:

```javascript
// Get DOM elements
const buttonSampleMusicVaeTrio = document
    .getElementById("button-sample-musicae-trio");
const canvasMusicVaePlot = document
    .getElementById("canvas-musicvae-plot");

// Starts the MusicVAE model and initializes it. When finished,
enables
// the button to start the sampling
async function startMusicVae() {
  const musicvae = new
mm.MusicVAE("https://storage.googleapis.com/" +
      "magentadata/js/checkpoints/music_vae/trio_4bar");
  await musicvae.initialize();
  window.musicvae = musicvae;
```

```
                buttonSampleMusicVaeTrio.disabled = false;
            }
```

The URL for the checkpoint is the same as the one we used in the previous chapter—Chapter 4, *Latent Space Interpolation with MusicVAE*. Refer to this chapter if you want more information on that checkpoint.

3. We now create a new Tone.js player to play the three generated sequences, as follows:

```
// Declares a new player that have 3 synths for the drum kit (only
the
// bass drum), the bass and the lead.
class Player extends mm.BasePlayer {

    bassDrumSynth = new mm.Player.tone.MembraneSynth().toMaster();

    bassSynth = new mm.Player.tone.Synth({
      volume: 5,
      oscillator: {type: "triangle"}
    }).toMaster();

    leadSynth = new mm.Player.tone.PolySynth(5).toMaster();

    // Plays the note at the proper time using tone.js
    playNote(time, note) {
      let frequency, duration, synth;
      if (note.isDrum) {
        if (note.pitch === 35 || note.pitch === 36) {
          // If this is a bass drum, we use the kick pitch for
          // an eight note and the bass drum synth
          frequency = "C2";
          duration = "8n";
          synth = this.bassDrumSynth;
        }
      } else {
        // If this is a bass note or lead note, we convert the
        // frequency and the duration for tone.js and fetch
        // the proper synth
        frequency = new mm.Player.tone.Frequency(note.pitch, "midi");
        duration = note.endTime - note.startTime;
        if (note.program >= 32 && note.program <= 39) {
          synth = this.bassSynth;
        } else {
          synth = this.leadSynth;
        }
      }
      if (synth) {
```

```
        synth.triggerAttackRelease(frequency, duration, time, 1);
    }
  }
}
```

This code extends the `mm.BasePlayer` class in Magenta.js, which is useful because we only need to implement the `playNote` method to play the sequences. First, we define three synths: `bassDrumSynth`, `bassSynth`, and `leadSynth`, described here:

- The **bass drum synth** only plays the bass drum, which is represented by the `note.isDrum` property and MIDI notes 35 or 36 and always plays a `C2` frequency for an 8-note length `8n`, using the `MembraneSynth` from Tone.js. Remember: in the MIDI specification for the percussion channel, the instruments (Bass Drum, Snare, etc.) are defined by the note's pitch—for example, pitch 35 is Acoustic Bass Drum.
- The **bass synth** only plays the programs from 32 to 39 inclusive, using the `Synth` from Tone.js with a triangle waveshape. Remember: from the MIDI specification, the program specifies which instrument should be played. For example, program 1 is Acoustic Grand Piano, and program 33 is Acoustic Bass.
- The **lead synth** plays the other programs, using the `PolySynth` from Tone.js with five voices.

One thing to notice for the bass and lead synths is that we first need to convert the MIDI note to a Tone.js frequency, using the `Frequency` class.

Another important thing to talk about is the **note envelope**, used on a synth in Tone.js with the `triggerAttackRelease` method. An envelope acts as a filter that will let the note be heard for a certain amount of time. You can think of a synthesizer as *always playing*, and the envelope—when closed—does not let the sound through. When opened, the envelope lets the sound be heard, using a certain **slope**, meaning the sound can come slowly (or fast), and end slowly (or fast). This is called, respectively, **the attack** and **the release** of the envelope. Each time we call the trigger method, the synth will be heard for the given duration, using a certain slope.

You might have already heard the term **Attack Decay Sustain Release** (**ADSR**) when talking about envelopes. In Tone.js, we are using a simplified version of this, using only the **Attack** and the **Release** of the envelope. With an ADSR envelope, we have more control over the resulting shape. For the sake of our example, we'll stick with the simplified version.

4. Let's now sample the MusicVAE model, as follows:

```
// Samples a trio of drum kit, bass and lead from MusicVAE and
// plays it repeatedly at 120 QPM
async function sampleMusicVaeTrio() {
  const samples = await musicvae.sample(1);
  const sample = samples[0];
  new mm.PianoRollCanvasVisualizer(sample, canvasMusicVaePlot,
      {"pixelsPerTimeStep": 50});

  const player = new Player();
  mm.Player.tone.Transport.loop = true;
  mm.Player.tone.Transport.loopStart = 0;
  mm.Player.tone.Transport.loopEnd = 8;
  player.start(sample, 120);
}
```

First, we sample the MusicVAE model using the `sample` method and an argument of 1, which is the number of required samples. We then plot the resulting note sequence, using an `mm.PianoRollCanvasVisualizer` in the previously declared `canvas`. Finally, we start the player with the sample at 120 QPM and loop the 8-second sequence, using the Tone.js `Transport` class. Remember that the MusicVAE models have fixed length, meaning that by using the 4-bar trio model, we generate 8-second samples at 120 QPM.

5. Finally, let's wrap up our example by binding the button to an action and initializing the MusicVAE model, as follows:

```
// Add on click handler to call the MusicVAE sampling
buttonSampleMusicVaeTrio.addEventListener("click", (event) => {
  sampleMusicVaeTrio();
  event.target.disabled = true;
});

// Calls the initialization of MusicVAE
try {
  Promise.all([startMusicVae()]);
} catch (error) {
  console.error(error);
}
```

First, we bind our button the `sampleMusicVaeTrio` method, then we initialize the MusicVAE model using the `startMusicVae` method. You can see here that we are using the `Promise.all` call that we previously introduced to launch our asynchronous code.

6. Now that we have our web application ready, we can test our code. Let's open the HTML page we've created using a browser. We should see a page similar to the one shown in the following screenshot:

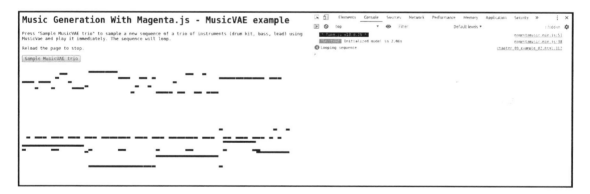

By pressing the **Sample MusicVAE trio** button, the MusicVAE should sample a sequence, plot it, and play it using the synths we've defined. The generated plot is rather basic, since it doesn't differentiate the three instruments and has no time or pitch marker, but it can be customized using the `PianoRollCanvasVisualizer` class.

To generate a new sequence, reload the page to start again.

Using a SoundFont for more realistic-sounding instruments

When listening to the generated sound, you might notice that the music sounds a bit *basic* or *simple*. That is because we've used the default synths in Tone.js, which have the advantage of being easy to use, with the downside of not sounding as good as more complex synths. Remember that the Tone.js synth can be customized to sound better.

Instead of using a synthesizer, we can also use a SoundFont. SoundFonts are recorded notes of various instruments, and we've been using them in FluidSynth since the beginning of this book. In Magenta.js, we can use the `SoundFontPlayer` for that purpose, instead of using the `Player` instance, as shown in the following code block:

```
const player = new mm.SoundFontPlayer("https://storage.googleapis.com/" +
    "magentadata/js/soundfonts/salamander"));
player.start(sequence, 120)
```

The list of the SoundFonts hosted by the Magenta team can be found in the Magenta.js music README (github.com/tensorflow/magenta-js/tree/master/music).

Playing generated instruments in a trio

Now that we have MusicVAE generating a three-instrument sequence and GANSynth generating audio, let's make the two work together.

 You can find this code in the `chapter_08_example_04.html` file in the source code of this chapter. There are more comments and content in the source code—you should go and check it out.

Since the code is similar to the last section, we won't be going through all the content, but we'll explain the major differences:

1. First, let's define the page structure and script imports, like this:

```html
<html lang="en">
<body>
<div>
  <button disabled id="button-sample-musicae-trio">
    Sample MusicVAE trio
  </button>
  <button disabled id="button-sample-gansynth-note">
    Sample GANSynth note for the lead synth
  </button>
  <canvas id="canvas-musicvae-plot"></canvas>
  <div id="container-plots"></div>
</div>
<script
src="https://cdn.jsdelivr.net/npm/@magenta/music@1.12.0/dist/magent
amusic.min.js"></script>
<script>
  // MusicVAE + GANSynth code
</script>
</body>
</html>
```

The page has the same structure as the previous section. We'll be filling in the code in the `MusicVAE + GANSynth code` comment.

2. Then, let's initialize both the MusicVAE model and the GANSynth model, as follows:

```js
// Get DOM elements
const buttonSampleGanSynthNote = document
    .getElementById("button-sample-gansynth-note");
const buttonSampleMusicVaeTrio = document
    .getElementById("button-sample-musicae-trio");
const containerPlots = document
    .getElementById("container-plots");
const canvasMusicVaePlot = document
    .getElementById("canvas-musicvae-plot");

// Starts the MusicVAE model and initializes it. When finished,
enables
// the button to start the sampling
async function startMusicVae() {
  const musicvae = new
mm.MusicVAE("https://storage.googleapis.com/" +
```

```
        "magentadata/js/checkpoints/music_vae/trio_4bar");
    await musicvae.initialize();
    window.musicvae = musicvae;
    buttonSampleMusicVaeTrio.disabled = false;
}

// Starts the GANSynth model and initializes it
async function startGanSynth() {
    const ganSynth = new
mm.GANSynth("https://storage.googleapis.com/" +
        "magentadata/js/checkpoints/gansynth/acoustic_only");
    await ganSynth.initialize();
    window.ganSynth = ganSynth
}
```

Here, we only enable the **MusicVAE sampling** button. The **GANSynth sampling** button will get enabled when MusicVAE has completed its generation.

3. We keep the same `plotSpectra` method (from the previous example).

4. We keep the same `Player` class (from the previous example) for the sound synthesis. We can set `leadSynth = null` because it will get replaced by the GANSynth generation, but it is not necessary.

5. We keep the same `sampleMusicVaeTrio` method (from the previous example), but we also set the instantiated player as a global variable using `window.player = player`, since GANSynth will need to change the lead synth later.

6. We rewrite the `sampleGanNote` method (from the previous example) to add a sample player, as follows:

```
// Samples a single note of 4 seconds from GANSynth and plays it
// repeatedly
async function sampleGanNote() {
    const lengthInSeconds = 4.0;
    const sampleRate = 16000;
    const length = lengthInSeconds * sampleRate;

    // The sampling returns a spectrogram, convert that to audio in
    // a tone.js buffer
    const specgrams = await ganSynth.randomSample(60);
    const audio = await ganSynth.specgramsToAudio(specgrams);
    const audioBuffer = mm.Player.tone.context.createBuffer(
        1, length, sampleRate);
    audioBuffer.copyToChannel(audio, 0, 0);

    // Plays the sample using tone.js by using C4 as a base note,
    // since this is what we asked the model for (MIDI pitch 60).
    // If the sequence contains other notes, the pitch will be
```

```
// changed automatically
const volume = new mm.Player.tone.Volume(-10);
const instrument = new mm.Player.tone.Sampler({"C4":
audioBuffer});
instrument.chain(volume, mm.Player.tone.Master);
window.player.leadSynth = instrument;

// Plots the resulting spectrograms
await plotSpectra(specgrams, 0);
await plotSpectra(specgrams, 1);
}
```

First, we sample a random instrument from GANSynth using `randomSample`, as in the previous example. Then, we need to play that sample in a Tone.js synth, so we use the `Sampler` class, which takes a dictionary containing a sample for each key. Because we sampled the model using the MIDI pitch 60, we are using a `C4` for the resulting audio buffer. Finally, we put that synth in our player using `window.player.leadSynth = instrument`.

7. Let's wrap up our example by binding the buttons to their corresponding actions and initializing the MusicVAE and GANSynth models, as follows:

```
// Add on click handler to call the MusicVAE sampling
buttonSampleMusicVaeTrio.addEventListener("click", (event) => {
  sampleMusicVaeTrio();
  event.target.disabled = true;
  buttonSampleGanSynthNote.disabled = false;
});

// Add on click handler to call the GANSynth sampling
buttonSampleGanSynthNote.addEventListener("click", () => {
  sampleGanNote();
});

// Calls the initialization of MusicVAE and GanSynth
try {
  Promise.all([startMusicVae(), startGanSynth()]);
} catch (error) {
  console.error(error);
}
```

This code will start the models, bind the buttons, and update the button states.

8. Now that we have our web application ready, we can test our code. Let's open the HTML page we've created using a browser. We should see a page similar to the one shown in the following screenshot:

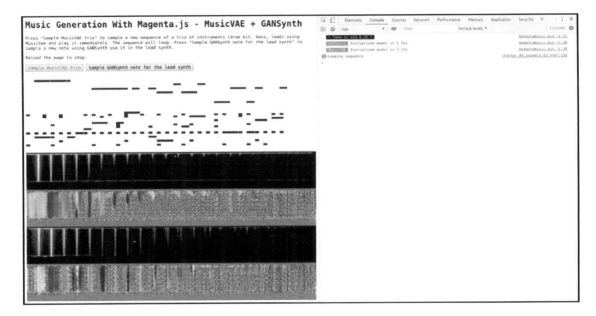

By pressing the **Sample MusicVAE trio** button, the MusicVAE should sample a sequence, plot it, and play it using the synths we've defined. Then, the **Sample GANSynth note for the lead synth** button can be used to generate a new sound for the lead synth, which can be used multiple times.

To generate a new sequence, reload the page to start again.

Using the Web Workers API to offload computations from the UI thread

As you might have noticed from the previous example when you use the **Sample GANSynth note for the lead synth** button, the audio freezes (you won't hear any sound coming from MusicVAE) while GANSynth generates its first sample.

This is because JavaScript's concurrency is built on the event loop pattern, meaning that JavaScript is not multithreaded, and everything is executed in a single thread called the **UI thread.** This works well because JavaScript uses non-blocking I/O, meaning most of its costly operations complete immediately, and return their values using events and callbacks. Nonetheless, if a long computation is synchronous, it will block the UI thread while it executes, which is what happens when GANSynth generates its sample (see the previous *Introducing TensorFlow.js for machine learning in the browser* section, for more information on how Tensorflow handles computations using WebGL).

One solution to this is the **Web Workers API** (`html.spec.whatwg.org/multipage/workers.html`), specified by the **Web Hypertext Application Technology Working Group (WHATWG)**, which enables offloading computations to another thread that won't affect the UI thread. A web worker is basically a JavaScript file that gets started from the main thread and executes in its own thread. It can send and receive messages from the main thread. The Web Workers API is mature and well supported across browsers. You can read more about web workers in the *Further reading* section.

 You can find this code in the `chapter_08_example_05.html` and `chapter_09_example_05.js` files in the source code of this chapter. There are more comments and content in the source code—you should go and check it out.

Unfortunately, at the time of writing, some parts of Magenta do not work well with web workers. We'll be showing an example using the MusicVAE model, but we can't show the same example using GANSynth, for example, because the model won't load in a web worker. We still provide this example, since it can serve as a base for later use:

1. Let's write the main page code. We'll include only the JavaScript code from the full HTML page since we've covered the other parts in the previous sections. Proceed as follows:

```javascript
// Starts a new worker that will load the MusicVAE model
const worker = new Worker("chapter_09_example_05.js");
worker.onmessage = function (event) {
  const message = event.data[0];
  if (message === "initialized") {
    // When the worker sends the "initialized" message,
    // we enable the button to sample the model
    buttonSampleMusicVaeTrio.disabled = false;
  }
  if (message === "sample") {
    // When the worked sends the "sample" message,
    // we take the data (the note sequence sample)
```

```
    // from the event, create and start a new player
    // using the sequence
    const data = event.data[1];
    const sample = data[0];
    const player = new mm.Player();
    mm.Player.tone.Transport.loop = true;
    mm.Player.tone.Transport.loopStart = 0;
    mm.Player.tone.Transport.loopEnd = 8;
    player.start(sample, 120);
  }
};
// Add click handler to call the MusicVAE sampling,
// by posting a message to the web worker which
// sample and return the sequence using a message
const buttonSampleMusicVaeTrio = document
    .getElementById("button-sample-musicae-trio");
buttonSampleMusicVaeTrio.addEventListener("click", (event) => {
  worker.postMessage([]);
  event.target.disabled = true;
});
```

We've already covered most of the code shown in the preceding block in the previous examples. Let's break down the new content, covering the web worker creation and the message passing between the web worker and the main thread, as follows:

- First, we need to start the worker, which is done by using `new Worker("chapter_09_example_05.js")`. This will execute the content of the JavaScript file and return a handle we can assign to a variable.
- Then, we bind the `onmessage` attribute on the worker, which will get called when the worker uses its `postMessage` function. In the `data` attribute of the `event` object, we can pass anything we want (see the worker's code described here next):
  - If the worker sends `initialized` as the first element of the `data` array, it means that the worker is initialized.
  - If the worker sends `sample` as the first element of the `data` array, it means the worker has sampled a MusicVAE sequence and is returning it as the second element of the `data` array.
- Finally, when the HTML button is clicked, we call the `postMessage` method on the worker instance (without arguments, but it needs—at least—an empty array), which will start the sampling.

Remember that the web workers have no shared state with the main thread, meaning all data sharing needs to happen using the onmessage and postMessage methods or functions exclusively.

2. Now, let's write the JavaScript worker's code (which sits at the same location as the HTML file), as follows:

```
importScripts("https://cdn.jsdelivr.net/npm/@tensorflow/tfjs@1.4.0/
dist/tf.min.js");
importScripts("https://cdn.jsdelivr.net/npm/@magenta/music@^1.12.0/
es6/core.js");
importScripts("https://cdn.jsdelivr.net/npm/@magenta/music@^1.12.0/
es6/music_vae.js");

async function initialize() {
  musicvae = new
music_vae.MusicVAE("https://storage.googleapis.com/" +
      "magentadata/js/checkpoints/music_vae/trio_4bar");
  await musicvae.initialize();
  postMessage(["initialized"]);
}

onmessage = function (event) {
  Promise.all([musicvae.sample(1)])
      .then(samples => postMessage(["sample", samples[0]]));
};

try {
  Promise.all([initialize()]);
} catch (error) {
  console.error(error);
}
```

The first thing you notice here is that we are using Magenta's ES6 bundle since we cannot import everything in a web worker. By importing Tone.js, for example, we would get an error such as **This browser does not support Tone.js**. Also, remember that Magenta.js is not fully compatible yet with web workers, meaning importing GANSynth might result in an error.

Since we've already covered most of the code shown in the preceding block, we'll just talk about the web worker additions, as follows:

- First, we need to send an `initialized` message to the main thread using `postMessage` when the model is ready to roll.
- Then, we bind on the module `onmessage` attribute, which will get called when the main thread sends the worker a message. Upon reception, we sample the MusicVAE model and then use `postMessage` to send the result back to the main thread.

This covers the basic usage of creating a web worker and making it exchange data with the main thread.

Using other Magenta.js models

As always, we cannot cover all models here, but the usage of other models will be similar to the examples we've provided. There are a lot of Magenta.js examples and demos on the internet, and some are very impressive music-generation web applications.

We provide resources to find examples and demos in the *Further reading* section.

Making Magenta.js interact with other apps

Because Magenta.js sits in the browser, it is a bit harder to make it interact with other applications such as a DAW than a Magenta application, but as web standards evolve, this will become easier.

Using the Web MIDI API

The Web MIDI API (`www.w3.org/TR/webmidi/`) is a W3C standard with a specification that isn't very mature, with the status of *W3C Working Draft March 17, 2015*. It isn't well supported across browsers, with Firefox and Edge having no support at all. It works pretty well in Chrome, though, so if you require your users to use that browser, your application might work. See the last section, *Further reading*, for more information.

 You can find this code in the `chapter_08_example_06.html` file, in the source code of this chapter. There are more comments and content in the source code—you should go and check it out.

We'll write a small example using the Web MIDI API, based on the previous example on MusicVAE and the trio sampling. You can copy the previous example and add the new content:

1. First, let's add a `select` element to our page, like this:

```
<label for="select-midi-output">Select MIDI output:</label>
<select disabled id="select-midi-output">
</select>
```

2. Then, in the `startMusicVae` method, let's initialize the list of available MIDI outputs, as follows:

```
// Starts a MIDI player, and for each available MIDI outputs,
// adds an option to the select drop down.
const player = new mm.MIDIPlayer();
player.requestMIDIAccess()
    .then((outputs) => {
        if (outputs && outputs.length) {
            const option = document.createElement("option");
            selectMidiOutput.appendChild(option);
            outputs.forEach(output => {
                const option = document.createElement("option");
                option.innerHTML = output.name;
                selectMidiOutput.appendChild(option);
            });
            selectMidiOutput.disabled = false;
        } else {
            selectMidiOutput.disabled = true;
        }
    });
window.player = player;
```

Here, we use the Magenta.js `MIDIPlayer` class, which makes usage of the `requestMIDIAccess` method easier than directly calling the Web MIDI API. Calling this method will return a list of `output` that we add, using the `name` attribute in the selection list.

3. Finally, in the `sampleMusicVaeTrio` method, we use the player to send the MIDI directly to that output, as follows:

```
// Gets the selected MIDI output (if any) and uses the
// output in the MIDI player
const midiOutputIndex = selectMidiOutput.selectedIndex;
if (midiOutputIndex) {
    player.outputs = [player.availableOutputs[midiOutputIndex -
1]];
```

```
        mm.Player.tone.Transport.loop = true;
        mm.Player.tone.Transport.loopStart = 0;
        mm.Player.tone.Transport.loopEnd = 8;
        player.start(sample, 120);
    }
    selectMidiOutput.disabled = true;
```

Here, we only need to set the `outputs` list with the element that was selected in the dropdown (if any).

4. To test our code, we can use our trusty FluidSynth, using the following:
   - **Linux:** `fluidsynth -a pulseaudio -g 1 PATH_TO_SF2`
   - **macOS:** `fluidsynth -a coreaudio -g 1 PATH_TO_SF2`
   - **Windows:** `fluidsynth -g 1 PATH_TO_SF2`

FluidSynth should start and show a terminal (notice we removed the `-n` and `-i` flags so that we can receive MIDI notes).

5. Now, let's open our web application. Once the model is initialized, we should see the FluidSynth MIDI input port in the **Select MIDI output**—select drop-down list. It should look like this: **Synth input port (17921:0)**. Choose the option, and then click on **Sample MusicVAE trio**. You should hear the sound coming from FluidSynth.

You'll notice that all the notes are played as a piano sequence, even if we have three instruments. This is because the `MIDIPlayer` is pretty basic and won't send the percussion on the drums channel, as specified in the MIDI specification.

Running Magenta.js server side with Node.js

Magenta.js can also be used server side, using Node.js. Using Node.js is nice because you can have the same (or almost the same) code running server side and client side. Communication between client and server can be handled using WebSockets.

The WebSocket API (`developer.mozilla.org/en-US/docs/Web/API/WebSockets_API`) is an API that makes it possible to open **two-way communications** between a client and a server. We won't be looking at WebSockets here, but they can be a good way of transferring the data back and forth between a server-side Magenta process (Magenta.js server side using Node.js, or Magenta in Python) and a client application. The easiest way of using WebSockets is to use a framework such as Socket.IO (`socket.io/`).

Another advantage of using Node.js is that our program is running server side, which means it isn't dependent on the browser's implementation. A good example of this is that we could use a Node.js package to handle sending MIDI to other processes, such as node–midi (`www.npmjs.com/package/midi`), which alleviates the necessity of using the Web MIDI API.

Let's show a simple example of Magenta.js running with Node.js. The code shown here is similar to what we've already covered in JavaScript:

 You can find this code in the `chapter_08_example_07.js` file in the source code of this chapter. There are more comments and content in the source code—you should go and check it out.

1. First, let's install Node.js (`nodejs.org/en/download/`)
2. Then, let's install Magenta.js, using the `npm` command, which is the Node.js dependency manager, like this:

   npm install --save @magenta/music

   This will install Magenta.js and its dependencies in the `node_modules` directory. When Node.js runs, it looks in this directory to find the script's dependencies, for each `require` call.

3. We can now create a JavaScript file to sample a sequence, as follows:

```javascript
const music_vae = require("@magenta/music/node/music_vae");

// These hacks below are needed because the library uses performance
// and fetch which exist in browsers but not in node.
const globalAny = global;
globalAny.performance = Date;
globalAny.fetch = require("node-fetch");

const model = new music_vae.MusicVAE(
    "https://storage.googleapis.com/magentadata/js/checkpoints/" +
    "music_vae/drums_2bar_lokl_small");
model
    .initialize()
    .then(() => model.sample(1))
    .then(samples => {
        console.log(samples[0])
    });
```

This code is similar to the previous examples, the only addition being the `require` method, which is used in Node.js to import a dependency module.

4. To execute your Node.js application, use the `node` command (replacing `PATH_TO_JAVASCRIPT_FILE` by a proper value), as follows:

```
node PATH_TO_JAVASCRIPT_FILE
```

The sample should show on the console because we've used `console.log`. You will also notice a couple of messages on the console, as follows:

```
This browser does not support Tone.js
Hi there. Looks like you are running TensorFlow.js in Node.js. To speed
things up dramatically, install our node backend, which binds to TensorFlow
C++, by running npm i @tensorflow/tfjs-node, or npm i @tensorflow/tfjs-
node-gpu if you have CUDA. Then call require('@tensorflow/tfjs-node'); (-
gpu suffix for CUDA) at the start of your program. Visit
https://github.com/tensorflow/tfjs-node for more details.
```

This reminds us that Tone.js cannot be run on Node.js, because the Web Audio API is implemented client side. It also reminds us that Node.js can use CUDA libraries for better performance.

Summary

In this chapter, we've looked at Tensorflow.js and Magenta.js, the JavaScript implementations of TensorFlow and Magenta. We've learned that TensorFlow.js is GPU accelerated using WebGL and that Magenta.js has a limited set of models available that can only be used for generation, not training. We've converted a Python-trained model from the previous chapter to a format that TensorFlow.js can load. We've also introduced Tone.js and the Web Audio API, which is used by Magenta.js to synthesize sound in the browser.

Then, we've created three music generation web applications. The first application used GANSynth to sample short audio notes. By doing so, we've learned how to import the required scripts, either using a big ES5 bundle or a smaller, split up, ES6 bundle. The second application used MusicVAE to sample a trio of instruments, with the drum kit, the bass, and the lead, and played the sequence in a loop. The third application used both models to generate sequences and audio together and introduced the usage of the Web Workers API to offload computations to another thread.

Finally, we've talked about how to make Magenta.js interact with other applications. We've used the Web MIDI API to send the generated sequences to another synthesizer—for example, FluidSynth. We've also used Node.js to run a Magenta.js application server side.

Magenta.js is a great project because it makes it easy to create and share music-generation applications using web technologies. There are other ways of making Magenta fit in a broader context, such as using Magenta Studio (which makes Magenta run in Ableton Live) and using MIDI, which is a good way of controlling all types of devices, such as software and hardware synthesizers. We'll be showing those subjects in the next chapter.

Questions

1. Can a model be trained using Tensorflow.js? Using Magenta.js?
2. What does the Web Audio API do, and what is the easiest way of using it?
3. What is the generation method in GANSynth? What is the argument that needs to be provided?
4. What is the generation method in MusicVAE? How many instruments does it generate?
5. Why is the Web Workers API useful in JavaScript?
6. Name two ways of sending MIDI from a Magenta.js application to another application.

Further reading

- **MagentaMusic.js demos**: A Magenta-maintained list of demos using the various models and core classes in Magenta.js (`tensorflow.github.io/magenta-js/music/demos/`).
- **Web apps built with Magenta.js**: A community-driven list of demos using Magenta.js, with lots of cool stuff (`magenta.tensorflow.org/demos/web/`).
- **Monica Dinculescu—Why you should build silly things**: Interesting talk on the importance of Magenta.js and sharing music-creation applications (`www.youtube.com/watch?v=DkiFjzQgJtg`).
- **Celebrating Johann Sebastian Bach**: A good example of a popular music-generation application (`www.google.com/doodles/celebrating-johann-sebastian-bach`).

- **WebGL Specifications**: The WebGL specification
  (`www.khronos.org/registry/webgl/specs/latest/`).
- **Platform and environment**: An interesting read on memory management and
  GPU computations using WebGL in TensorFlow.js
  (`www.tensorflow.org/js/guide/platform_environment`).
- **Web Audio API**: The Web Audio API specification from the W3C
  (`webaudio.github.io/web-audio-api/`).
- **Web Audio API**: An introduction to the Web Audio API
  (`developer.mozilla.org/en-US/docs/Web/API/Web_Audio_API`).
- **Web Workers**: The Web Workers API specification from the WHATWG
  (`html.spec.whatwg.org/multipage/workers.html`).
- **Concurrency model and the event loop**: An introduction to the event loop
  pattern in JavaScript (`developer.mozilla.org/en-US/docs/Web/JavaScript/EventLoop`).
- **Using Web Workers**: An introduction to the Web Workers API
  (`developer.mozilla.org/en-US/docs/Web/API/Web_Workers_API/Using_web_workers`).
- **Web MIDI API**: The Web MIDI API specification for the W3C
  (`webaudio.github.io/web-midi-api/`).
- **Web MIDI (MIDI Support in Web Browsers)**: An introduction to the Web MIDI
  API from the MIDI Association, with examples of applications using it
  (`www.midi.org/17-the-mma/99-web-midi`).

Making Magenta Interact with Music Applications

9

In this chapter, we'll see how Magenta fits into a broader picture by showing how to make it interact with other music applications such as **Digital Audio Workstations** (**DAWs**) and synthesizers. We'll explain how to send MIDI sequences from Magenta to FluidSynth and DAWs using the MIDI interface. By doing so, we'll learn how to handle MIDI ports on all platforms and how to loop MIDI sequences in Magenta. We'll show how to synchronize multiple applications using MIDI clocks and transport information. Finally, we'll cover Magenta Studio, a standalone packaging of Magenta based on Magenta.js that can also integrate into Ableton Live as a plugin.

The following topics will be covered in this chapter:

- Sending MIDI to a DAW or synthesizer
- Looping the generated MIDI
- Using Magenta as a standalone application with Magenta Studio

Technical requirements

In this chapter, we'll use the following tools:

- The **command line** or **Bash** to launch Magenta from the Terminal
- **Python** and its libraries to write music generation code using Magenta
- **Magenta** to generate music in MIDI and synchronize with other applications
- **Mido** and other MIDI tools to send MIDI notes and clock
- **FluidSynth** to receive MIDI from Magenta
- A **DAW** of your choice (Ableton Live, Bitwig, and so on) to receive MIDI from Magenta
- **Magenta Studio** as a standalone application or Ableton Live plugin

In Magenta, we'll make the use of the **MIDI interface** to send MIDI sequences and MIDI clock to other music applications. We'll cover its usage in depth, but if you feel like you need more information, the Magenta MIDI interface, README.md, in the Magenta source code (github.com/tensorflow/magenta/tree/master/magenta/interfaces/midi) is a good place to start. You can also take a look at Magenta's code, which is well documented. We also provide additional content in the *Further reading* section at the end of this chapter.

We'll also make the use of the **Magenta Studio** project on which you can find more information on its GitHub page at github.com/tensorflow/magenta-studio.

The code for this chapter is in this book's GitHub repository in Chapter09 folder, located at github.com/PacktPublishing/hands-on-music-generation-with-magenta/tree/master/Chapter09. The examples and code snippets will assume you are located in this chapter's folder. For this chapter, you should go to cd Chapter09 before you start. Check out the following video to see the Code in Action: http://bit.ly/2RGkEaG.

Sending MIDI to a DAW or synthesizer

Since the start of this book, we've been generating MIDI as physical files and then listening to them using either MuseScore or FluidSynth. This is a good way of composing music, generating new sequences, keeping the ones we like, and generating more based on them. But what if we'd like the MIDI notes to play continuously as the model generates them? This is a good way of making an autonomous music generation system, where Magenta is the composer, and an external program is a player, as it plays the notes it receives using instruments.

In this section, we'll be looking at how to send MIDI from Magenta to synthesizers or DAWs. We'll also show how to loop the sequences that are generated in Magenta and how to synchronize our Magenta program with the application it is sending the sequences to.

Introducing some DAWs

Producing music using a DAW has many advantages over simple synthesizers such as FluidSynth:

- Recording and **editing MIDI** sequences
- Recording and **editing audio**, either for the master track or single (instrument) track
- Creating our own **synthesizers** using oscillators, envelopes, filters, and so on
- Using **effects** such as reverb, delay, saturation, and so on
- Applying **EQ** and **mastering** to the audio tracks
- Cutting, merging, and mixing **audio clips** to produce a whole track

There are many DAWs on the market, but unfortunately, not many of them are open source or free to use. We'll give a small tour (which is not extensive by any means) of some DAWs that we think are interesting to use with Magenta:

- **Ableton Live** (`www.ableton.com` – *not free*) is a well known product in the music industry and has been around for a long time. Ableton Live is one of the most complete DAWs on the market but is sold at a hefty price for all of the features. It works only on Windows and macOS.
- **Bitwig** (`www.bitwig.com` – *not free*) is also a very complete product, similar to Ableton Live, and is a bit less pricey than its counterpart. It is a good DAW with many features and is available on all platforms, Windows, macOS, and Linux.
- **Reason** (`www.reasonstudios.com/` – *not free*) is a DAW that focuses on instruments and effects rather than composition. It works really well when integrated with another software for the MIDI sequencing, such as Ableton Live or Magenta. It works only on Windows and macOS.
- **Cubase** (`new.steinberg.net/cubase/` – *not free*), from Steinberg, a renowned company making all sorts of audio software and hardware, is one of the oldest DAWs out there. It works only on Windows and macOS.
- **Cakewalk** (`www.bandlab.com/products/cakewalk` – *free*) by Bandlab is a complete and easy-to-use DAW. This is the only non-open source DAW that is free to use. It works only on Windows, unfortunately.

- **SuperCollider** (`supercollider.github.io/` – *free and open source*) is a platform for audio synthesis and algorithmic composition, enabling the development of synthesizers and effects using code, with a language called `sclang`. It works on all platforms and is open source.
- **VCV Rack** (`vcvrack.com/` – *free and open source*) is a DAW that reproduces the joys of modular synthesis in software form. It works on all platforms and is open source.

We'll be giving our examples using Ableton Live, but all DAWs have similar features when it comes to receiving MIDI, so the examples should work well for all software. We'll highlight caveats when possible, such as handling MIDI routing on Linux.

Looking at MIDI ports using Mido

First things first, we need to find what MIDI ports are available on the machine, if any, to send MIDI messages between applications, such as Magenta to FluidSynth or a DAW. There is a great library called Mido, MIDI Objects for Python (`mido.readthedocs.io`), that is really useful in finding MIDI ports, creating new ones, and sending data over.

Since Magenta has a dependency on Mido, it is already installed in our Magenta environment.

 You can follow this example in the `chapter_09_example_01.py` file in the source code of this chapter. There are more comments and content in the source code, so you should go check it out.

Let's look at the MIDI ports that are available on our machine:

```
import mido
print(f"Input ports: {mido.get_input_names()}")
print(f"Output ports: {mido.get_output_names()}")
```

This should produce an output similar to the following:

```
Input ports: ['Midi Through:Midi Through Port-0 14:0']
Output ports: ['Midi Through:Midi Through Port-0 14:0']
```

On Linux and macOS, one input port and one output port should already be present, as in the preceding output. On Windows, the list is either empty, because the OS doesn't create any virtual MIDI ports automatically, or contains only `Microsoft GS Wavetable Synth`, a MIDI synthesizer like FluidSynth.

Let's have a look at how to create new ports for our applications to communicate.

Creating a virtual MIDI port on macOS and Linux

What is nice about FluidSynth is that it opens a Virtual MIDI port automatically at launch. Unfortunately, it doesn't work on Windows, so we'll be looking at how to create Virtual MIDI ports works first.

A Virtual MIDI port is a MIDI port that can be created for **applications to send MIDI messages between them**. This is essential for all music production applications. For Magenta to send MIDI data to another program such as a DAW, we'll need to open a virtual port for them to communicate.

Like we saw in the previous example, Virtual MIDI ports are either **input** ports or **output** ports. That means we can create an input port named `magenta` and an output port named `magenta`. More often then not, it is clearer to use two different names when doing this, for example, `magenta_out` for the output port, and `magenta_in` for the input port. It is also simpler when mapping the ports in a DAW.

We'll be choosing the port names from Magenta's perspective, meaning `magenta_out` is named as such because Magenta is sending information.

On macOS and Linux, creating new virtual ports is easy, since Mido supports the RtMidi backend that can create them. Using `MidiHub` in Magenta, we can provide a string for each of the input and output, for the virtual port names we want to create:

```
from magenta.interfaces.midi.midi_hub import MidiHub

# Doesn't work on Windows if the ports do not exist
midi_hub = MidiHub(input_midi_ports="magenta_in",
                   output_midi_ports="magenta_out",
                   texture_type=None)
```

This will create two virtual ports, `magenta_in` and `magenta_out`, if they don't exist, or use the existing ones if they do. Using only Mido, we can use the following:

```
import mido

# Doesn't work on Windows if the ports do not exist
inport = mido.open_input("magenta_in")
outport = mido.open_output("magenta_out")
```

Note that an input port has a `receive` method and an output port has a `send` method. When printing the ports, we should see this:

```
Input ports: ['Midi Through:Midi Through Port-0 14:0', 'RtMidiOut
Client:magenta_out 128:0']
Output ports: ['Midi Through:Midi Through Port-0 14:0', 'RtMidiIn
Client:magenta_in 128:0']
```

The named virtual ports are now available, until restart, for applications to use.

However, depending on the DAW, this might or might not work. For example, Bitwig in Linux doesn't work well with ALSA virtual ports, so opening one with RtMidi is not sufficient; you'll have to look at the documentation for a workaround using **JACK Audio Connection Kit (JACK)**. Other DAWs on Linux, such as VCV Rack, will work properly and show the virtual ports.

Creating a virtual MIDI port on Windows using loopMIDI

On Windows, we can't create virtual ports using the code provided earlier. Fortunately, we have the **loopMIDI** software (www.tobias-erichsen.de/software/loopmidi.html), a small and rather old program that is a godsend when using MIDI on Windows. The only thing it does is that it creates named virtual MIDI ports on the machine.

Once installed, launch the software and create two new ports named `magenta_in` and `magenta_out` using the name field at the bottom and the plus button:

The virtual ports named `magenta_in` and `magenta_out` should now be available both for Ableton Live and Magenta to communicate. When creating a new port, **loopMIDI** always creates both the input port and the output port, meaning we can both send and receive MIDI from the `magenta_in` port. We'll be keeping both ports separate for simplicity.

On Windows, if you have to the following error when launching the Magenta `MidiHub`, this is because you haven't properly created or named your virtual ports:

```
INFO:tensorflow:Opening '['magenta_out 2']' as a virtual MIDI port for
output.
I1218 15:05:52.208604  6012 midi_hub.py:932] Opening '['magenta_out 2']' as
a virtual MIDI port for output.
Traceback (most recent call last):
  ...
NotImplementedError: Virtual ports are not supported by the Windows
MultiMedia API.
```

Notice the port name, `magenta_out 2`, also contains the port index, `2`. This is important when referring to ports in Windows, as they are named using the format: name index. This is kind of a pain because the port index might change if you create new ports (or plugin new MIDI devices) that shift the indexes.

To fix that issue, we make sure we filter the ports using string contains and not exact matching (all of our provided examples work properly in this matter).

Adding a virtual MIDI port on macOS

On macOS, we can either use the previous method described in the *Looking at virtual MIDI ports* section or use the built-in macOS interface to create a new virtual port. Using the built-in interface is easy:

1. Launch the **Audio MIDI Setup**.
2. Open the **Window** menu and click on **Show MIDI Studio**.
3. Choose the **IAC Driver** icon.
4. Activate the **Device is online** checkbox.

We can then create named virtual ports using the + button.

Sending generated MIDI to FluidSynth

To send generated MIDI from Magenta to FluidSynth, we'll take one of the first examples we wrote in `Chapter 2`, *Generating Drum Sequences with the DrumsRNN*, and add some code to send the MIDI messages directly to the software synthesizer.

> You can follow this example in the `chapter_09_example_02.py` file in the source code of this chapter. There are more comments and content in the source code, so you should go check it out.

This is similar to what we did in the previous chapter when we used the Web MIDI API to send MIDI notes to FluidSynth from the browser:

1. First, we'll start FluidSynth using one of the following:
   - Linux: `fluidsynth -a pulseaudio -g 1 PATH_TO_SF2`
   - macOS: `fluidsynth -a coreaudio -g 1 PATH_TO_SF2`
   - Windows: `fluidsynth -g 1 -o midi.winmidi.device=magenta_out PATH_TO_SF2`

Note the −o flag in the Windows command, which tells FluidSynth to listen to this MIDI port because, on Windows, it doesn't open up a port automatically.

Also, notice how we aren't using the −n and −i flags this time since we want to keep incoming MIDI messages and use the synth command line. The program should stop in the command-line interface and should have created a new input MIDI port automatically (or will use the provided one).

 On Windows, if you see the following error message upon starting FluidSynth: **fluidsynth: error: no MIDI in devices found** or **Failed to create the MIDI thread**, this means you either misspelled the MIDI port or didn't open **loopMIDI**.

On macOS and Linux, you can run the previous example code again, you should see an output similar to this:

```
Input ports: ['Midi Through:Midi Through Port-0 14:0',
'RtMidiOut Client:magenta_out 128:0']
Output ports: ['FLUID Synth (7171):Synth input port (7171:0)
129:0', 'Midi Through:Midi Through Port-0 14:0', 'RtMidiIn
Client:magenta_in 128:0']
```

Here, the FLUID Synth (7171): Synth input port (7171:0) 129:0 port is the FluidSynth port. We also have the magenta_out and magenta_in ports from the previous example.

On Windows, running the previous example code again should give you this:

```
Input ports: ['magenta_in 0', 'magenta_out 1']
Output ports: ['Microsoft GS Wavetable Synth 1', 'magenta_in
2', 'magenta_out 3']
```

The FluidSynth input port that we'll use is the magenta_out 3 port, which should match the −o midi.winmidi.device=magenta_out flag provided to FluidSynth.

2. Then, we'll copy the chapter_02_example_01.py example:

```
import argparse

parser = argparse.ArgumentParser()
parser.add_argument("--midi_port", type=str, default="FLUID Synth")
args = parser.parse_args()

def generate(unused_argv):
  # The previous example is here
```

```
    . . .

    # Write the resulting plot file to the output directory
    plot_file = os.path.join("output", "out.html")
    pretty_midi = mm.midi_io.note_sequence_to_pretty_midi(sequence)
    plotter = Plotter()
    plotter.show(pretty_midi, plot_file)
    print(f"Generated plot file: {os.path.abspath(plot_file)}")

    # Write the code to send the generated "sequence" to FluidSynth
    pass

    return 0

if __name__ == "__main__":
    tf.app.run(generate)
```

We add a `--midi_port` flag to change the MIDI output port (remember the input and output terminology is from Magenta's perspective) easily for our examples. We'll be writing the code to send the MIDI content (which is in the `sequence` variable) at the end of the `generate` method.

3. We find the provided output port and initialize `MidiHub` using the port:

```
import mido
from magenta.interfaces.midi.midi_hub import MidiHub

# We find the proper input port for the software synth
# (which is the output port for Magenta)
output_ports = [name for name in mido.get_output_names()
                if args.midi_port in name]

# Start a new MIDI hub on that port (output only)
midi_hub = MidiHub(input_midi_ports=[],
                   output_midi_ports=output_ports,
                   texture_type=None)
```

We then start a new MIDI hub on that port; it will serve as a communication interface between our app and the synth. It is useful because it enables us to use `NoteSequence` objects directly without the need of converting them by hand.

The `midi_hub` module is located in Magenta in the `magenta.interfaces.midi` module and contains useful utilities for handling MIDI.

4. Next, we'll get a player instance from the hub and set the playback channel to 9:

```
import music_pb2

empty_sequence = music_pb2.NoteSequence()
player = midi_hub.start_playback(empty_sequence,
allow_updates=True)
player._channel = 9
```

Remember that GM 1 compatible synthesizers will play the drums sound bank if the MIDI channel is 10 (but the channel is zero-indexed in Magenta MIDI hub so we have to use 9). We'll be starting the playback on an empty sequence, allowing the update of the sequence later.

5. Now we can play our sequence, but we need to adjust it first so that the player knows when it starts:

```
import time
from magenta.interfaces.midi.midi_interaction import
adjust_sequence_times

wall_start_time = time.time()
sequence_adjusted = music_pb2.NoteSequence()
sequence_adjusted.CopyFrom(sequence)
sequence_adjusted = adjust_sequence_times(sequence_adjusted,
                                          wall_start_time)
```

The MIDI player will play sequence according to wall time, but our sequence starts at 0 (the wall time is the time since epoch). For example, if the wall time (which is given by time.time()) is 1564950205, then we need to update the start of the sequence forward by that amount. We do that by keeping our current sequence intact and making a copy that will be given to the player. We use the adjust_sequence_times function from Magenta to do that.

Notice here the usage of the CopyFrom method, which is present on Protobuf message objects. You can always go check the methods on the google.protobuf.message.Message class to find useful methods for NoteSequence.

6. Now that we adjusted our sequence to the proper time, let's play it! We use the update_sequence method on the player to do this, which is the equivalent of play:

```
player.update_sequence(sequence_adjusted,
start_time=wall_start_time)
```

```
try:
  player.join(generation_end_time)
except KeyboardInterrupt:
  return 0
finally:
  return 0
```

We also give the `start_time` argument to the player `instance`, which is equal to the start of our adjusted (shifted forward) sequence.

Since `player` is a thread, we need to wait for it to finish before exiting or the program will exit before the sequence has played. We do that by using the `join` method on the player instance, which is present on any thread class. That method will block until the thread finishes, but because the player thread never stops, this call will block indefinitely. By adding a timeout of `generation_end_time`, which is the length of the generated sequence, the call will return after the end of the sequence being played. A blocked join call can always be interrupted by pressing *Ctrl + C*, which can be caught using the `KeyboardInterrupt` exception class.

7. We can now launch the program by using the following on Linux and macOS:

   > **python chapter_09_example_02.py**

   By keeping the default `--midi_port` flag, it will use the port started by FluidSynth.

   Or we can use the `magenta_out` MIDI port on Windows:

   > **python chapter_09_example_02.py --midi_port=magenta_out**

You should now hear your music play from FluidSynth! When executing the code, you might see the following warning:

WARNING:tensorflow:No input port specified. Capture disabled.

This is because the MIDI hub can also receive a MIDI message, but we haven't provided any MIDI port to do so. This is only a warning and shouldn't be an issue.

Sending generated MIDI to a DAW

Sending MIDI to FluidSynth is nice, but you probably want to use another software for producing music. We won't be looking at every DAW, but we'll show examples that can be applied for most music production software.

Now that we have Virtual MIDI ports opened for transferring MIDI from our Magenta application, let's try it out in Ableton Live. You can also try this in any other DAW that has MIDI functionalities.

You can find the Ableton Live set (with the .als file extension) in the chapter_09_example_02.als file in the source code of this chapter.

You can use this Ableton set along with the Python code we've shown in the previous example, chapter_09_example_02.py.

Let's configure the magenta_out port in Ableton Live that will be also used by the Magenta app:

1. First, in Ableton, go to **File** > **Options** > **Preferences...** > **Link MIDI** and find the magenta_out input:

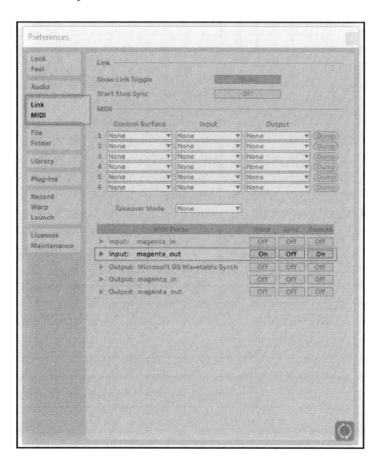

We need to activate both **Track** and **Remote** to **On** to receive the MIDI notes.

2. Now that the MIDI input is activated, we can create a new MIDI track by right-clicking in the **Drop Files and Devices Here** section and choosing **Insert MIDI track**.

3. In the new track, we see the following **MIDI from** section:

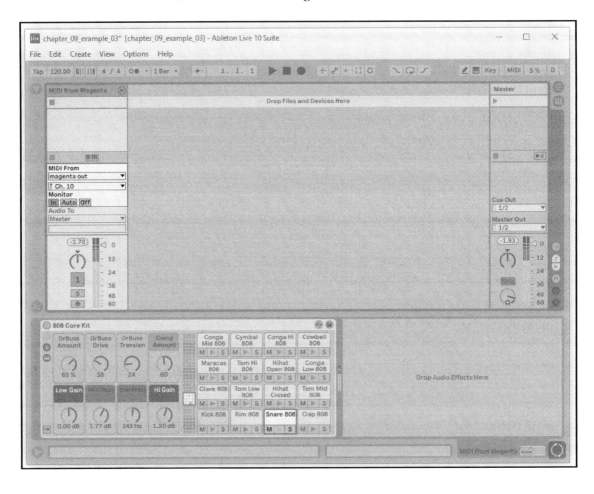

In the screenshot, we highlighted three parts:

- The **MIDI From** section, which is available for a MIDI track, where we can now select the `magenta_out` MIDI port. We also selected **Ch. 10** for the drum channel 10 and **Monitor** to **In**.
- The **third octave** on the 8-octave strip that represents all of the 127 possible MIDI values, where the **808 Core Kit** is defined. This corresponds to MIDI notes 36 to 52 and you can see note 38 is currently playing.
- The currently playing note, the **Snare 808**, in the **808 Core Kit** instrument.

On the top-right corner, a yellow indicator shows whether there is incoming MIDI or not, which is useful for debugging.

4. Now that we have our Ableton Live setup, we can launch our application by using this:

```
> python chapter_09_example_02.py --midi_port="magenta_out"
```

You should receive MIDI in Ableton Live and hear the **808 Core Kit** play the percussion.

Using NSynth generated samples as instruments

In the previous `Chapter 5`, *Audio Generation with NSynth and GANSynth*, we talked about using our generated samples by sequencing them using the generated MIDI from Magenta. Since we can now dynamically send the generated MIDI to a DAW, now is a good time to test this out.

In Ableton Live, in the **808 Core Kit** section, we can drag and drop a generated sample to replace an existing drum kit sample. For example, we could change the **Cowbell 808** instrument with one of our samples, for example, `160045_412017`:

When double-clicking on the new sound, the sampler interface will open, which lets you modify the start and the end of the loop, as well as the volume. We choose that sample because it has a strong attack (the sound envelope goes up fast), which is perfect for a percussive sample. Go ahead and experiment with your own samples.

When mapping drum sounds on channel 10, remember the percussion instrument is chosen according to the MIDI pitch note. In the previous figure, the 16 instruments in the grid are mapped to the MIDI pitches as follows:

48	49	50	51
44	45	46	47
40	41	42	43
36	37	38	39

Here, pitch 36 corresponds to **Kick 808**, pitch 37 to **Rim 808**, pitch 51 to our `160045_412017` sample, and so on. You can compare that grid with the MIDI plot that is outputted by our program (in `output/out.html`).

This works well for drum elements. But if you are sending a melody to your DAW, you will want to use a sampler, which will change the pitch of the sound, depending on the incoming note. To do that, in Ableton Live, follow these steps:

1. Create a new MIDI track by right-clicking in the **Drop Files and Devices Here** section and choosing **Insert MIDI track**.
2. Find the **Sampler** instrument by choosing **Instruments** > **Sampler**.
3. Drag and drop the **Sampler** in the **Drop Audio Effects Here** at the bottom (in the new MIDI track).
4. Drag and drop the `412017_83249` generated sample (or another of your choice) in the **Drop Sample Here** at the bottom (in the **Sampler**).

We've chosen the 412017_83249 generated sample since the cat sound makes a good (and funny) note when played as a melody. You should have the following interface:

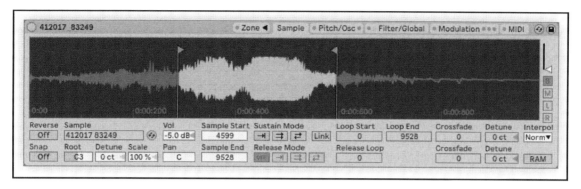

Now when you send a melody from your Magenta program, you will hear the sample, 412017_83249, getting played and pitched up and down, following the melody notes pitch.

Looping the generated MIDI

Now that we can send generated MIDI to a DAW, let's have a look at how to loop the generated MIDI. This opens up many different use cases, such as building a system that **generates music continuously**. We'll first have a look at how to loop NoteSequence. We'll also cover how to synchronize Magenta with a DAW using a MIDI clock, which is important in long-running live music systems.

Using the MIDI player to loop a sequence

In this example, we'll be using the player instance from Magenta to loop a generated NoteSequence, by copying the sequence and playing it at a later time, before the player ends its playback.

You can follow this example in the chapter_09_example_03.py file in the source code of this chapter. There are more comments and content in the source code, so you should go check it out.

Let's take our previous example and make the sequence loop indefinitely:

1. First, let's find the period, which is equivalent to the loop time in seconds:

```
from decimal import Decimal
from magenta.common import concurrency

period = Decimal(240) / qpm
period = period * (num_bars + 1)
sleeper = concurrency.Sleeper()
```

Here, we want a period (in seconds) of 4 bars, which is the loop length. Using 240/QPM, we get the period for 1 bar (for example, 2 seconds at 120 QPM). We then multiply that by 4 bars (`num_bars + 1`), which is our loop length. Also, we are using the `Decimal` class, which doesn't have rounding errors like the built-in `float`, for increased accuracy for the timing.

We make use of the `Sleeper` class from Magenta, which implements a more precise version of `sleep` than the one present in the `time` module, so it should wake up more consistently with proper timing.

2. Let's now define the main loop, which will copy the current sequence, adjust it in time, and play it using the player:

```
while True:
  try:
    # We get the next tick time by using the period
    # to find the absolute tick number (since epoch)
    now = Decimal(time.time())
    tick_number = int(now // period)
    tick_number_next = tick_number + 1
    tick_time = tick_number * period
    tick_time_next = tick_number_next * period

    # Update the player time to the current tick time
    sequence_adjusted = music_pb2.NoteSequence()
    sequence_adjusted.CopyFrom(sequence)
    sequence_adjusted = adjust_sequence_times(sequence_adjusted,
                                             float(tick_time))
    player.update_sequence(sequence_adjusted,
                           start_time=float(tick_time))

    # Sleep until the next tick time
    sleeper.sleep_until(float(tick_time_next))
  except KeyboardInterrupt:
    print(f"Stopping")
    return 0
```

Let's break the code down a bit:

- On each loop start, we get the current time since epoch (in `now`).
- We get the current tick number, by dividing the current time by the period (in `tick_number`). The tick number corresponds to the current index in a separation of the time from epoch to now in intervals of `period`.
- We get the current tick time by multiplying the period with the tick number (in `tick_time`).

For example, if the start time is `1577021349`, we have a ticking time of `1577021344` and a next tick time of `1577021352` (for a period of 8 seconds). In this case, we are on the first iteration of the loop, which is why there is such a big difference between the start time and the ticking time. On the second loop, the start time will be `1577021352` (approximately) because the thread will wake up with proper timing.

Because of the start time difference on the first loop, this means that when the player starts, it might start in the middle of the generated sequence. If we want to make it start at the beginning of the sequence, we need to subtract the start time when calculating the tick number. See the `Metronome` class in the `magenta.interfaces.midi.midi_hub` module for a more complete implementation.

Finally, we update the sequence and the player using `tick_time` and we sleep until `tick_time_next`.

3. We can now launch the program by using this:

```
> python chapter_09_example_03.py --midi_port="magenta_out"
```

You should now hear a 4-bar loop of 8 seconds at 120 QPM playing in the DAW you are using.

Synchronizing Magenta with a DAW

Synchronizing devices when playing instruments is important. Two instruments that are in sync will have the **same QPM** (**tempo**) and start on the **same beat** (**phase**). Addressing those problems is simple on the surface, but good sync is hard to achieve because precise timing is difficult.

Syncing our Magenta application with a DAW has many usages, such as recording the MIDI sequences in a DAW with proper timing (tempo and phase), or playing multiple sequences at the same time, some coming from Magenta and the others coming from the DAW.

Sending MIDI clock and transport

In this example, we'll synchronize Magenta with a DAW using a MIDI clock and transport (start, stop, and reset) information. The MIDI clock is one of the oldest and more popular ways of synchronizing devices, which is available for pretty much every instrument and music software.

We'll be giving the example in Ableton Live, but you can also try this in any DAW that has MIDI clock functionality.

 You can follow this example in the `chapter_09_example_04.py` file in the source code of this chapter. There are more comments and content in the source code, so you should go check it out.

To sync our Magenta program to Ableton Live, we'll launch a metronome thread that wakes up on every beat and sends a clock message:

1. First, let's declare the `Metronome` class that extends the `Thread` class:

```
import mido
from decimal import Decimal
from threading import Thread

class Metronome(Thread):

  def __init__(self, outport, qpm):
    super(Metronome, self).__init__()
    self._message_clock = mido.Message(type='clock')
    self._message_start = mido.Message(type='start')
    self._message_stop = mido.Message(type='stop')
    self._message_reset = mido.Message(type='reset')
```

```
    self._outport = outport
    self._period = Decimal(2.5) / qpm
    self._stop_signal = False

def stop(self):
    self._stop_signal = True

def run(self):
    # Run code
    pass
```

At instantiation, we use Mido to define the following messages (see the last section, *Further reading*, for more documentation on the messages supported by Mido and to what they correspond in the MIDI specification):

- The `clock` message, which is sent every beat
- The `start` message, which is sent when the sequence starts
- The `stop` message, which is sent when the sequence ends, or when the program exits
- The `reset` message, which is sent before the start message, making sure that the synced device restarts from the beginning in terms of beat count
- The `continue` message, which we won't use, but can be used to restart the playback without resetting the beat count

We also define the period, which is the exact time between each thread wake up. The thread needs to wake up at each beat, so in 4/4 time at 120 QPM, it needs to wake up every 0.5 seconds, which is the period.

Here, we choose to synchronize both applications using one message (or pulse) per beat, which is our period, since it is easy to do. In the MIDI specification (www.midi.org/specifications/item/table-1-summary-of-midi-messag e), another synchronization period is described, which is called **24 Pulses Per Quarter Note (24 PPQN)**, which is more precise than what we are implementing here.

One pulse per beat and 24 PPQN are both used in many DAWs and instruments. There are other synchronization pulses, however, such as 48 PPQN for Korg instruments. There are also other ways of synchronizing instruments, such as the **MIDI Time Code (MTC)**, which we won't see here.

Depending on the software or hardware you are trying to sync, make sure to check what type of synchronization pulse they are configured to handle. If this doesn't work, it is probably because you are sending an unexpected pulse rate.

2. Let's now implement the run method in the `# Run code` comment:

```python
import time
from magenta.common.concurrency import Sleeper

def run(self):
  sleeper = Sleeper()

  # Sends reset and the start, we could also
  # use the "continue" message
  self._outport.send(self._message_reset)
  self._outport.send(self._message_start)

  # Loops until the stop signal is True
  while not self._stop_signal:
    # Calculates the next tick for current time
    now = Decimal(time.time())
    tick_number = max(0, int(now // self._period) + 1)
    tick_time = tick_number * self._period
    sleeper.sleep_until(float(tick_time))

    # Sends the clock message as soon it wakeup
    self._outport.send(self._message_clock)

  # Sends a stop message when finished
  self._outport.send(self._message_stop)
```

The following list further explains the code:

- When the thread first starts, it sends a `reset` message followed by a `start` message, meaning Ableton Live will reset its beat count to 0, and then start the playback.
- Then, we calculate the next tick time and make the thread sleep to that time (see the previous section explanation on the ticking time). At wake up, we send the `clock` message, which will happen at every beat.
- Finally, if the `stop` method is called, `self._stop_signal` is set to `True`, which will exit the loop, sending the `stop` message.

3. Let's initialize the thread and launch it:

```
import argparse

parser = argparse.ArgumentParser()
parser.add_argument("--midi_port", type=str, default="magenta_out")
args = parser.parse_args()

def send_clock():
  output_ports = [name for name in mido.get_output_names()
                  if args.midi_port in name]
  midi_hub = MidiHub(input_midi_ports=[],
                     output_midi_ports=output_ports,
                     texture_type=None)
  outport = midi_hub._outport

  # Starts the metronome at 120 QPM
  metronome = Metronome(outport, 120)
  metronome.start()

  # Waits for 16 seconds and send the stop command
  metronome.join(timeout=16)
  metronome.stop()

  return 0


if __name__ == "__main__":
  send_clock()
```

The following list explains it further:

- The code is similar to our previous example. The first thing we change is that we keep a reference to the `midi_hub._outport` port so that we can send the MIDI clock to it.
- Then, we initialize the `Metronome` class using `outport` and start it using `start`. This will execute the `run` method in the thread.
- We then `join` on the thread with a timeout of 16 (seconds), meaning we'll play 8 bars before exiting and calling the `stop` method. We do this solely to show the stop usage and its impact on Ableton Live.

4. In Ableton Live, we need to make sure that the **Sync** button is **On** for the `magenta_out` port:

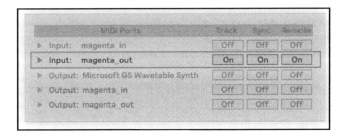

5. Once we've done that, we need to make sure that the **Ext** button on the top-left of the screen is activated:

The **Ext** button, short for **External**, means that Ableton won't use its internal clock, but rather rely on an external source for the clock.

Most DAWs and hardware synths have a similar **External** option but this is often deactivated by default. Make sure to check how to activate that for the software or hardware you are trying to sync.

On the right of the **Ext** button, two indicators show incoming and outgoing MIDI clock messages, which is useful for debugging. We've also highlighted the following:

- The **QPM indicator**, which will get updated to 120 during playback (currently at 110 QPM for testing purpose)
- The **Arrangement position** section, that shows **9.1.1**, which is the value the beat count will be at when our Python program exists and sends the `stop` message (because we stop after 8 bars)
- The **Transport section** with the start, stop and record buttons, which will update when we start and stop the program

We can now send the MIDI clock to Ableton Live.

6. Finally, let's launch our Magenta application:

```
> python chapter_09_example_04.py --midi_port="magenta_out"
```

In Ableton Live, you should see the BPM change to 120 QPM. It might take time to get there, and it might oscillate up and down while it stabilizes, but it should converge to 120 QPM. After 16 seconds, Ableton Live should stop, with a final beat count of 8 full beats (shown as **9.1.1**).

Using MIDI control message

Sending the MIDI clock is the most common way of synchronizing devices because all devices support the MIDI clock. Another way of synchronizing Magenta with a DAW would be to use **MIDI control messages**.

A MIDI control message is a message that sends `control` and `value`. For example, we could be using the following Mido message to send MIDI control: `mido.Message(type="control_change", control="...", value"...")`. Let's define some control message for the actions we want to make:

- **Start/stop**: This is to start and stop the transport, which will be used to synchronize the phase (using `control="1"` and `control="2"`, respectively).
- **QPM**: This is to set the tempo before the transport starts (using `control="3"`).

This is just an example of control values; you can use whatever value you want, as long as it is properly mapped on the DAW side. In most DAWs, mapping a control message to input is easy. Often, a `learn` function is provided, which, once activated, will map the selected input in the DAW to whatever MIDI message comes next.

Let's try this in Ableton Live:

1. Activate the MIDI mapping mode using the **MIDI** button in the upper-right corner (all of the mappable inputs in Ableton will turn to purple).
2. Select the input you want to map (**QPM**, for example) and then send the corresponding MIDI control message (see the previous code snippet), which will map the input to the control message.
3. After the MIDI control message is received, the input in Ableton will be mapped to it.
4. Exit the MIDI mapping mode, then send the same MIDI control message. The mapped input should activate.

Once all of our inputs are mapped, we can send the corresponding messages from our Magenta application, to start, stop, and change the QPM when needed. For example, the Magenta application can send the QPM before starting, and then when sending the first MIDI note, send the MIDI control message **start** at the same time.

The downside of this approach is that if any of the two applications become desynced, there isn't any way of syncing the applications back together without stopping and restarting the playback. MIDI clock, on the other hand, is constantly syncing the devices together.

Using Ableton Link to sync devices

Ableton Link (`github.com/Ableton/link`) is an open source standard aimed at synchronizing software devices. It enables auto-discovery across a local network and is easy to use. A lot of DAWs now support Ableton Link, which is yet another way of syncing our Magenta application to a DAW but necessitates implementing the specification.

Sending MIDI to a hardware synthesizer

Sending MIDI to a hardware synthesizer is very similar to what we've been doing in the previous sections, with the exception that the hardware synthesizer should open a new MIDI port by itself (just like FluidSynth) so we don't need to create a virtual port for it.

We'll be using an Arturia BeatStep Pro for our example, but this should work with any MIDI-enabled device:

1. First, we need to install the drivers for the synthesizer, which might or might not be necessary, depending on the synth and the platform.

2. Then, we connect the synthesizer using USB to the computer and run the first example to find what are the declared MIDI ports. For the Arturia BeatStep Pro on Windows, we have the output port, `MIDIIN2 (Arturia BeatStep Pro) 1`.

3. Now, we can run our previous example, by changing the Magenta output port with the synthesizer input port:

   ```
   > python chapter_09_example_03.py --midi_port="MIDIIN2 (Arturia
   BeatStep Pro) 1"
   ```

This should send the MIDI directly to the hardware synthesizer.

This example sends MIDI using USB MIDI, which is not available on all synthesizers. Some synthesizers only support MIDI using a MIDI cable, not a USB cable, which means you'll need a sound card or a USB to MIDI converter. The procedure is still the same, but you'll have to go through the sound card or the converter.

Using Magenta as a standalone application with Magenta Studio

Magenta Studio is the closest you can get to a Magenta standalone application, in the sense that it doesn't require any installation and any knowledge of technologies to make it work. This is especially important, because Magenta and the technology that powers it is complex, but in the end, it is **important that everybody can use it**.

We'll be looking at how Magenta Studio works and find many elements we've already covered in the previous chapters. Magenta Studio comes in two packagings:

- As **Ableton Live Plugins** (`magenta.tensorflow.org/studio/ableton-live`), which integrates Magenta into Ableton Live using the Max for Live integration and Magenta.js applications (supported on Windows and macOS)
- As **Standalone Applications** (`magenta.tensorflow.org/studio/standalone`), which are Electron applications (supported on all platforms)

We won't be talking about the standalone applications too much because we've already covered everything we need to know about them. Indeed, an Electron application is a Node.js application packaged with its runtime and a Chromium browser, so we've already covered that content in the previous `Chapter 8`, *Magenta in the Browser with Magenta.js*.

Looking at Magenta Studio's content

Since both packagings are based on Magenta.js, they both contain the same features:

- **CONTINUE** makes use of MusicRNN (LSTM based), either the DrumsRNN model or the MelodyRNN model depending on the usage, to continue a sequence from a primer.
- **GENERATE** makes use of the MusicVAE model, using a 4 bar model for the drums or the melody generation.
- **INTERPOLATE** also makes use of the MusicVAE model.
- **GROOVE** makes the use of the GrooVAE model to add groove to a quantized sequence.
- **DRUMIFY** uses the GrooVAE tap model to convert a **tap sequence** into a **drum sequence**.

When downloading the standalone version, you'll be able to install (using `.exe` or `.dmg` depending on the platform) any of the five applications. When installed and launched, the applications are shown as follows:

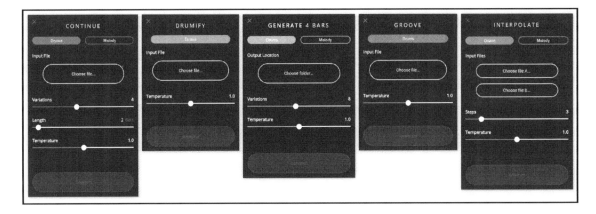

You can find many parameters we already talked about: temperature, length, variations (number of generated sequences), steps (number of interpolations), and so on. The difference between the standalone and the Ableton packaging is how they integrate with our music tool: the standalone application can work with files on disk (as shown in the previous screenshot, with the **Choose file...** button) and the Ableton Live plugin can directly read and write clips in the **Session View**.

Let's have a look at the Ableton Live Plugins integration.

Integrating Magenta Studio in Ableton Live

The Magenta Studio plugin integration in Ableton Live is nice because it corresponds to the idea of a **machine learning augmented** music production environment. In general, the integration of Magenta in existing tools is important, and Magenta Studio is a good example of that.

It is interesting to understand how the Ableton Live plugins are designed since it is quite clever. In Ableton Live, you can integrate a Max MSP application as a plugin or device. Max MSP (`cycling74.com/products/max-features/`) is a powerful visual programming language for music. The Ableton Live Plugins works as follows:

1. Ableton Live launches the `magenta.amxd` patch, which is a Max MSP program.
2. The Max MSP program shows a UI in Ableton Live, in which we can choose any of the **Continue**, **Generate**, and other programs.
3. When chosen, the Max MSP program will launch a Node.js process, containing the Magenta.js application (which is the same as the standalone application).
4. Using the Max MSP API, the Magenta.js application can see the Ableton Live **Session View** content, including clips and tracks, and write content.

For now, Magenta Studio integrates only in Ableton Live. Other DAWs might be integrated in the future, as Magenta Studio's implementation has nothing specific to Ableton Live.

> For this example to work, we need Ableton Live 10.1 Suite since the integration of Max For Live (only in the **Suite** version) is necessary for Magenta Studio to work. You can try the demo at `www.ableton.com/en/trial/` if you don't have the program handy.

Let's go through a complete example using the **Continue** application:

1. From `magenta.tensorflow.org/studio/ableton-live`, download the Max MSP patch using the **Download** button for your platform, which should download the `magenta_studio-VERSION-windows.amxd` file.

2. Open Ableton Live, create a new MIDI track, and drag and drop the file in the MIDI track devices (it might take a while to load):

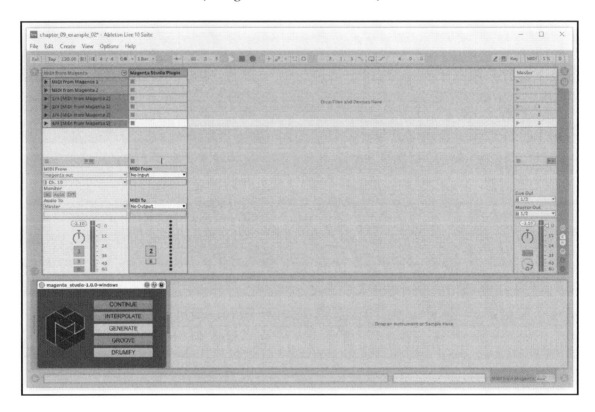

In the previous screenshot, we see that we recorded two MIDI clips from our previous example, **MIDI from Magenta 1** and **MIDI from Magenta 2**, which we'll use to generate new content using the **Continue** plugin. We can see the Magenta Studio patch in the **Magenta Studio Plugin** track, which shows at the bottom.

3. Now, let's click on **CONTINUE** in the Magenta Studio Plugin. You should see the **Continue** Node.js application start:

In the **Input Clip** section, we've added from the **MIDI from Magenta** track the **MIDI from Magenta 2** MIDI clip, which will be used by the DrumsRNN model for its primer. The four variations will be added automatically to Ableton Live after the primer clip, with the name x/4 [MIDI from Magenta 2], with *x* being the index of the generated clip.

Summary

In this chapter, we've covered the interaction of Magenta with established music production software.

First, we have shown how to send MIDI from Magenta to DAWs or synthesizers. We started by looking at MIDI ports using Mido, a powerful Python library to handle MIDI operations. We've shown examples of how to loop MIDI in Magenta, which requires proper timing and threading tools. We also looked at synchronization between Magenta and a DAW using various methods, most notably using the MIDI clock messages and transport messages. We finished the MIDI section by showing how Magenta could send MIDI directly to hardware synthesizers, such as keyboards.

Finally, we introduced Magenta Studio, both as a standalone application and as an Ableton Live plugin. We looked at its integration in Ableton Live and the importance of integrating Magenta in existing music tools.

Looking at Magenta's integration in a music production ecosystem is the perfect closing chapter. It reminds us that Magenta is not an end by itself, but rather a tool that needs to be used in conjunction with other music production tools to be truly useful. Magenta is becoming more usable by a broader, non-technical audience, by developing projects such as Magenta.js and Magenta Studio.

There is still a lot that can be done for Magenta to grow in terms of usability for everybody. This is, however, the start of a great music production tool.

Questions

1. What is the difference between a software synthesizer, such as FluidSynth, and a DAW, such as Ableton Live?
2. Why is opening MIDI virtual ports required to make music software interact with each other?
3. Write the code based on `chapter_09_example_03.py` that, instead of looping the four bars sequence, generates a new sequence every four bars.
4. Why is syncing based on the MIDI control message not robust?
5. Why is Magenta Studio such an important project in the music composition ecosystem?
6. What are the technologies behind Magenta Studio Plugins and Magenta Studio Standalone?

Further Reading

- **Learn Live (Ableton Live)**: Amazing tutorials on Ableton Live, which are far the best tutorials available on music production in general, with advanced content on many topics that can be used in many DAWs
  (www.ableton.com/en/live/learn-live/)

- **Session View (Ableton Live)**: More information on Ableton Live's **Session View** which is a useful view for using Magenta Studio
  (www.ableton.com/en/manual/session-view/)

- **Community Learning (Bitwig)**: Good tutorials for Bitwig
  (www.bitwig.com/en/community/learning.html)

- **Tutorials (Reason)**: Tutorials for Reason in the form of blog posts
  (www.reasonstudios.com/blog/category/tutorials)

- **Getting Started With SC (SuperCollider)**: The best way to get into SuperCollider and its programming language, sclang—the examples are also bundled with the software when downloaded
  (doc.sccode.org/Tutorials/Getting-Started/00-Getting-Started-With-SC.html)

- **VCV Rack Manual (VCV Rack)**: VCV documentation along with the developer API if you want to write code for the software (vcvrack.com/manual/)

- **Ports**: Mido documentation on Virtual MIDI ports differences between platforms
  (mido.readthedocs.io/en/latest/ports.html)

- **Summary of MIDI Messages**: List of MIDI messages, including the MIDI clock and transport message we're using
  (www.midi.org/specifications/item/table-1-summary-of-midi-message)

- **Message Types**: Supported message types in Mido from the MIDI spec
  (mido.readthedocs.io/en/latest/message_types.html)

- **Magenta Studio**: Blog post from the Magenta team on Magenta Studio
  (magenta.tensorflow.org/studio-announce)

Assessments

Chapter 1: Introduction to Magenta and Generative Art

1. Randomness.
2. Markov chain.
3. Algorave.
4. **Long short-term memory (LSTM)**.
5. Autonomous systems generate music without operator input; assisting music systems will complement an artist while working.
6. Symbolic: sheet music, MIDI, MusicXML, AbcNotation. Sub-symbolic: raw audio (waveform), spectrogram.
7. "Note On" and "Note Off" timing, pitch between 1 and 127 kHz, velocity, and channel.
8. At a sample rate of 96 kHz, the Nyquist frequency is 96 kHz/2 = 48 kHz and the frequency range is 0 to 48 kHz. This is worse for listening to audio since 28 kHz of audio is lost on the ear (remember anything over 20 khz cannot be heard), and that sampling rate is not properly supported by much audio equipment. It is useful in recording and audio editing though.
9. A single musical note, A4, is played for 1 second loudly.
10. Drums, voice (melody), harmony (polyphony), and interpolation and manipulation.

Chapter 2: Generating Drum Sequences with the Drums RNN

1. Given a current sequence, predict the score for the next note, then do a prediction for each step you want to generate.

2. (1) RNNs operate on sequences of vectors, for the input and output, which is good for sequential data such as a music score, and (2) keep an internal state composed of the previous output steps, which is good for doing a prediction based on past inputs, not only the current input.

3. (1) First, the hidden layer will get $h(t + 1)$, which is the output of the previous hidden layer, and (2) it will also receive $x(t + 2)$, which is the input of the current step.

4. The number of bars generated will be 2 bars, or 32 steps, since we have 16 steps per bar. At 80 QPM, each step takes 0.1875 seconds, because you take the number of seconds in a minute, divide by the QPM, and divide by the number of steps per quarter: 60 / 80 / 4 = 0.1875. Finally, you have 32 steps at 0.1875 seconds each, so the total time is 32 * 0.1875 = 6 seconds.

5. Increasing the branch factor reduces the randomness, since you have more branches to choose from when selecting the best branch, but increasing the temperature will increase the randomness. Doing both at the same time will cancel out each other, we just don't know in what proportions.

6. At each step, the algorithm will generate four branches and keep two. At the last iteration, the beam search will search for the best branch in the graph by checking the remaining two nodes at each level multiplied by the number of steps of the generated graph (also the height of the tree), which is three. So we go through 2 * 3 nodes = 6 nodes.

7. `NoteSequence`.

8. The MIDI notes maps to the following classes: 36 maps to 0 (kick drum), 40 maps to 1 (snare drum), 42 maps to 2 (closed hi-hat). The resulting index is calculated with $2^0 + 2^1 + 2^2 = 7$, so the resulting vector will be $v = [0, 0, 0, 0, 0, 0, 1, 0, ...]$.

9. The bit representation of index 131 is `10000011` (in Python, you can use `"{0:b}".format(131)` to get that). This is represented as $2^0 + 2^1 + 2^7$, which gives us the following classes: 0 (drum kit), 1 (snare drum) and 7 (crash cymbal). We then arbitrarily take the first element of each class: *{36, 38, 49}*.

Chapter 3: Generating Polyphonic Melodies

1. Vanishing gradients (values get multiplied by small values in each RNN step) and exploding gradients are common RNN problems that occur when training during the backpropagation step. LSTM provides a dedicated cell state that is modified by forget, input, and output gates to alleviate those problems.

2. **Gated recurrent units** (**GRUs**) are simpler but less expressive memory cells, where the forget and input gates are combined into a single **update gate**.

3. For a 3/4 time signature, you need 3 steps per quarter note, times 4 steps per quarter note, which equals 12 steps per bar. For a binary step counter to count to 12, you need 5 bits (like for 4/4 time) that will only count to 12. For 3 lookbacks, you'll need to look at the past 3 bars, with each bar being 12 steps, so you have *[36, 24, 12]*.

4. The resulting vector is the sum of the previous step vectors, each applied with the attention mask, so we have 0.1 applied to *[1, 0, 0, 0]*, plus 0.5 applied to *[0, 1, 0, x]* giving *[0.10, 0.50, 0.00, 0.25]*. The value of x is 0.5, because 0.5 times 0.5 equals 0.25.

5. A C major chord of one quarter note.

6. In Polyphony RNN, there are no note end events. If no `CONTINUED_NOTE` is used for a pitch in a step, it stops the note. In Perfomance RNN, a `NOTE_END 56` event would be used.

7. (1) Expressive timing using `TIME_SHIFT` events, present in all Performance RNN models, for example in the `performance` configuration, and (2) dynamic play using `VELOCITY` events, present in the `performance_with_dynamics` configuration.

8. It will change the number of iterations during the RNN steps call. A bigger number of notes per seconds will ask for more RNN steps during the generation.

Chapter 4: Latent Space Interpolation with MusicVAE

1. The main use is dimensionality reduction, to force the network to learn important features, making it possible to reconstruct the original input. The downside of AE is that the latent space represented by the hidden layer is not continuous, making it hard to sample since the decoder won't be able to make sense of some of the points.

2. The reconstruction loss penalizes the network when it creates outputs that are different from the input.

3. In VAE, the latent space is continuous and smooth, making it possible to sample any point of the space and interpolate between two points. It is achieved by having the latent variables follow a probability distribution of P(z), often a Gaussian distribution.

4. The KL divergence measures how much two probability distributions diverge from each other. When combined with the reconstruction loss, it centers the clusters around 0 and makes them more or less close to one another.

5. We sample the normal distribution using `np.random.randn(4, 512)`.

6. Calculate the direction between two points in the latent space.

Chapter 5: Audio Generation with NSynth and GANSynth

1. You have to handle 16,000 samples per second (at least) and keep track of the general structure at a bigger time scale.

2. NSynth is a WaveNet-style autoencoder that learns its own temporal embedding, making it possible to capture long term structure, and providing access to a useful hidden space.

3. The colors in the rainbowgram are the 16 dimensions of the temporal embedding.

4. Check the `timestretch` method in the `audio_utils.py` file in the chapter's code.

5. GANSynth uses upsampling convolutions, making the training and generation processing in parallel possible for the entire audio sample.

6. You need to sample the random normal distribution using `np.random.normal(size=[10, 256])`, where 10 is the number of sampled instruments, and 256 is the size of the latent vector (given by the `latent_vector_size` configuration).

Chapter 6: Data Preparation for Training

1. MIDI is not a text format, so it is harder to use and modify, but it is extremely common. MusicXML is rather rare and cumbersome but has the advantage of being in text format. ABCNotation is also rather rare, but has the advantage of being in text format and closer to sheet music.

2. Use the code from `chapter_06_example_08.py`, and change the `program=43` in the extraction.

3. There are 1,116 rock songs in LMD and 3,138 songs for jazz, blues, and country. Refer to `chapter_06_example_02.py` and `chapter_06_example_03.py` to see how to make statistics with genre information.

4. Use the `RepeatSequence` class in `melody_rnn_pipeline_example.py`.

5. Use the code from `chapter_06_example_09.py`. Yes, we can train a quantized model with it since the data preparation pipeline quantizes the input.

6. For small datasets, data augmentation plays an essential role in creating more data, because sometimes you just don't have more. For bigger datasets, it also plays a role by creating more relevant data and variations on existing data, which is good for the network training phase.

Chapter 7: Training Magenta Models

1. See `chapter_07_example_03.py`.

2. A network that underfits is a network that hasn't reached its optimum, meaning it won't predict well with the evaluation data, because it fits poorly the training data (for now). It can be fixed by letting it train long enough, by adding more network capacity, and more data.

3. A network that overfits is a network that has learned to predict the input but cannot generalize to values outside of its training set. It can be fixed by adding more data, by reducing the network capacity, or by using regularization techniques such as dropout.

4. Early stopping.

5. Read *On Large-Batch Training for Deep Learning: Generalization Gap and Sharp Minima*, which explains that a larger batch size leads to sharp minimizers, which in turn leads to poorer generalization. Therefore it is worse in terms of efficiency, but might be better in terms of training time, since more data is processed at the same time.

6. A bigger network is a network that will be more precise in its prediction, so maximizing that should be important. The network size should also grow with the size (and quality) of the data. For example, a network that's too big for its data will likely overfit.

7. It helps with the exploding gradients problem because the weights will be multiplied by smaller values, limiting the possibility of having big gradients. Another way of doing this is by reducing the learning rate.

8. It can be used to launch training on more powerful machines and to launch multiple training sessions at the same time. Unfortunately, using cloud providers have a cost, meaning the more training time and power we use, the more costly our training will get.

Chapter 8: Magenta in the Browser with Magenta.js

1. We can train models using TensorFlow.js, but we cannot train models using Magenta.js. We need to train the models in Magenta using Python and import the resulting models in Magenta.js.

2. The Web Audio API enables audio synthesis in the browser using audio nodes for generation, transformation, and routing. The easiest way to use it is to use an audio framework such as Tone.js.

3. The method is `randomSample` and the argument is the pitch of the generated note. As an example, using 60 will result in a single note at MIDI pitch 60, or C4 in letter notation. This is also useful as a reference for pitching the note up or down using Tone.js.

4. The method is `sample` and the number of instruments depends on the model that is being used. In our example, we've used the `trio` model, which generates three instruments. Using a `melody` model will generate only one lead instrument.

5. Since JavaScript is single threaded, long synchronous computations that are launched in the UI thread will block its execution. Using a web worker makes it possible to execute code in another thread.

6. Using the Web MIDI API in the browser, which is not well supported at the moment, or using Magenta.js in a Node.js process on the server side, making it easier to send MIDI to other processes.

Chapter 9: Making Magenta Interact with Music Applications

1. A DAW will have more functions geared towards music production such as recording, audio, MIDI editing, effects and mastering, and song composition. A software synthesizer like FluidSynth will have less functionalities, but have the advantage of being lightweight and easy to use.

2. Most music software won't open MIDI ports by themselves, so to send sequences back and forth between them we have to manually open ports.

3. See the code in `chapter_09_example_05.py` in this chapter's code.

4. Because syncing two pieces of software that have desynced requires restarting them. A MIDI clock enables syncing once per beat.

5. Because Magenta Studio integrates with existing music production tools such as DAWs and doesn't require any technical knowledge, it makes AI-generated music available to a greater audience, which is ultimately the goal of Magenta.

6. Magenta Studio plugins and Magenta Studio standalone are both based on Magenta.js, packaged using Electron. Magenta Studio Plugins uses the Max MSP integration in Ableton Live to execute inside it.

Other Books You May Enjoy

If you enjoyed this book, you may be interested in these other books by Packt:

Hands-On Generative Adversarial Networks with PyTorch 1.x
John Hany, Greg Walters

ISBN: 978-1-78953-051-3

- Implement PyTorch's latest features to ensure efficient model designing
- Get to grips with the working mechanisms of GAN models
- Perform style transfer between unpaired image collections with CycleGAN
- Build and train 3D-GANs to generate a point cloud of 3D objects
- Create a range of GAN models to perform various image synthesis operations
- Use SEGAN to suppress noise and improve the quality of speech audio

Advanced Deep Learning with Python
Ivan Vasilev

ISBN: 978-1-78995-617-7

- Cover advanced and state-of-the-art neural network architectures
- Understand the theory and math behind neural networks
- Train DNNs and apply them to modern deep learning problems
- Use CNNs for object detection and image segmentation
- Implement generative adversarial networks (GANs) and variational autoencoders to generate new images
- Solve natural language processing (NLP) tasks, such as machine translation, using sequence-to-sequence models
- Understand DL techniques, such as meta-learning and graph neural networks

Leave a review - let other readers know what you think

Please share your thoughts on this book with others by leaving a review on the site that you bought it from. If you purchased the book from Amazon, please leave us an honest review on this book's Amazon page. This is vital so that other potential readers can see and use your unbiased opinion to make purchasing decisions, we can understand what our customers think about our products, and our authors can see your feedback on the title that they have worked with Packt to create. It will only take a few minutes of your time, but is valuable to other potential customers, our authors, and Packt. Thank you!

Index

reference link 178
  using, for audio content 178
NSynth generated samples
  using, ad instruments 305, 306, 307
  using, as instrument notes 161
NVIDIA CUDA drivers
  installing 247, 248

O

one-hot encoding 74
output size 49
overfitting
  about 227, 228
  fixing 229, 230

P

pen and paper generative music 11, 12, 13
performance music
  MAESTRO dataset, using for 177
Performance RNN
  configuring, with performance music 103, 104, 105
  example 105, 106
  used, for generating polyphony 97, 98
pipelines
  used, for preparing data 203
polyphonic encoding 101, 102, 103
Polyphony RNN
  used, for generating polyphony 97, 98
polyphony
  about 84
  generating, with Performance RNN 97, 98
  generating, with Polyphony RNN 97, 98
pre-trained models
  overview 134
PrettyMIDI 175
Protocol Buffers (Protobuf) 18
Pulse Code Modulation (PCM) 20
Python environment
  creating, with Conda 27, 29, 30
Python
  Drums RNN, using in 66, 67

Q

quantization 62
quarter 57
Quarter-notes Per Minute (QPM) 57

R

raw audio 144
reason
  URL 293
reconstruction loss 111
Recurrent Neural Networks (RNNs)
  about 15, 80
  defining 50, 51, 52
  right terminology, using for 52
  sequence of vectors, operating on 49, 50
  significance, in music generation 48
RNN models
  dataset, creating 222, 223, 224
  evaluation, launching 224, 225
  TensorBoard, launching 225, 226, 227
  training 222
  training, launching 223, 224
RNN types, representation ways
  many-to-many 49
  many-to-one 49
  one-to-many 49
  one-to-one 49

S

same beat (phase) 310
same QPM (tempo) 310
sample method 138
score transformation
  with GrooVAE model 115, 116
  with MusicVAE model 115, 116
Seq2Seq models 25
sequence of vectors 49
Sequence-to-Sequence (Seq2Seq) 25
sequence
  generating, from trained model 236, 237
  humanizing 128
sheet music
  MuseScore, installing for 36, 37
Sketch-RNN 25

Made in the USA
Las Vegas, NV
28 September 2021